Pilgrim in the Palace of Words

Pilgrim in the Palace of Words

A Journey Through the 6,000 Languages of Earth

Glenn Dixon

DUNDURN PRESS
TORONTO

Editor: Michael Carroll
Design: Courtney Horner
Printer: Webcom

Library and Archives Canada Cataloguing in Publication

Dixon, Glenn, 1957-
    Pilgrim in the palace of words : a journey through the 6,000 languages of earth / by Glenn Dixon.

Includes bibliographical references and index.
ISBN 978-1-55488-433-9

1. Dixon, Glenn, 1957- --Travel. 2. Sociolinguistics. 3. Language and languages--Philosophy. 4. Voyages and travels. I. Title.

P40.D59 2009   306.44   C2009-903002-0

1   2   3   4   5   13   12   11   10   09

  Conseil des Arts
du Canada   Canada Council
for the Arts   Canada   ONTARIO ARTS COUNCIL
CONSEIL DES ARTS DE L'ONTARIO

We acknowledge the support of the **Canada Council for the Arts** and the **Ontario Arts Council** for our publishing program. We also acknowledge the financial support of the **Government of Canada** through the **Book Publishing Industry Development Program** and **The Association for the Export of Canadian Books**, and the **Government of Ontario** through the **Ontario Book Publishers Tax Credit program**, and the **Ontario Media Development Corporation**.

The Sappho translation on page 57 is reprinted by permission of the publisher and the Trustees of the Loeb Classical Library from *Greek Lyric Poetry: Volume 1, Sappho and Alcaeus*. Loeb Classical Library Volume 142, translated by David A. Campbell, Cambridge, MA: Harvard University Press, 1982. Copyright by the President and Fellows of Harvard University.

Care has been taken to trace the ownership of copyright material used in this book. The author and the publisher welcome any information enabling them to rectify any references or credits in subsequent editions.

J. Kirk Howard, President

Published by The Dundurn Group
Printed and bound in Canada.

www.dundurn.com

Dundurn Press	Gazelle Book Services Limited	Dundurn Press
3 Church Street, Suite 500	White Cross Mills	2250 Military Road
Toronto, Ontario, Canada	High Town, Lancaster, England	Tonawanda, NY
M5E 1M2	LA1 4XS	U.S.A. 14150

 Mixed Sources
Product group from well-managed forests, and other controlled sources
FSC   www.fsc.org Cert no. SW-COC-002358
© 1996 Forest Stewardship Council

The limits of my language mean the limits of my world.

— Ludwig Wittgenstein

Contents

PART ONE

At the Gates of the Western World

1

Climbing the Tower of Babel

The airport security guard hauled me into a back room. "Step behind the curtain, please, and take off your clothes."

"What do you mean?" I asked helplessly. "Everything?"

"Everything."

I stripped clumsily, my two pale feet hopscotching behind the thin curtain. Outside I could hear the guard flipping through my passport. I was sure he was eyeing the stamps from the Muslim countries I'd been to, and could well imagine his lips pursing in disapproval.

It's not so easy getting into Jerusalem. The whole place can be something like a war zone. The guard returned, took a quick look, and then asked me to dress and come out to identify my belongings. My backpack had already been hauled out of the plane and its contents had been placed on a long metal table. There was my toothbrush and my underpants neatly stacked in front of me. I'd flown in on the Israeli national airline — El Al — and it wasn't taking any chances. El Al has yet to have an "accident," and these extreme measures were one of the reasons why.

The plane had landed at Ben Gurion Airport in the desert past Tel Aviv. It's not actually near anything, so it's somewhere you want to get out of as soon as possible. Actually, any airport is a place you want to leave quickly. I snatched my backpack off the table and hustled toward the buses.

Ψ

I've been travelling now for more than ten years, slipping in and out of countries, poking my nose into where I probably shouldn't be. I've been attacked by wild dogs on a high mountain pass. I've heard jaguars roar in the deep jungle foliage. And once, in the calm blue waters above a coral reef, a shark angled in at me. But in every case the wildlife was protecting its territory, and I was the one who didn't belong.

Humans, of course, tend to section off their land with borders, guns, and barbed wire. But these are only surface markers. In reality we claim our territory with a much more powerful and ancient tool. We mark our place in the world, and even ourselves, with language.

About six thousand languages are spoken around the globe today, and each is a whole world in itself. Before I went off travelling, I was studying linguistics. In fact, I'd been doing graduate work and had just been accepted to do my doctorate.

I turned the offer down.

Languages, as one philosopher said, are the Houses of Being. And I wanted to journey to these houses. I wanted to strut up their sidewalks. I wanted to knock on their doors and peek in their windows. I wanted to see what they were hiding in their basements ... even if it meant a little bit of trouble.

ع

The bus took me into Tel Aviv, the most modern city in the Middle East. It sits on a long beach and could easily pass for a metropolis on California's coast except that here people carry even more guns than Californians. I saw a young man and his girlfriend walking along a tree-lined street. They were holding hands and obviously much in love, and the whole picture would have made me sigh were it not for the Uzi machine guns draped over their shoulders.

Near the bus station I found a bank to change my money into shekels. In the line something quite strange happened. The windows of the bank began to rattle quite noticeably. It felt as if a minor earthquake was shaking the ground. Then it stopped, and five minutes later it started again. Very odd.

When I got to the cashier, I asked her what had happened. "Oh," she said, "that means a jet has just broken the sound barrier." Somewhere ten thousand metres above us the cutting edge of military technology was knifing through the slipstream, arcing over some of the most ancient cities on Earth.

But listen, *shekels*, can you believe it? I know it's only a name, but it conjures up a world that's long gone, something quite old. I miss such things in Europe now that the European Union countries have gone over to the euro. Euros themselves are dull pieces of paper adorned with nondescript images. I miss counting out drachmas in Greece. I miss the schillings of Austria. I miss the drawing of the little prince on the fifty-franc note in France. When the world becomes homogenized, something is lost. Even if it's only a name, we lose a little part of the soul of that place.

No matter. There I was on the doorstep of Jerusalem, hands dripping with shekels. I caught another bus that took me into the Judean hills, up into one of the world's most disputed regions.

ℸ

And so ... Jerusalem ... *Jeru-salam*. The name rolls off the tongue like a poem. Five thousand years of history in four short syllables. A Canaanite city is mentioned in an ancient Egyptian papyrus scroll dating from the second millennium B.C. Then, in ancient Semitic, it was called Ursalem.

My first glimpse of the old city was of its massive walls gleaming in the sunlight. Everyone must feel like a pilgrim here. It's impossible not to. I'm not very religious, but this city wallops you on the chest and really gets to you.

I spent a few days clambering down dark passageways, finding my way from one holy site to another. One early morning I went up to see the Temple Mount long before the crowds arrived. Even that early, sunlight splashed onto the stones and in the desert air, the blue tiles of the Dome of the Rock standing out vividly. The roof of the Dome is coated in gold and shimmers and dazzles.

The first and second Jewish Temples stood here. Christ was whipped here. Muhammad ascended to heaven here. All of it here in an area no larger than a soccer pitch. These are events people kill and die for — and they have for thousands of years in great numbers on this very spot.

On this particular morning, though, I had the whole place to myself except for one old Palestinian man who was sweeping the steps. I wandered aimlessly for a while around the geometric tiles of the Dome and eventually made my way to the back wall where a small set of steps dropped to the Golden Gate. Of the eight gates in the walls of Jerusalem, this is the only one that is sealed and permanently closed. The door has been bricked in because of an ancient legend that says the Jewish messiah will arrive through this gate. So the current keepers of the Temple Mount have blocked it up.

The Golden Gate was one of the ancient entrances to Jerusalem, and almost certainly Jesus Christ, on his first palm-waving entry into Jerusalem, accessed the city here. So I stood and gazed at the steps, the very ones Jesus would have strolled up. They were roped off, but soon enough the old man who had been sweeping came over. At first he said it was forbidden to go closer, to actually walk down the steps and touch the fabled gate, but after looking both ways he removed the rope and swept his arm forward in invitation. I descended and placed my hand on the gate. It was cold. In the dark shadows, however, there was only decaying masonry and the acrid smell of urine.

When I came back up the steps, the old man held out his hand for *baksheesh*. This translates as a kind of a tip. If someone has done a service for you, you're obliged to reciprocate by giving *baksheesh*, usually in the form of money. I didn't begrudge him, and he seemed perfectly happy with the single shekel I doled into his old broom-callused hand. He flashed a cracked-tooth grin, and I left the Temple Mount, disappointed because, in the heart of three of the world's major religions, I hadn't felt anything.

Ω

The streets of old Jerusalem are narrow and dark. Spice shops and *halal* butchers line the alleyways, and in one doorway I spied two elderly shopkeepers arguing with each other. Standing nose to nose, they shook their fists in the air, then, after a few hot moments, ambled down the street arm in arm. I watched them disappear around a corner, and I couldn't understand it. How could they go from confrontation to friendship so quickly?

I was forgetting that their House of Being, their Palace of Words, was different. In English we frame arguments within the metaphor of a battle. We "defend our positions." We "shoot down" the ideas of others. It's a metaphorical fight, and the whole point is that there will be winners and losers. It's not necessarily like that in Arabic. Different languages work under different metaphors. An argument could, for example, be a performance, or a dance, if you like. There are steps to be learned. It's a delicate interplay of give and take, a thing to be engaged in and even enjoyed.

All in all, Arabic has received a bad rap in the West. We tend to think of it as a harsh language filled with crackling, angry consonants. The truth is that these consonants float on a bed of honey. They drip with vowels.

Most Arabic words are constructed from three-letter "roots." For example, k-t-b conveys the idea of writing. The addition of other sounds before, between, and after the roots produces a whole family of related words such as book (kitab) and writer (katib). Kataba forms the past tense, and yaktuba yields the future. And maktub takes everything a step farther. It carries the concept of fate, the hand of Allah, and a whole way of being. Literally, it means "it is written."

In English we, too, have words that shift meaning, or at least tense, with the change of a vowel: drink, drank, drunk; sing, sang, sung. I once taught English to a student who did well on these irregular verbs. For sit she wrote sat. For swim she wrote swam. For think she paused for a moment, confused, and then pencilled in the word thank.

My favourite triad in Arabic consists of the letters s-l-m. From these you get the word salam or peace. All through the Muslim world you are greeted with salam aleikum — "peace be with you."

If you listen closely, you'll hear salam everywhere. Even the very word Islam comes with these fine sounds: I-salam. Quite often Islam is translated in English as "surrender to God," and a Muslim mu-salam is "one who surrenders to God." But to me those English translations are loaded with baggage. We're still

16

working here with negative connotations. Another translation I often hear is "submission." That's even worse. It carries the idea that Muslims are forced into something, which isn't true. All these translations only serve to reveal the West's own prejudices and ignorance.

Among the *alim* — the scholars of the Quran — there is much discussion about such subtle distinctions. A proper understanding of the word *Muslim* must carry the flavour of the word *salam*, so that in English it should translate as something along the lines of "one who is pacified by God," or even "one to whom God has brought peace."

And I like that very much.

Φ

Now imagine a voice … deep and resonant, biblical even. "Behold," it booms, "the whole Earth had one language and one speech … and it came to pass that the people found a plain and they dwelt there.

"Then they said to one another, 'Come, let us make bricks and bake them thoroughly. Let us build ourselves a city, and a tower whose top is in the heavens. Let us make a name for ourselves, lest we be scattered abroad over the face of the whole Earth.'"

The above passage concerns the Tower of Babel, of course, the story of the formation of languages. It's found in Genesis 11:1–9.

Babel almost certainly refers to Babylon, though the forgotten scribe who wrote this particular tale had probably never seen that fabled city. He would have lived somewhere in ancient Israel, quite likely in Jerusalem, and anyway, he was already writing about something long ago and far away.

"Let us make a name for ourselves," the people of Babel said. That was arrogance, obviously, and it didn't go unnoticed by God. He didn't like the idea of people coming up to see him. In fact, he didn't like it at all.

"Behold," said God, "they are one people and they have one language and this is only the beginning of what they will do." He considered the tower. "Nothing that they propose to do will now be impossible for them." This worried God greatly, and after deep deliberation, he made his plan: "Come, let us go down and there confuse their language that they may not understand one another's speech."

Confuse in the ancient Hebrew texts is the word balal, an archaic root that actually means "to overflow or spill." And that's what God let loose. He turned up the heat until the pot spilled over, mixing up the languages of these first people and "scattering them from there over the face of all the Earth." After that, God thought, the troublesome creatures wouldn't be a problem.

Boy, was God wrong!

$$\Psi$$

18

Today there seems to be a sort of reverse Tower of Babel effect. Of the six thousand languages spoken around the world, it is estimated that only five hundred will be left by the year 2100, and even then only about twenty will still be in solid shape. The rest will have simply withered away. And another century after that the world may be down to three or four superpower languages and a handful more that have simply refused to die.

Arabic is one of the Big Twenty. It's spoken by almost two hundred million people in more than twenty-two countries, though it has separated into a number of dialects that vary greatly from nation to nation. The Arabic spoken in Morocco, for example, is virtually incomprehensible to Saudis.

The written language is the same, however, and that's what anchors everything. The Quran retains the seventh-century Arabic script of Muhammad, and according to Islamic thought, it simply can't be translated without losing something. The sacred book of Islam can only be read in the original Arabic. Even in

Muslim countries such as Malaysia and Pakistan where Arabic isn't spoken, the faithful must learn the old Arabic. The Quran can't be reproduced in Malay or Urdu. Something of the nuance would be lost, it's claimed, or something of its power — a very interesting idea indeed.

Of course, one can translate even the most complex of ideas from one language into another. That's a fact. But it's true that something more subtle might well be lost. Imagine William Shakespeare translated into Chinese. The plot would certainly remain, but the colour of Shakespeare's words, the very thing that gives them their beauty, their identity, would surely be lost.

The Christian world, however, freely translates the Bible. Some factions even pride themselves on how many languages they've translated it into — Swahili and Blackfoot, Finnish and Korean. But for me the colour of the Bible is always in the *thees* and *begats* of the King James Version. "Thou shalt be scattered over the face of the Earth" — there's a certain power in that kind of voice, a terrible magic. It's so powerful that it's easy to get confused and imagine that the original texts must have sounded like that. The original Hebrew, Greek, or Aramaic must somehow have had that sort of flavour. But did they?

In the Quran there's no doubt. That book sings only in Arabic.

ع

I'd been staying for a week in a dirty little pension in the Armenian quarter of Jerusalem. I shared a room with Arno and Berhitte, a Dutch couple. Arno fancied himself a photographer. One day he took three hundred pictures. We would go our separate ways, and in the evening we'd meet for beer and discuss our photographic exploits, each trying to outdo the other.

One afternoon, knowing full well I could challenge Arno with the adventure, I climbed a wall in the Arab quarter. I'd seen some Israeli soldiers sitting on the edge of a roof. They were watching

19

the crowds below, and I figured if I climbed the wall and stuck my head above the far side of the roof they were on, I could get a great shot of them silhouetted against the Dome of the Rock.

I figured out all the angles and scampered up for the shot. It's only now, in retrospect, that I realize how foolish I was. Sneaking up on two soldiers armed with machine guns isn't a smart thing to do. But I went, anyway, and snapped the photo without the pair ever realizing I was there. I still think about it. What if a chunk of rock had broken off under my feet? What if I had startled them? Sometimes, I guess, you think that because you're a tourist, you're bulletproof and not really part of what's going on.

One evening, poring over maps with Arno and Berhitte, we came up with our craziest escapade. We decided to tunnel under Jerusalem. That's not as daft as it sounds — a tunnel really does exist. There aren't many references to it, but we managed to find it. We were going to go through Hezekial's Tunnel.

Okay, I thought, *here we go.* It was a sort of metaphor for the whole trip. A tunnel, all Freudian analysis aside, is a dark place through which one emerges into the light. The real Hezekial's Tunnel begins at a pool of water, and it was there, at that pool, that Jesus is said to have washed the eyes of a blind man and made him see again. That's the metaphor exactly: to come through the tunnel into the light, to see clearly, to understand.

In King Hezekial's time the water supply of Jerusalem was outside the city walls. No river runs through Jerusalem and never has. Instead, the first settlements were built around a little artesian well, a pool of water that has bubbled faithfully up from the ground throughout the long years of the city's existence.

Now, when King Hezekial got word that an Assyrian army was advancing on his city, he wisely ordained that a tunnel should be built to bring water to a reservoir inside the walls. Work on the tunnel commenced. One party dug in from the pool, while another dug out from inside the city walls. And almost thirty centuries ago water flowed through the tunnel for the first time, the Assyrians were thwarted, and Jerusalem, the city of peace, survived to live another day.

The tunnel is still there, carrying a stream of water through its dark shaft. Outside St. Stephen's Gate an unmarked path winds down into a valley. Arno, Birhitte, and I descended it wordlessly, and at the bottom of the path, still within sight of the city walls, we saw an unremarkable concrete building. Inside it was the ancient spring.

There, too, a group of young Palestinian boys appeared from nowhere and began pulling at our sleeves. "You go? You go?" They held flashlights so that we knew we had reached the place. Hezekial's Tunnel starts at the bottom of a decrepit set of concrete stairs, and the boys' faces quickly reflected disappointment when we declared forcefully that we would go through it without guides.

Berhitte, though, took one look at the pitch-black entrance and chickened out. She couldn't do it, she said. Too claustrophobic. Big Arno glanced at her sheepishly. I'd like to think he was feeling a little doubtful himself. "Berhitte," he said, "I can't leave you here by yourself. It's not safe." He was probably right. I'd already seen one young woman being followed ominously by a man with less than honourable intentions. The tunnel's entrance wasn't a safe place for a lone woman. Arno shrugged and said to me, "I can't leave her alone."

"It's okay," I said. "I'll do it myself."

"You are sure?"

For a moment I, too, was unsure. I hadn't really planned on going solo, but there I was and there it was.

Berhitte and Arno said they'd meet me at the other end, and I ventured forward into the water, switching on my flashlight. The boys were still calling, their voices echoing in the darkness. Within a few steps the water was around my knees, gurgling and splashing as it has for three thousand years. The stone resembled unpolished marble, and the thin lance of my flashlight swept over rock that was a gentle pink like the hue of a seashell's interior.

I could see how the tunnel was carved out by hand chisels. The marks were still visible in the rock, and again I wondered how anyone could possibly have managed the feat. The water was crystal-clear, and the only sound was my own breathing and the slosh of my two pale legs, diffracted and determinedly striding beneath the surface. Literally, I was tunnelling through history, plunging deep below the meaning-heavy city above.

At first the ceiling was a full metre over my head, and I could extend both arms and touch the walls on either side. Farther into the tunnel the walls began to squeeze in and the roof descended. Then, of course, the water was forced higher, and I had to crouch with only my head and shoulders and desperately precious flashlight free of the flowing stream.

Somewhere above Christ had been crucified. Somewhere above Muhammad had ascended to heaven on a silvery steed. The tunnel stretched on, seemingly winding and bending toward the very roots of the world.

In time I came to the point where the two parties of diggers had met all those years ago. There was once an inscription here in archaic Hebrew. It had read simply: BEHOLD ... THE EXCAVATION.

I continued on, a heartbeat from panic, knowing there were hundreds of tonnes of rock overhead. Hurrying, I tipped my flashlight occasionally to see if something was in the water. I didn't know what I expected to see lurking in the depths — perhaps something unknown and terrifying, something scuttling along the bottom in the murk.

There were also rumbles several times as if the earth was still settling around me. I hustled a bit more, jittery at the thought of being trapped in a cave-in. The thundering, I rationalized later, must have been the noise of trucks passing overhead — either that or more jets breaking the sound barrier.

Finally, the tunnel started to weave back and forth, and it seemed that the ceiling was growing higher. I turned another bend and heard a voice calling. It was indistinct, but I had little choice but to forge toward it. Then I realized my name was being shouted. It was Berhitte. She was quite worried. I'd been underground for maybe forty-five minutes. Her voice became louder until all at once I emerged at the Pool of Siloah and into the light.

A gang of boys was there, as well, but they were older than those at the entrance. They offered to take my picture as I arrived, but I didn't trust them with my camera. These boys had a menacing air, laughed at my soaked T-shirt, and probably wondered why anyone would want to clamber through a three-thousand-year-old tunnel.

I shook them off, and Arno slapped my back and grinned. Together we three trudged back up to re-enter Jerusalem by the Dung Gate, which was given its unpleasant name because ancient villagers had once tossed their refuse there.

Today the Dung Gate leads into one of the most famous of all the sites of Jerusalem. In my wet clothes I was alarmingly out of place among the long white beards and black robes rocking gently in prayer. Directly in front was the legendary Wailing Wall.

23

뎌

A few hundred metres away, in the Arab quarter, one is greeted with *"Salam aleikum,"* but at the Wailing Wall only Hebrew is heard, and for Israelis the salutation is that most Jewish of words — *shalom.*

Salam, shalom — they are brother words from an ancient Semitic root. The name of the city, Jerusalem, literally means City of Peace. Now there's a misnomer.

In 1947, when the United Nations mandated Israel into existence, a number of things happened with amazing speed. A war broke out, of course, but also the beginnings of a most remarkable language story occurred. Across Central and Eastern Europe a Jewish language, Yiddish, had already been in place for hundreds of years. For a while it was assumed Yiddish would become the official tongue of the new Israel. In those heady early days it was even proposed that Albert Einstein should become the first prime minister. Neither of these two things came to pass.

Yiddish is a Germanic language related to Old German with a smattering of Slavic thrown in. We know Yiddish for such words as *putz*, *verklemmt*, and *schmooze*, which evoke something of the world of those lost northern Jews, a hint of the colour, rhythm, and humour of their lives.

During the Holocaust, several million Yiddish speakers perished, and the language has never fully recovered. So in 1948, in one of the first sessions of the new Israeli parliament, a most extraordinary decision was made: the official language of the new state would be Hebrew. However, for almost two thousand years hardly a living soul had spoken that language in everyday situations. It's true that Hebrew was well-known in its biblical context, but for people on the street it had about as much use as Latin. That meant it was a fossil language, a remnant of a long-ago time.

Nevertheless, the movement to revive Hebrew has been incredibly successful in Israel. In fact, even before the United Nations mandate, groups of people had been working on adapting Classical Hebrew to the twentieth century. They certainly had some problems describing technology. Bicycles, for example, are most definitely not mentioned in the Torah. And how about airplanes?

To deal with such modern inventions, Hebrew has adopted the word מטוס, written in the Roman alphabet as *matos*. The root *ma* basically means "a tool." If we attach it to the verb *to move* (pronounced *lanor*), we get the word for machine (*manor*), and if we wed it with the verb *to fly* (*latus*), we wind up with *matos*, or *airplane*.

Languages are pliable entities. They're infinitely creative in their solutions to problems such as dealing with new ideas and new ways of thinking. Hebrew is a perfect example. Resurrected when it was all but extinct, it's now spoken as a mother tongue by nearly six million people. Remarkable.

One reason for the success of today's Hebrew is that the flood of Jewish immigrants to Israel hailed from many different language groups — a sort of Tower of Babel in reverse. Moreover, while the choice of Hebrew as the official language was initiated by the Israeli government, it was the heartfelt choice of the people, as well. The language is as intimately linked to the Jewish religion as Arabic is to Islam, and therefore it became one's duty to learn Hebrew and to pass it on to children, not only as a language of religion but as the language employed for all things.

So for me this story is one of the most powerful of all in the annals of language. It is the one and only time in history that a language has been successfully resurrected from the dead, not just as a museum piece but as a fully functioning modern tongue.

Ω

25

In West Jerusalem, the new city, there's a museum that holds the Dead Sea Scrolls. When I went to see them, I merged behind a group of people on a tour. Not that I like organized tours. It was just a cheap way of getting a free guided commentary.

The little guide was a passionate fellow, and at one point we stood in front of a large fragment of the Scrolls. Most of the group's members were Israeli, I think, and could read ancient Hebrew. The guide told us to go ahead and read the fragment, and I studied it solemnly as if I could actually decipher it.

"What is this text?" he finally asked after a few moments of silence. Some keener in the crowd said it was from Isaiah, and the guide beamed. "That's right. This piece of sheepskin is two thousand years old. It's almost a thousand years older than any previously known copy of the Book of Isaiah. And what do you notice about it?"

Again I stood shamefaced, hoping the guide wouldn't notice I didn't have a clue. Those around me seemed a bit confused, as well. "Do you remember," he continued, "when you were children and played the whispering game?"

The whispering game?

"Yes, where children get in a line and the teacher gives something to whisper in the ear of the first. That first child whispers to the next and then that one to the next. The fun is when you see how much it changes. 'I want French perfume for my birthday' eventually becomes 'I wore frog pajamas that burned my dog.' Now what do you notice here?" His hand swept over the glass-enclosed manuscript. He paused dramatically, then answered himself. "There's no change. Two thousand years of copying and there's no change at all. Look, you can read it yourself."

The first Dead Sea Scrolls were discovered by a Bedouin shepherd named Muhammad Ahmed el-Hamed. One of his goats climbed into a cave along the Dead Sea to escape the searing heat, and he picked up a rock and threw it in to get the animal out. When he tossed in the stone, he heard the tinkle of pottery breaking. Up there in the caves he found the Scrolls hidden in ceramic jars. This, our guide told us, happened on the same day the United Nations created the State of Israel. "Now you can believe whatever you want about such a coincidence," he said, "but I know what I believe."

Φ

My last day in Jerusalem was a Friday which, as it happens, is when Franciscan monks walk in procession down the Via Dolorosa, the Way of Sorrows. Arno and I got our cameras ready, Berhitte sighed, and off we went.

The winding path of the Via Dolorosa leads from the Temple Mount to a Crusader church built over the site where it's thought Christ was crucified. On July 15, 1099, the knights of the First Crusade entered Jerusalem and slaughtered almost all of the inhabitants. Forty thousand people, Jews and Muslims alike, were cut down until the streets were knee-deep in blood. And then the Crusasders built the Church of the Holy Sepulchre over the place where Christ was said to have died for humanity's sins — one more profoundly ironic bit of history in Jerusalem where meanings easily become tangled, where belief sometimes obscures reality.

There are some wonderful accounts of the Muslim reaction to this First Crusade. There was a sense of confusion and dismay. The city had been open to everyone and was peaceful for five hundred years. One Muslim writer, in an attempt to make sense of these acts of barbarism, set out to understand what had happened, so he read the Christian books. In Islam, of course, there's only one god, but in reading about the Holy Trinity, it seemed to him that the Crusaders worshipped three divinities: a father, a son, and a holy ghost. Moreover, Christians appeared to cannibalize their god — eating his body and drinking his blood. To top it off, this same god created his own mother who then created him ... immaculately. No wonder the scholar was confused. All of this demonstrates how difficult it is to truly understand the nuances of another culture. It doesn't help, either, when that new culture is intent on slaughtering you and all of your family.

27

The Church of the Holy Sepulchre is somewhat gaudy, which I admit is a terrible pun, but it's true. The building is ornate to a fault and is run by six different sects, which is a big problem. The different sects are often not on speaking terms, and the church is strictly divided into areas of influence. Changing a light bulb or even moving a carpet a few centimetres can spark fistfights between monks from the different groups. Up on the roof, out of the fray, is the Ethiopian sect. It laid claim to the top of the church and has, in fact, lived in crumbling wooden shacks on the roof for more than a hundred years.

Christ himself spoke a language called Aramaic. It's neither Hebrew nor Arabic but a cousin of the two. *Salam* in Aramaic, for example, is *shela'm* (the apostrophe denotes a glottal stop, a sort of gulping pop of breath). Aramaic began as a pidgin language in the Middle East a few hundred years before Christ and had become the standard tongue in Jerusalem by the first century of the current era.

On the main floor of the Church of the Holy Sepulchre is a little grotto. Visitors line up to go into it because only a half-dozen people can fit at a time. It was dark when I entered. Candles flickered in the shadows, and an old priest, Greek Orthodox by the look of his clothes, stood guard. Behind him was a small rocky space, smooth with all the hands that have reached out for it. It is said to be the tomb of Christ. I waited for a moment, hoping for a revelation. I waited for the light of understanding to hit me, but there was nothing. Not for me at least. I still couldn't feel a thing.

Later that same afternoon, sick of the crowds, dirt, and heat, I went for a walk outside the old city walls. There, up ahead, was a garden, almost a park. I could see the tree branches poking above the dusty walls, and in this desert land I was drawn toward the greenery. The only problem was that an old nun was standing at the gate. What belief system was she going to foist on me? I wondered. I walked up, still desperate to sit among the flowers, and she smiled and simply said, "Welcome." That was it. I actually hesitated, expecting her to say more. Didn't she want to ask if I'd found Jesus in my heart? Didn't she want to tell me that fire and brimstone would rain down on me for eternity?

Well, apparently, she didn't. She invited me in with a graceful movement of her hand, didn't say another word, and continued to smile.

The place is called the Garden Tomb. Charles Gordon, a British general, discovered it in 1883. He had come to Jerusalem with some doubts about the true location of the religious sites. Golgotha, in ancient Hebrew, means "place of the skull," and Gordon couldn't help but notice a strange rock formation outside the old walls several hundred metres from the Church of the Holy Sepulchre. And here, in the Garden Tomb, I saw it, too. On a little rise there is a tumble of rocks and a crevice that looks like the eye sockets and jawbone of a skull. At the bottom there is, indeed, another small tomb carved out of the rock. There is no church here, only a garden, but of all my time in Jerusalem, this was the first occasion I actually felt something click. That was what I'd been waiting for. Not enough to make me become celibate perhaps. Not enough to inspire me to wander into the desert for forty days and forty nights. But there it was.

Something, finally, had touched me. For all the anger and turmoil of this holy city, for all its guns and wars and violence, for all its crowded, desperate clawing for territory, there is something grand here. Something like the sense of wonder a child feels gazing into a starry sky for the first time. Jerusalem really is like no other place on the planet. Elie Wiesel, the writer, survivor of the Holocaust, and Nobel Prize laureate, said: "You don't go to Jerusalem. You return to it."

That means, I guess, a part of us has always been there. Metaphorically, at least, our hearts are all in the same place, and though we've been "scattered across the face of the Earth," though our languages have been "confused" so that we can no longer understand one another, we need to find our way back. We need to understand one another again. We need to start building a new Tower of Babel.

29

2

At the Gates of the Western World

I got on the wrong bus. All the signs were in Greek, and the lettering was indecipherable to me. Ironic, considering that the Greek letters *alpha* and *beta* make up the English word *alphabet*. In Hebrew they are *aleph* and *bet*; in Arabic *alif* and *ba*. It didn't make any difference, though. I couldn't read any of it.

When I bought a ticket to Athens, the man in the booth waved me generally in the direction of a row of buses behind him. I hoisted my backpack and trudged toward them, squinting at the cardboard signs displayed on their windshields. Finally, after a little deliberation, I got on the bus whose sign read: Δελφοί. As it turned out, I should have gotten on the one that read: Αθηνα.

I tried to check that I had the right bus, but when I asked the driver, I got completely confused. To say *yes* in Greek, one says *né*, which to me sounded a lot like *no*. And to further complicate matters, *no* in Greek is *okhi*, which sounds suspiciously like *okay*. So when I asked the driver if his bus was going to Athens, he said, "Okay," and waved his head at me.

After I climbed on, we took off in approximately the right direction. It wasn't until we'd been travelling for an hour that I knew something was wrong. We came to a broad stretch of water, and I was pretty sure we weren't supposed to be crossing anything like that. With a sinking heart I glanced around the bus for someone who might speak English. I found a middle-aged woman from France. "But, of course, we're not going to Athens," she said. "Unless you want to go the long way." She laughed cruelly. "*Mais oui* ... a very, very long way."

I sat with her, anyway. For an hour or two she lectured me on the geometric period in ancient Greek pottery shards, often breaking into French when her English wouldn't do. It turned out she was a professor in Paris and looked down on the world over a long, aquiline nose. I tried to keep up, but mostly it was beyond me. Our bus puttered into the green mountains past almond trees and olive groves until we stopped at a little town on the edge of the Gulf of Corinth. We had arrived at Itea, just down from Δελφοί, or what turned out to be the legendary ruins of Delphi.

Back behind the town a huge mountain, Parnassus, reared up, and we waited a while for the connecting bus that would carry us to a natural amphitheatre in the rock that held Delphi, home of the legendary Oracle.

Delphi is where the human world touches the divine. Zeus, it is said, released two golden eagles. One flew west and the other soared eastward. They circled the globe, and where they met again was Delphi, the centre of the world, the navel of the universe.

I had come to Greece to search for beginnings, so perhaps I hadn't made a mistake getting on that bus, after all. Maybe it was fate, since there was little doubt that I had come to the right place.

Ψ

No one really knows how languages began. Somewhere in the primordial jungle a system of sounds developed. A particular shout, "yeeee," for example, might have alerted our ancestors to a predator that was on its way, while another, "yaaaa," might have told them that a snake was coiled in a tree. And that, in a nutshell, is what language is: a random set of sounds to which we've affixed meanings. Simple as pie.

Languages developed almost organically, so much so that we can talk about them in terms of families. We can build the lineages for most of them, tracing their relationships and their roots farther back than one might think. Joseph Greenberg, one of the grand old masters of linguistics, hypothesized a proto-language for the Earth's tongues. By reverse engineering from a mountain of data, he and his colleagues came up with a list of twenty-seven words from this presumed initial language.

The sniffing out of bloodlines, a favourite pastime of linguists, is usually based on the study of cognates, which are similar-sounding root words in different languages. *Salam* in Arabic and *shalom* in Hebrew are good examples and clearly demonstrate a common ancestry. Cognates, typically, tend to show up in the roots of the most basic concepts: kin relationships such as mother, brother, sister, father; and words for the most fundamental descriptions of nature — hand, bird, cat, tree.

Greenberg's team hunted for cognates that would pertain to every language on the planet. *Tik*, for example, is what Greenberg claims is the first word for *finger*. It's *daktulos* in Greek and *digitus* in Latin. These come to us in the English form *digit* (and from that, *digital*), and that's how cognates tend to work. Languages tumble around, swapping, quite predictably, a *t* for a *d*, or a *b* for the pop of a *p*. Phonetic changes over time, in fact, are so predictable that they provide a sort of carbon-dating for languages.

We can tell fairly accurately when Old English split from High German. We can surmise when Norwegian diverged from Icelandic and when Portuguese hived off from Spanish. Greenberg simply pushed this research as far as he could. Some say he shoved it too far. While claiming that he had found cognates for the word *finger* across all of the language families, he also posited as many related concepts as he could imagine. For example, if he didn't find the word for *finger*, he would look at the words for *hand* or *thumb*, or in quite a lot of cases, the number *one*, which according to him is described in most languages by holding up a single finger.

Greenberg's theories are highly controversial, and talk of a single proto-language is largely downplayed in academic circles today. In fact, most linguists find it a load of bunk. It was a brave idea and obviously a hell of a lot of work, but unfortunately the truth probably leans more toward the opposite dynamic. Whereas there are now some six thousand languages spoken on Earth, chances are there were as many as fifteen thousand before written language appeared. So the languages we speak today aren't the result of a Tower of Babel phenomenon. They probably didn't all come from a single source. More likely, a multitude of languages sprang up around the same time independent of one another, and today, sadly, most of them have already disappeared.

ξ

The French professor and I strolled to a little hostel that had staggering views over the Gulf of Corinth. She was put into a room with Chantal and Valérie, two young women who also spoke French. As it turned out, they were from Quebec, my country … more or less. I was in the next room, and the girls soon escaped the professor's dry lectures and found their way over to my balcony. A couple of cheap bottles of Greek wine appeared, and far from home we talked about Canada.

Chantal and Valérie were from Quebec City, though Chantal had born in the Province of Quebec's Eastern Townships. She was from the little town of Notre-Dame-du-Portage, which has, she insisted, one of the most beautiful sunsets in the world. The sun dips into the wide St. Lawrence River, and the colours, she told me, are *magnifique.*

Valérie pursed her lips in agreement, and I couldn't help but remember a woman I once worked with. This woman always claimed that before she spoke French she had to make her face "go French." It sounds ridiculous, but there's actually something to her contention. Speaking a language is a whole way of being. You can feel it in the very sounds of the words (French, phonetically, tends to be a bit more forward in the mouth than English). And that's even before you get to the meanings, the ways languages describe the world. Languages are direct reflections of ourselves. We think in them. We dream in them. We exist in them.

I could come at language from a linguistic point of view. I could describe noun clauses and verb stems, but I didn't live the language the way Chantal and Valérie did. Chantal shook her head at me. "You don't understand. You see French on your cornflakes."

"My cornflakes?"

"Yes. You see the French. On the box. The translation. But you don't really understand."

"That's true," I said, sloshing some wine onto the floor of the balcony.

Chantal tugged at her floppy woollen hat and smiled. She saw that I at least understood that, even if I could speak a few words of a language, I didn't know what it was like to be "in" that language … to live it. And that, for Chantal and Valérie, was a start.

ꓭ

I spent the next few days with Chantal and Valérie, traipsing around the ruins of Delphi. The most famous one is the Temple of Apollo. It lies halfway up a cliff, and in a little grotto at its foot there once sat the famous Oracle. The Oracle was always a woman, and it's generally agreed that there must have been some fissure in the rock that leaked a kind of gas that put the Oracle into her trance. An earthquake closed up the whole thing a thousand years ago, but scientists now say it was methane gas with traces of ethylene. Essentially, the poor woman was sniffing a hallucinogen.

In ancient times the Oracle's ruminations were considered the height of wisdom. Pilgrims came from distant lands to ask questions. The Oracle's answers, of course, were enigmatic, but there were legions of priests on hand to interpret them. Monarchs and emperors frequently sought advice, and one of the many famous tales is that of King Croesus of Asia Minor. He was set to attack Persia and asked the Oracle if he would be victorious.

In her gas-induced trance the Oracle answered that once Croesus crossed the river a great empire would fall. The king understood this to mean that once his troops crossed the Euphrates River into what was then Persia, victory would indeed be his. Unfortunately, the reverse was true, and he suffered a devastating defeat. Years later the broken king returned to Delphi to pose a second question. "Why didn't you tell me the truth?" he cried.

"I did," the Oracle said. "The great empire that fell was your own."

Ω

When we approached the Temple of Apollo, we looked around, but I couldn't see either a grotto or a fissure. They had long ago disappeared. As we wandered around, we were caught in a sudden cloudburst and got soaked to the skin. The temple is only one of many on the hill, and we still had a long way to walk. Chantal glanced at her watch. "The time is short."

"Sounds like something the Oracle might say," I ventured.

"Are you having fun with my English?" Chantal looked at me sternly from beneath her floppy hat.

"No, no … your English is a hell of a lot better than my French."

"That's right," she said. "A hell."

Later, ploughing wetly back to our hostel, we spotted something bizarre. A single black cloud clung to the top of the cliff. It broiled darkly and was lit up repeatedly by small explosions of sheet lightning.

"Look," Valérie said, "do you think we've angered the Oracle?"

I snickered. "Do you think she's mad about the 'time is short' thing?"

"Don't laugh about these things." Chantal was serious. Time wasn't something to be messed with.

Φ

The family groupings of European languages are well understood. That's no surprise. Until recently, most linguists have been English, American, German, or French, and they've been more interested, of course, in how their own languages evolved. Still, over the years, Western linguists have discovered a lot more than they bargained for.

In 1786 Sir William Jones, a British judge and scholar working in India, noticed strange resemblances between Latin and ancient Sanskrit. Like Greenberg, Jones began matching up cognates. Some were fairly obvious like the Sanskrit word for *king* — *raj*. In English we have the cognates *regent* and *royal*, both deriving from the Latin *regina*. There's also the Latin *diva*, meaning "god," from which we get the word *divine*.

However, my all-time favourite cognate is *Buddha*. It stems from Pali, a dialect of ancient Sanskrit, and literally means "to awake." But the only tattered remnant we have of this particular cognate, in English at least, is the word *bed*. It's amazing how a concept can take different directions. I'm even tempted to say that a culture gets what it deserves. While the ancient wise men of India and the Far East became enlightened, well, we were ... sleeping.

Sanskrit was the language of the ancient Hindu and Buddhist texts and spread its wings across most of Asia. It spawned languages such as Hindi, Punjabi, the Urdu of Pakistan, Bengali, Kurdish, and Persian ... and the list goes on and on. All of these languages seemed to have a common ancestor, the same as European tongues. The evidence this time was simply overwhelming. We now believe that this ancestor language, what today is unimaginatively called Proto Indo-European, was spoken about five thousand years ago by a small band of hunter-gatherers. By an incredible fluke of history, it survived, prospered, and spread even as countless languages around it died out.

More recently the search for this ancient and unwritten Proto Indo-European language has become even more focused. Among the cognates for animals and trees there are only a few that run through all of the hundreds of languages descended from Proto Indo-European. *Salmon* is one. The cognate here is actually *lok*. The Old English is *leax* from which we derive just *lake*. German has *lachs* and Yiddish, of course, has *lox*. The Greek is σολομός or *solomos* where you can find both the English *salmon* and an appendage of the old root word in the middle syllable: *lo*.

The only other cognate that features in all Indo-European languages is the word for beech tree. With a little insight it was realized that Proto Indo-European must have arisen among a people who lived on the banks of a salmon-spawning river in an area where beeches grew. This observation narrowed the search to the plains of what is now eastern Germany and Poland. There a small tribe of wanderers spoke a tongue that forms the basis for the languages of more than two billion people today, about one-third of the Earth's population.

$$\Psi$$

Have I mentioned hell journeys? Have I referred to marathons in cramped buses sitting squeezed and stiff for ten or twelve long, impossible hours? Sometimes there's no other way to get where you're going. In this case I was headed into the northern reaches of Greece. I'd already veered off track, and there was one thing up there that I thought I might as well see.

I'd been on the road for a full day already when I tucked into the city of Thessaloniki. From there I should have had a short jaunt over the border and into Turkey, but it wasn't that easy.

Greeks and Turks hate each other passionately. The Greeks on their side of the border warn travellers not to venture into Turkey. "They eat babies over there," they say. "Don't go. It's terrible." On the Turkish side, meanwhile, they say much the same thing. "What do you want to go there for? They're monsters ... horrible, horrible."

Such antipathy no doubt dates back to the Turkish occupation of Greece for hundreds of years, but the discord really heated up in the 1920s when the present borders between the countries were set. Vast numbers of both populations were forced to relocate, sometimes leaving the places their families had lived in for centuries. There were tens of thousands of deaths, and what happened then hasn't been forgotten by either side.

I arrived in Thessaloniki in time to learn that I had missed the sole train across the border. There was only one other option — a bus that departed from the train station at three in the morning. This seemed to be typical: you could travel from one country to the other, but it would be as inconvenient as possible.

After idling away the rest of the day, I tried to sleep, and when I finally got to the bus at the ungodly hour of a quarter to three in the morning, I discovered it was pretty much full. There were no tourists here. Most of the people appeared to be local. This was a chicken-on-your-lap bus. Everyone glanced at me as I got on, wielding my backpack as I buffaloed down the aisle. Their eyes followed me to see what I would do, since it was apparent there was only one place free. A small space was vacant on a bench near the back, but the other person sitting there was one of the largest human beings I'd ever seen, and I don't mean he was fat. This guy was African, well over two metres tall, at least one hundred and forty kilograms of muscle, and was draped in gold chains. I shuffled in beside him, and every head in the bus swivelled to see what would happen next.

"How do you do?" the huge man asked. His hand enveloped mine, and I shook it.

"Uh … I'm okay. How are you?"

"I'm fine, thank you. My name's Cole."

Cole was from Nigeria and turned out to be exceptionally polite. He was soft-spoken and remarkably thoughtful. In fact, he had just finished his Ph.D. in economics at the University of Athens. He talked a lot about his own country. Nigeria had a lot of oil, he said, but nasty things were occurring there, and he fervently hoped he could put his education to use to help the nation extricate itself from corruption and dictatorship. "Two hundred languages are spoken in Nigeria," he told me. "Did you know that?"

"Is that right?"

"I'm afraid it is. We're a divided community, sometimes quite fiercely."

We talked until just before dawn and then I slept a little, huddled into my corner of the seat. The bus stopped often, and most of the passengers got off at little towns before the Turkish frontier. When we arrived at the border, a full twelve hours later, Cole and I were almost alone on the bus.

Cole was travelling on to Istanbul, but I planned to head south along the coastline. He had a bit of time, though, and walked with me to the next bus. It was kind of fun striding through the streets with this towering giant. I was in a country once more where the shopkeepers were quite persistent, always trying to bully tourists into their stores. They didn't bother us, however. The hawkers shrank into their doorways, faces pale and alarmed. At my next bus I said goodbye to Cole, shook his massive hand, and wished him well on his return to Nigeria.

ξ

Besides the Indo-European family of languages, there are at least a couple of dozen other groupings. Most of the languages in Nigeria, for instance, are part of a family called Niger-Kordofanian. The Sino-Tibetan languages, which include Mandarin and all other Chinese dialects, boast about a billion speakers.

Most of the language families, though, are much smaller, such as Uralic, which includes a pocket of languages — Estonian, Finnish, and Hungarian — that are European but not Indo-European. There are oddities such as Khoison, which features the clicking languages — the !Kung of the Kalahari Desert's Bushmen, for example — but the real peculiarities of the linguistic world are the isolate languages. There are only a few of them, perhaps a hundred or so, and they exist completely by themselves. As far as anyone can tell, these isolate languages aren't related to any other languages on the planet.

Of course, all this categorization of languages is a bit academic. The fact is that one can make a very good case, and some philosophers have, that languages don't really exist at all. A language, quipped the linguist Max Weinreich, is only a dialect with an army and a navy. And he was correct. Languages shade into one another subtly. There are rainbows of dialects, and when one rises to take precedence, when one is called a language and the rest are termed dialects, well, that's often a political distinction more than a linguistic classification.

ᐱ

On a nameless hill, on a long anonymous plain, stands the broken city of Troy. There's not much to see, just a few leaning rock walls and a couple of archaeological trenches, but this literally, figuratively, and chronologically is the beginning of the Western world.

I had always wanted to visit Troy. So, with a dog-eared copy of Homer in my backpack, I slipped across the Dardanelles into what is now Turkish territory. The sea today is far away, the land having silted up over the millennia. Gazing across a long plain of grass with an old broken wall slightly angled, just as the mighty walls of Troy had been described in *The Iliad*, I knew that from these battlements a war had indeed been waged circa twelfth century B.C.

Travelling home from this war was Odysseus. I've always considered his exploits, as recounted in Homer's other great epic, *The Odyssey*, to be the first real travel writing. In Latin he is Ulysses because, of course, the Romans later appropriated everything that was great about Greece. Even the name Homer is actually a Latin derivative. The name in Greek is Omeris.

Here, in the ancient tongue of the Greeks, is a whopping good story of love and misfortune, of adventure and endless travel. "Sing to me," Homer began, "of the man ... the wanderer. Under the wide ways of earth, caught in the teeth of the gods." The translation I have is by Robert Fitzgerald, my favourite, because it rings and strides like William Shakespeare. Read aloud around a flickering campfire, it booms and thunders like a war drum. "Of mortal creatures, all who breathe and crawl ... the earth bears none frailer than man."

I love that stuff. It's still some of the finest writing I've ever come across, except that in reality Homer never wrote it at all. He was illiterate, if indeed there was a man named Homer at all. The fact is that whoever came up with these tales couldn't actually read a thing. *The Iliad* and *The Odyssey* are oral texts — remembered stories with all the colour and tangle of the spoken word.

This then is the borderline between oral and written cultures. We've been speaking languages for perhaps a hundred thousand years, but the writing down of them is relatively recent. Starting about five thousand years ago, we made lists of things, and around the time of Homer (sometime in the ninth century B.C.) written words began recounting the great stories.

It's important to remember that languages, in essence, are merely arbitrary sounds to which we've attached meanings. With writing we took everything a step farther. We assigned random marks to these arbitrary sounds. But it all made sense. It was a way of encoding the world. It was a meaning system we had been working on for a very long time.

Scholars are divided about how Homer's words found their way into print, how they at last became a written reality. Some say Homer, or someone else, dictated *The Iliad* and *The Odyssey* to a scribe. Others speculate that the stories were passed down orally with a few changes here and there for many more generations until they finally settled into their accepted texts. By the sixth century B.C., it's certain *The Iliad* and *The Odyssey* had become the central books of ancient Greece — and by extension of our modern world.

Homer's telling of the tales probably took place over many nights and numerous cups of wine. The storyteller might have accompanied himself on a stringed instrument, tweaking at the hearts of listeners with a swell of chord and melody. But what's really important here is that somehow, somewhere, someone began to write it all down. The earliest Greek texts had lines that wove down the page. The first line was read left to right, as you're reading this, but then the line after that would be read right to left, as in Arabic or Hebrew, so that the eye literally zigzagged down the page. And though this at first seems absurd, at least one modern theorist has wondered why this manner of reading and printing never caught on. It really does seem to make much more sense.

At any rate, none of that really matters. What's important is that someone wrote the stories down. Writing crystallizes language. It catches it, holding it like an insect in a fossilized drop of amber.

And now here I was, almost three thousand years later, taking in something Homer himself had never actually seen. I wondered how a blind man could have been so precise with his descriptions. Scratching my own poor stories onto paper, I'm still humbled and inspired by his eloquence.

Ω

For the next four weeks I followed Homer's sweet trail of words back into Greece. I plunged into his wine-dark seas. I slept on the deck of a half-dozen rusting and anonymous ferries, chugging southward from island to island across the placid Aegean Sea, and whenever I could I read a line in *The Odyssey* and came upon the very real place being described.

On Crete I hiked up to the ancient ruins of Knossos. Odysseus brushed past here on his way to the Land of the Lotus Eaters. Knossos is a Minoan palace a thousand years older than classical Greek civilization. It has been largely reconstructed by a French archaeological team, and walking around its ruins, I could feel how impressive it must have once been.

Here one of the very earliest writing systems was unearthed. The Linear B script was discovered on a number of broken clay tablets, but it wasn't until 1953 that it was finally deciphered. The script is a form of archaic Greek dialect and is based mostly on syllabic signs, a fair number of logograms (where a single symbol represents a whole word), and a base ten number system, the forerunner of our own mathematics. Most of the tablets are simply lists, a kind of accounting of tools, animals, and materials, but they provided the basis for the written language to come. The letters would soon relax and blossom into the call of Sirens and Cyclops, and over time would record the tale of Odysseus, shining among the deathless gods, sailing to his one true love on the distant shores of Ithaca.

Φ

The south coast of Crete faces Africa. A dusty bus ride gets you there — eventually. Over the backbone of the island I bounced along, heading for a little seaside village named Matala.

In the 1960s, Matala was on the hippie trail. Jimi Hendrix came through here. Cat Stevens stopped by on his way to India. Joni Mitchell lived in one of the caves in the cliffs. Nowadays police sweep through the caves in the evening and eject anybody trying to recapture their youth. The caves are ancient Minoan tombs and stare down over a bright beach, flooded during the day with travellers. I met no one here except for a bedraggled, eccentric old woman. She was from Germany originally, she said, but had lived in Greece for years. The woman cackled, hacked, and told me about the bonfires that used to roar on the beach decades ago. She spoke about the young men with their guitars, about their long hair and their dreams, and the crashing surf that comes in from Africa.

So one dark night, under the starry dome, I went down to sit on the beach. Far off in front of me were the coasts of Egypt and Tunisia. This was the end of the known world for ancient Greek wayfarers. Beyond this was only the strange, the curious mention of elephants, and spices.

I sat on the cool sand and thought about the Rosetta stone, which was used to first decode ancient Egyptian hieroglyphics. They hadn't been read for a couple of thousand years, but when the Rosetta stone was unearthed by a troop of Napoleon's soldiers in the dunes along the Nile River, it was immediately recognized as the needed missing linguistic link.

The Rosetta stone is just a big flat rock with inscriptions describing the coronation of Pharaoh Ptolemy V. The uppermost lines are unreadable hieroglyphics. The middle lines are demotic (a cursive form of glyphs and a forerunner to Arabic), and the bottom lines are Greek. There were plenty of scholars who could translate the ancient Greek, and since the hieroglyphics carried exactly the same message, well ... for the first time in two thousand years the Egyptian pictographs unfolded and all the long stretch of history was revealed.

The above, though, isn't what I intended to write about. I meant to fashion the old German woman into a modern-day Oracle. I meant to dig up some more on Jimi Hendrix. I meant to go drinking in the Mermaid Tavern, but somehow my thoughts on that beach diverted me and I found myself wading through a deeper history.

45

Napoleon lost the stone to the British, and they carried it off to London to the confines of the British Museum. I touched it once, this magical Rosetta stone, a gesture very much like blasphemy to a museum curator. Strange, actually, because moments later an urgent siren wailed, and a legion of uniformed guards swept into the large room out of nowhere.

They didn't head directly for me, though surely the colour of my face had blanched into a pale and guilty white. No, they herded everyone into a group and pushed us out an unmarked door. One minute I was brushing my hand against the Rosseta stone and the next I was standing in a parking lot. What really happened is that someone had phoned in a bomb scare. Obviously, the guards were used to such eventualities and were highly trained. Rightly so, because in a place like the British Museum, a repository of the world's greatest treasures, the damage an explosion would cause would be a blow against all of humanity.

In any event, through Greek we know the ancients. Those who could write Greek began to record everything. Much of the Bible has come to us through Greek. So have our first solid glimpses of science, medicine, and philosophy. From Athena, the grey-eyed goddess of wisdom, we have the first intimations of what we would become.

Ψ

From Crete I sailed to the Cycladic Islands. Dolphins danced in the ship's wake, and in a few hours' time we were under the cliffs of Santorini, the first of the islands. Everyone aboard moved outside to stand at the railings and gawk. Santorini is spectacular. The cliffs rise five hundred metres straight out of the water, and at their very top, miraculously clinging to the rocks, is the whitewashed town of Thera.

The ferry pulled into a little port at the base of the cliffs. We poured onto a bus that then laboured up a switchbacking road. Up and up we went in the swaying bus, stopping sometimes to reverse when a truck rumbled down the other way, loaded with tomatoes or watermelons.

At the rim of the cliff the terraces of the town overlook the frothing ocean far below. The houses are painted in traditional Greek colours — white with blue windowsills and doorstops. From here I could see that the cliffs swept around in a crescent moon shape, forming the one remaining wall of a vast volcanic cauldron. Down below there were smaller islands of black lava, some still steaming with the fury of the Earth's core.

On the other end of Santorini, in the opposite crook of the crescent, is Oia, another tiny village. The tourists come here to watch the sunset. Busload upon busload arrives as the sun starts to dip. They line the cliffs and watch the sun boil red and dip at last into the sea. On the day I was there perhaps a thousand people actually broke into applause at the sunset. That was something I had never experienced before. They were clapping as if they had just seen a theatrical performance, and an old man beside me turned my way and smiled wryly. He was from somewhere in England.

"By George," he said, "that's the second most beautiful sunset I've ever seen."

He appeared to be well into his seventies, so I imagined he had watched plenty of sunsets. I wondered, in fact, if he had seen Chantal's fine sunset in the Eastern Townships of Quebec. Of course, I couldn't help but ask, "So where is the most beautiful sunset in the world?"

"Oh ... I don't know. I haven't seen it yet. You see, I just like to leave room for improvement."

ξ

The language Homer spoke was only one of a multitude of Greek dialects used in the ninth century B.C. The Greek that's spoken today comes down to us from only a single one of these many dialects, something we owe largely to Alexander the Great. He was a pupil, we're often reminded, of Aristotle, who also came from the northern reaches of Greece. But Alexander, thundering across the far plains of Asia, conquering most of the known world, decided there would be only one language for communication in his vast empire. And for this he chose the dialect of Athens.

Attic Greek, as it's called, wasn't Alexander's mother tongue, so his decision was brave and enlightened. He was wise enough to see that in Athens something spectacular was happening. A new world was being forged, and Attic was its language.

Alexander's decision is a monumental turning point in history, one that's had a vast effect on humanity. It's much like the spread of English throughout the world today. English, of course, travelled across the globe under the fist of the British

Empire, the one the sun never set on. And in the dissolution of that empire a detritus of English was left in pockets around the planet.

Twenty-five hundred years ago the same was true of Attic Greek. Throughout Europe and the Middle East it became the language of commerce, politics, and religion. Our first democracy and much of the kick-start of Greek philosophy rode on the tails of this one little dialect.

Alexander called this notion of a standard tongue a *koine*, meaning "to imprint," in this case a common language stamped upon the various peoples of his empire (from which we get not only the word but the concept of "coining a phrase"). Today Attic roots, largely through the Latin and then the French side of our linguistic ancestry, account for about 30 percent of all English words. And what words they are: *tragedy* and *triumph*, *poetry* and *parable*, *history* and *tyranny*. We have *narcotic*, *embryo*, and *skeleton*. We have *arithmetic* and *paradox*. All of these are direct cognates from Attic Greek. Even the name *Europe* comes from the old Greek tongue. *School* and *music* and *theatre* and *symphony* and *theory* and *Catholic* and *character* and *astronaut* — all from the vast encyclopedia that is Greek.

That evening I caught a ferry that would finally take me to Athens. I slept on the deck once more, and in the grey-eyed dawn came to the port of Piraeus. Athens itself is a few kilometres inland. The ferry dumped us off at the dockyards, and I hoisted my backpack once more and ventured up toward the buses.

When I finally arrived in Athens, I was sorely disappointed. I'd taken a huge roundabout, a circling of the entire Aegean Sea, to get here, and what I found was a vast sprawl of ugly concrete apartment blocks. Ten million people live in Athens under a perpetual cloud of exhaust fumes. It's not a pretty city, and there's an almost constant barrage of traffic noise.

What was it about this place? Why had I come here?

Way back in graduate school I studied a rather obscure little field in linguistics. I immersed myself in language consciousness. I looked at what it meant to think in one language as opposed to thinking in another. The field was obscure — mostly because everyone else had given up on it. Language consciousness wasn't politically correct anymore. Anything that could be said or thought in one language could, most surely, be said or thought in another. Wasn't that true?

Yes, but I still can't stop thinking that there's something more to languages, something about them that deeply defines us. I thought about Chantal and Valérie. They had talked about "living" in a language. It was the House of Being thing again, a palace filled with treasures.

I had come to Greece to see the birthplace of the Western world, the place where a whole new way of thinking, a whole new world view, was invented. Gazing around Athens, it was hard to imagine that anything special ever happened here. But it did. One rocky promontory still pushes above the clammer and clatter. It's sadly awash with tourists, of course, here to snap photos and cross one more destination off their lists. And it's too bad, because this really is the heart of everything. This is the Acropolis, the stony outcropping that's been inhabited in one way or another for five thousand years. It is a sacred place, an island on the vast Attic plain. Most important, it is the earthly seat of Athena, the goddess of wisdom.

Ω

I managed to find a little pathway around the northern edge of the Acropolis. There are some old houses — painted in the traditional fashion. Bougainvillea flowers drape down the walls, and birds chirp in the foliage.

The pathway skirts around the back of the Acropolis away from tour buses and snapping cameras. It overlooks the Agora, a large field of rocks that is, or was, the ancient marketplace of Athens. I wandered into a little museum there, mostly to find some shade. There were the inevitable statues, broken and fragmentary. Old, wise eyes stared at me from marble perches. But one small glass case caught my eye. In it a tangle of metal scraps, like a hairball, looked up at me, but I couldn't tell what it was.

Nails, the plaque said, cobbler's nails from the shop of Simon, the shoemaker. The nails were fused together by age, but I read further. It is known, the inscription said, that Socrates often frequented Simon's little shop. Likely, he held among the first of his lectures here. So, I gathered, this was one of the first informal settings of the Academy of Athens. A young Plato might well have sat beside Simon, helping him to cut leather for shoes while they listened to the great teacher.

For Socrates the great business of life was dialogue. He spoke with many of the citizens of Athens, switching, within a few sentences, from the mundane and trite observations of weather and shopping that usually pepper our talk, to a deep engagement with thought itself. In one of his first dialogues, as related by Plato, Socrates took on some of the philosophers that had come before him. He was particularly interested in the ancient Greek word *arete*. Now *arete* refers to the purpose of something, but more than that it's the measure of how well something performs its required purpose, the measure of its excellence.

The Pre-Socratics had spent long hours attempting to define this *arete*. Everything has its own measure of *arete*, they claimed. The *arete* of a chimney, for example, consists in how well it draws smoke up and out of a room and how well it reflects heat back into a room. Odysseus displayed his *arete* in his unquenchable thirst to return home, to battle even the gods in his desire to make it back to Ithaca.

But Socrates came to a different conclusion. Just as the purpose of a chimney is to draw smoke up and out of a room, the purpose of a human being is to seek knowledge. Through reason, Socrates said, an individual can free himself from the dark cave of the unknown. Through reason we can unravel the mysteries of the world and venture beyond oracles, gods, and fate.

And that surely smacks of a world view.

Now, of course, it would be foolish to imagine that the whole Western world grew from this single word *arete*. I only point out that sometimes a single word can contain vast, sprawling ideas. New ideas. And it's not that these words are untranslatable. It's not that no one else can understand them. It's just that they emerged here first, that they were believed here first ... in this language.

I glanced up from the little pile of nails. Had they heard the voice of Socrates? Had these small nails rolled about on the floor while his ideas came into being? Outside, the sun beat relentlessly on the stones. The Acropolis towered blackly above me, and I knew I was onto something. I didn't completely understand it, but I knew then that languages can contain whole worlds. And I wanted to go and see them.

51

Ψ

After a few days in Athens, I caught the train for Patras, a port city on the west coast of Greece. From there I would go to Italy. The train moved across the backbone of Greece, out over the Corinth Canal, across the top of the Peloponnese.

It was evening when I left Patras. The ferry to Italy chugged along so slowly that we didn't seem to move at all. We inched into the Adriatic Sea. The wide island of Cephalonia eventually reared up, and just north of that was a smaller island, green and double-humped. Something about it kept me on deck. The sun was growing larger and pinker in its descent, and the sea was truly wine-dark for an instant. Then I realized which island I was looking at. This was Ithaca, home of Odysseus. The trip from Troy had taken him ten long years, but in the telling of that journey a whole new world was created.

A single star emerged in the moonless night. I stood for a few moments longer on deck, then ducked back in through a hatchway. I needed rest, so I curled up in a corner and fell asleep to the soft murmur of the sea.

3

And Empires, Too, Shall Splash Across These Pages

The ferry pulled into Brindisi on the heel of the boot of Italy, and I stepped off, having had enough of sea travel for a while. Stars still hung in the east, but the harbour was already alive with touts and merchants. Brindisi is better known among travellers as "Brain Disease." Sorry, but it's true. There's a mind-numbingly long wait there between the time ferries pull in and when trains leave to take you up the coast. And there's nothing to do but sit around the featureless docks trying to safeguard your valuables from hordes of vendors and pickpockets.

When I finally did get on a train, however, it was headed for Rome, the Eternal City. All around me in the cramped compartment people spoke Italian. It's a beautiful Romance language that dances on the tongue. Of course, that doesn't mean it's a language for sweeping women off their feet, though it can. Calling it a Romance language means that it's a remnant of ancient Rome. It's one of the children of Latin, the tongue of the Roman Empire.

I found myself a little pension not far from the Spanish Steps in Rome. In a square near there I saw a Japanese couple swarmed by Gypsy children. None of the children were older than ten, and the youngest might have been six. They surrounded the couple, a mob of them, tearing at their pockets, at her purse and his camera. An old lady, dressed entirely in black, had been sitting at the fountain, and at this commotion she suddenly stood and began to blow on a whistle. Then, all along the street, shopkeepers came running out of their stores. It must have been a sort of vigilante system they had set up for the neighbourhood. The Gypsy kids bolted, leaving the poor Japanese tourists confused.

Afterward I sat with the old woman, who I thought was very brave. She spoke a bit of English and told me a story I'll never forget.

"You go to Colosseum?" she asked.

"Yes, of course. I'll see it this afternoon."

"You see the cats, yes?"

I had heard of them. The ancient Colosseum of Rome, an immense building that still towers almost jarringly over the centre of the city, crawls with cats.

The old woman pointed at her chest. "I go to feed the cats."

"You feed them?"

"*Sì.*" She heaved herself up and sighed. "In the war Mussolini ... you know?" She made a face.

I chuckled. "Yes, Mussolini."

"A very bad time. No food." She looked me hard in the eye. "No food, so we eat ... anything. You understand?"

I saw where she was going. During the worst of the war, the people ate wild cats. There was no choice.

"I was little girl," she said, "but I remember. I cried. And then we, all people of Rome, we made a ... what you call it ... a promise to the cats. We said, you helped us and we never forget, so we give the Colosseum to them. You understand? Forever, we go there and give them food."

"That's only fair."

"Yes, only fair."

Later I did go to the Colosseum. It's impressive, though the area below it, the famous Roman Forum, seat of one of the greatest empires that ever existed, is a rather sad two blocks of dirt and rubble. Only with the expert knowledge of a guide can one understand what was once there, since there's really not a lot to see. Somewhere in these ruins Julius Caesar was murdered. Somewhere here Nero fiddled while Rome burned. Somewhere here the last of the Roman emperors huddled in the dark with the barbarians at the gates.

On a fallen pediment, however, I saw a bit of chiselled writing, something I could read. The letters were familiar, all capitals perhaps, but the script was as plain as the text in front of you now. I was reading a word that was almost two thousand years old. And then, as if to break the spell, a skinny little kitten skittered onto the marble slab. It pawed the air where a bright blue butterfly fluttered by, and I had to smile. The empire had come to this, as all empires are destined to do. Then the kitten flicked a paw at the air and hopped into the shadows between the fallen stones.

ξ

I found once in an old book a fragment of a poem from Sappho:

ΔΕΔΥΚΕ ΜΕΝ Α ΣΕΛΑΝΝΑ
ΚΑΙ ΠΛΗΙΑΔΕΣ. ΜΕΣΑΙ ΔΕ
ΝΥΚΤΕΣ. ΠΑΡΑ Δ'ΕΡΧΕΤ' ΩΡΑ.
ΕΓΩ ΔΕ ΜΟΝΑ ΚΑΤΕΥΔΩ

55

That's Greek, of course, but look at the passage when it's put into Latin:

DEDUKE MEN A SELANNA
KAI PLEIADES. MESAI DE
NUKTES. PATA D'ERKHET' ORA.
EGO DE MONA KATEUDO

If you heard the above spoken aloud in either language, you would never know they were related. The written text, though, especially in uppercase letters, shows an astonishing resemblance. Quite obviously the written Latin borrowed heavily from the Greek.

It's a pattern. Some languages muscle their way across continents. They travel first on the feet of soldiers, pillaging and plundering. Then, if things go well, they float on the light winds of trade. After that they're unstoppable.

Languages can be powerful things. The stronger ones quite simply bulldoze the weaker ones, assimilating whatever is useful and discarding the rest. It doesn't take long. Even the speakers of the weaker language, or their children, anyway, soon start conversing in the more powerful tongue. People are quick to take up any language that will give them greater access to material advancement. It's survival of the fittest.

Empires are as much about language as they are about conquest. Today the three largest language populations in the world — English, Spanish, and Mandarin — are that way because they're the shells of past empires that inundated other languages, drowning them with power. Latin isn't on that list only because it died in a dusty armchair as a happy old man. It had already given the world a host of powerful children that includes Spanish and English.

The above fragment by Sappho, by the way, translates as:

The Pleiads have left the sky, and
The moon has vanished. It's midnight
The time for meeting is over
And me — I am lying, lonely.

۶

The train to Florence passes through lovely rolling hills. Cypress trees, rising like solidified whirls of smoke, stand in long, solemn rows. This is the legendary landscape of Tuscany, heart of the Italian Renaissance.

In Florence I'd arranged to meet with Lesley, an old friend of mine. She's a doctor from England and speaks three languages, Italian included. Funny enough, though, this was her first real trip to Italy. She had learned Italian in school and had never been to a place where she could actually use it.

The first thing to know about Florence is that the name is only our clumsy English approximation. Here they call it Firenze, a moniker with fire in its belly. And it's true. Five hundred years ago Florence burned with a collection of geniuses the world will probably never see again — Galileo, Leonardo da Vinci, Michelangelo. This city was at the heart of an explosion, the shifting of gears between the old world and the new.

It was the Renaissance, of course, literally the rebirth, not so much of the Roman Empire but of the ideals of long-ago Greece. And it was the dialect spoken here in Florence that finally replaced ancient Latin to become the language we now know as Italian. Most of that was due to the work of Dante Alighieri, another Florentine genius.

Never mind that Dante was exiled from Florence. It was he who went on to write *The Divine Comedy*, one of the great books of history, in the Florentine dialect. He made it plain for all to see that here was a dialect of great delicacy. In the rush and sweep of

57

his almost endless imagination he let loose a language that trips from the tongue like no other.

Walking down the ancient medieval streets, I made up a little game. Lesley and I were off to see Michelangelo's *David*, and though I was as usual completely inept at the language, I so badly wanted to try it out that I started making stuff up.

"Fettuccine?" I asked her, pointing at some luxurious old building.

"What?"

"Botticelli," I continued somewhat more insistently. "Paparazzi."

"Don't be such a tosser."

"Right ... sorry."

Lesley, as I've said, really was fluent in Italian and managed to get me safely through numerous transgressions. Once, in fact, she literally opened a door for us with this most beautiful of languages. One afternoon in Florence we went to see the Medici Chapel. The tombs there were sculpted by Michelangelo. I set up my camera on a tripod, but as usual in places like this, people weren't allowed to use flashes. So I diligently opened the f-stop for a long exposure.

A female security guard accosted me immediately. She waved her finger in my face and made it crystal-clear that I wasn't allowed to use a tripod. Her hands flew through the air, circling and swooping as she chewed me out. The woman was as ferocious as a pit bull, so I meekly folded my tripod and limped off to lick my wounds. Lesley and I gazed at the marbles for a while, then I reminded her of something I'd read in my guidebook. There are sketches by Michelangelo here, it said. Ask to see them.

Well, this place wasn't an art gallery. It was a chapel filled with tombs, and I couldn't see anything resembling sketches. Lesley glanced around. There was no one else there except the pit bull security guard, now standing in the corner and eyeing us suspiciously.

"Shall I ask her then?" Lesley questioned.

"I guess so."

She went over and spoke Italian to the pit bull. Instantly, the guard erupted, her hands gesturing madly. Lesley translated the barrage for me. "It's impossible," she was saying. "You must obtain permission from the front desk in writing. It takes six months to be approved."

Then the woman looked at us, and her attitude melted a bit. We had been unfailingly polite to her as only the British and Canadians can be, so she recanted. Glancing both ways as if to make sure the coast was clear, she put a finger to her lips and swore us to silence. Then she motioned us to follow her down a hallway off to the side. I think now that it was Lesley's Italian that tipped the scales. Perhaps the pit bull felt badly about verbally mauling us twice. So we followed her along the narrow passageway, and in the shadows she stopped and reached down to a latch on the floor. It was a trap door. She opened it and pointed. "*Vai la giu*," she said. "Go down there." A ladder poked up out of the opening, and Lesley and I exchanged looks.

We climbed into something like a cellar, a whitewashed space maybe the size of a small bedroom. The woman didn't accompany us down the ladder, and as our eyes gradually adjusted, I saw marks all over the walls. I peered more closely. Here there was a delicately rendered hand slightly turned, there a half-finished profile — a bearded god-like figure. They were drawings that were unmistakably the work of a master. *The master*. Here were the sketches of Michelangelo. He had stood in this little room and had left his mark on these walls.

It's something we all tend to do, though few of us can do it like Michelangelo. Still, we all like to mark where we've been. We all want to say simply, "I was here."

Afterward, I tried to find prints of these drawings, photos in books, postcards, anything, but I've never seen them reproduced anywhere. They were, it seems, done while

Michelangelo was in hiding. He sheltered here during a siege of the city in 1530. The troops of Charles V, the Holy Roman emperor, had surrounded Florence and were shelling it with cannons. Michelangelo stayed in this cellar for a month, doodling on the walls with charcoal. They were among the last drawings he ever did. Not long after the siege he fled to Rome and lived out the last years of his life there, never again to return to his beloved Firenze.

The drawings were only discovered again in 1975. The little cellar is still closed to the public and all but a handful of restoration scientists and historians. But somehow we were allowed in. The doors were unlocked for us, and we were allowed a glimpse of the sublime sketches of a frail and frightened genius.

Ω

We all make our marks in various ways. Humans are experts at creating and manipulating marks or symbols. Language is just one of these systems of symbols. We also use mathematics and spatial orientation. Humans can think in music or even with kinesthetic intelligence, a sort of muscle memory that might be used to choreograph a ballet or map a strategy for winning a football game. All of these are called semiotic systems, semiotics being the study of how humans represent things, how we assign symbols as stand-ins for much more complex ideas.

Humans are very good at symbols, much better than gorillas, for example. The most famous gorilla to use symbols was named Koko, who was taught to recognize and employ more than a thousand, even becoming proficient enough to name a kitten she had acquired for a pet. Koko named it All Ball, perhaps referring to the fact that the cat was an excellent playmate. But even if you buy the supposition that Koko truly understood what she was doing, with a thousand symbols she was working at about the level of a three-year-old human child.

The point is that humans tend to think in a variety of semiotic systems, representing things with symbols — topographical lines on a map, a percentage sign, holding up our middle finger at the guy who cuts us off in traffic — but the most powerful, most efficient, most versatile of these semiotic systems is undoubtedly language.

For one thing languages constantly change. They always evolve to meet our needs. Anyone can see the difference between Shakespearean English and our modern version. We've lost *thou* and *thee*, but that's four hundred years of change and easy to see.

The fact is that no matter what the various protectors of grammar say, languages relentlessly mutate. They borrow words and ideas from other languages. They change their pronunciation, and over time they even lose bits and pieces of their grammar. I suspect, for instance, that the adverb suffix *ly* will disappear from English in another fifty years. As shocking as it might appear to English teachers, sentences like "I tried to get there quick" will become perfectly grammatical.

61

Yes, languages are as organic as we are. And so Latin got old and eventually fossilized. It remains with us in a jumble of scientific phylums, though it rarely escapes the bonds of the written page any longer. The spoken variations, however, continue to grow and move and spring up into new dialects. Latin has already spawned not only Spanish, Portuguese, French, and Italian, but also Catalan, Provençal, and even far-off Romanian.

Language can get very complicated. The mythical lines between actual tongues and their dialects become blurry and confused. In Italy, for example, so many dialects came out of Latin that it wasn't until 1979 that what we commonly refer to as Italian, the Tuscan dialect, became the one spoken at home by more than 50 percent of all Italians. And, like many other countries, there are still pockets of other dialects spoken across Italy, including Sicilian, Umbrian, and Corsican.

That's how the Tower of Babel works. New dialects continually emerge from a mother tongue, usually the language of an empire. They blossom into dozens of other tongues, often leaving the host language a mere museum piece. They form families with all manner of odd uncles and drunken cousins.

Perhaps this is strange to us in North America where you can travel for hundreds and even thousands of kilometres without hearing any major differences in speech patterns. But we are the anomaly. That situation exists nowhere else in the world.

Φ

I was attacked in northern Spain by a pack of wild dogs. Well, okay, it was only two dogs, but one of them was a German shepherd and the other was a Rottweiler. They were big dogs, and the German shepherd had three legs. It was a real mean son of a bitch, so in my mind I was definitely assaulted by a pack of dogs. They ripped and tore at me, but why? Because I was on their turf.

I was staying in San Sebastian, a small city on the northern coast of Spain. It's set in a beautiful bay on the Atlantic Ocean. The entrance to the bay is guarded by two small mountains, and on one of them a statue of Jesus Christ glowers over the city.

I had come to San Sebastian quite by chance during yet another major festival — Semana Grande, "The Big Week." It's really an enormous drunk. Deep into the night I wound through the ancient streets sloppily cavorting from tapas bar to tapas bar. It was a lot of fun.

After a few sweet nights of this, my liver was beginning to shut down, and I needed to get away from the mayhem. So I moved to a quiet hostel high in the mountains behind the city. The views over the bay were spectacular, and all around there was a deep and tranquil forest.

One evening my responsibility was to get the wine for dinner, which meant a trip to the village at the foot of the mountain. I set off, half walking, half jogging along a narrow path that wound through the trees. And that was when it happened. About halfway down, the dogs came out of the trees ahead of me, snarling and growling. I was jogging at this point, and I thought I could loop around them. That was a mistake.

I felt their teeth rip into my legs, and I realize now that if I had tripped and fallen it might have been all over for me. For some reason, though, I halted, turned, and yelled at them, even as they were tearing at my legs like piranhas. It was only a wordless howl of protest, but to my surprise the dogs backed off a step or two. My jeans were shredded, and I could feel warm blood dripping down my left leg. The German shepherd with three legs continued to snarl and bark, white flecks of saliva spraying from its mouth. The Rottweiler, though, had edged farther back. It was barking at me, too, but without much enthusiasm.

I continued down to the village with a bloodied leg and torn jeans. I didn't resume my mission out of a sense of responsibility. It was more like I really didn't know what else to do. When I returned to the hostel, everyone gathered around in concern. I called up Lesley, who was now back in England, and according to her instructions, we cleaned the wound, though I've still got a nasty scar there. I'm kind of proud of it. That was the leg the German shepherd got hold of. On the other, the pant leg was ripped, but the Rottweiler didn't break the skin. I'll remember that in future: four legs good, three legs bad.

Of course, I had no right to charge out of the trees at the dogs. That was their place, their turf, their empire. I should have understood immediately, since there's no animal more territorial, more vicious, or more self-possessed than humans. We mark our turf emphatically, we raise our legs and piss around our borders, and we do it with language. Our accents and inflections, and the way we write, speak, and understand, indelibly mark us and the territory to which we belong.

63

Ψ

In San Sebastian there was a large poster on the wall outside the station. It read in English: TOURISTS, YOU ARE NOT IN SPAIN. YOU ARE IN BASQUE COUNTRY.

San Sebastian is all about turf and language. This is Basque country — a fiercely separatist region. In fact, no one here would even call the city San Sebastian. In Basque it's called Donostia.

The Basques are a curiosity. They speak a language called Euskara in their own tongue. It's an isolate language, meaning that it's completely unrelated to any other language on the planet. They're very rare these isolates. There are only a handful of them on Earth, and the Basques take great pride in the fact that their language is one of them.

Euskara, for the most part, is a cacophony of *k*'s, *r*'s, and *x*'s. Here, for example, is a random sentence from a pamphlet I picked up: *"Zuraren askotariko erabilerak giro bat sortu dugu orduko bizimoduaren kutsua emateko."* Try saying that three times fast.

The Basques believe they were actually the first inhabitants of Europe. They have a saying: "Before rocks were rocks, before God was God … the Basques were Basques."

A couple of hundred kilometres north of Donostia are the famous prehistoric caves of Lascaux whose rock walls dance with red ochre bisons and antelopes. The paintings date back almost fifteen thousand years, and to some degree they're not much different from Michelangelo's marks in that little cellar in Florence. The prehistoric people were marking territory, calling their mountainous world their own. The Basques believe the caves were painted by their direct ancestors, and there's a good possibility they're right.

A series of genetic tests seem to indicate that the Basques are the only pre-Neolithic population left in Europe, which means they might well be the first people to have arrived there. Undoubtedly, Euskara derives from something very ancient, something much older than Spanish or even Latin, older even than Indo-European. At the very least it's distinctly different. There are still about eight hundred thousand people fluent in Euskara and another two million who speak at least a little of it. Even though the language has been surrounded by Spanish for a thousand years, even though it was banned completely under the fascist dictatorship of Generalissimo Francisco Franco, it has somehow managed to survive.

The Basques have been pushed into corners of Spain and France where the Pyrenees protect them. But they've been able to hold on to that bit of turf. They are and always will be something apart, something different, something that came before.

ξ

When I was studying linguistics at university, there was one name that kept popping up — Noam Chomsky. In 1957 he produced a work called *Syntactic Structures*, and my field of study has never been the same.

Chomsky claimed that our brains are hardwired to produce language. We all have certain built-in mechanisms, sort of behind-the-scenes cogs and wheels that spin out our languages. The hardware in the brain is the same for all of us. It's only the software, or "wetware," that differs from language to language. What that means is that the grammars of all languages are simply variations on a basic underlying foundation. With a bit of imagination you can take that to mean there really is only one language and that everything you hear around the world, all six thousand languages and tens of thousands of dialects, are simply variations of a fixed template.

It's something like taking a mathematical formula, say $(a + b)^2$, and imagining it as a grammatical sentence in one language.

In another language the grammatical structure might look like $a^2 + 2ab + b^2$. But, if you remember high-school mathematics, you realize that it's actually the same formula. It's just been factored in a different way, or as Chomsky would say, the deep structure is the same.

I've never really liked this sort of mathematical model, though, this computer metaphor that seems so popular in academic circles. It's too cold, too sterile. It's like defining water as a molecule wherein two hydrogen atoms are bonded with an oxygen atom. That's all quite accurate, but it tells you nothing about the shimmering, splashing, gurgling properties of water.

In my own graduate work in linguistics I'd been taught how to map out noun phrases. I'd been educated to decipher the rules by which a transitive verb might be able to move to a different part of the sentence. We spent great gobs of time looking at different grammar.

Blah, blah, blah, I thought. What about the toot and whistle of all the tongues of the Earth? What about the way language snaps and sparkles? What about poetry? What about philosophy?

What about the way a language makes you feel? What about the way it makes you think? What about the way it makes ... you?

I took the long train down into Spain proper to Madrid, the capital. On the train I met Mark from South Africa. He had been a tour guide leader for three years all over Spain.

"Have you ever been to a real bullfight?" he asked after we arrived in Madrid. He had taken it upon himself to show me Spanish culture and had quickly pointed out the bullfight posters in the train station. I admit I was intrigued, though slightly alarmed. I didn't want to see any animals killed for sport.

"You can't understand Spain," Mark said, "until you've seen a bullfight."

"But —"

"There's a famous young matador appearing tonight. We should go."

And so we did, but it was sickening.

"What did you think of that?" Mark asked after the first bull was killed.

"It's awful." I'm sure my face was pale.

"You eat meat, don't you?"

"Yeah," I said, unsure where he was going with this conversation.

"Well, the cows you eat are penned up and force-fed. They live a miserable life. These *toros* —" he swept his hand over the arena "— they live their whole lives on the open range."

"And then they die a horrible death."

"No," he said. "That's exactly where you're wrong. They die a noble death. They die fighting."

"A death all the same," I argued.

"Have you read Hemingway?"

"Yeah, well ... some of his stuff."

"Then you must read *Death in the Afternoon* if you want to understand."

And I did want to understand. For hundreds of years the Spanish have been flocking to see this spectacle. It's as deeply ingrained in their culture as Catholicism. So why was it, to me, a sickening and disgusting affair?

One of the important features to know about a bullfight is that in Spain every bull is killed one way or another, which doesn't seem fair. They stick things in the back of the bull, for God's sake. Eventually, they slide a razor-sharp sword into the bull's neck. Properly done, the sword severs the aorta, and the bull dies instantly. That almost never happens, however. The sword bounces off ribs and slides between organs. It usually takes a minute or two for the beast's knees to buckle. Blood spews out of the bull's mouth, and then when the animal finally buckles,

67

the matador takes something resembling an ice pick and slams it into the creature's forehead. The bull's legs quiver once and then the animal is still. The carcass is dragged away after that, and though I'm told the meat is divided up and eaten, I was still shocked at the brutality of everything.

Mark shook his head sadly. "You don't understand. Perhaps foreigners never do." He seemed to have forgotten that he was a foreigner, too. "All things die," he continued. "Even you'll die one day. The whole thing's a metaphor."

Another bull was entering the ring.

"It's not unusual for a matador to be gored and horribly wounded even in this day and age." Mark looked hard at me. "I can see that this is what you're hoping for. You're cheering for the bull now, but you're wrong. All things must die. That's not open for debate. The real question is how we live. Do we live bravely? With courage?" He paused and took a deep, self-satisfied breath. "The matador lives and dies bravely, and so does the bull. It's all about *pundonor*."

"What?"

"*Pundonor*. In Spanish it means honour, but it's something more than just honour. It's also courage, self-respect, and pride all in one word. *Pundonor* to a Spaniard is as 'real as water, wine, or olive oil.'" Mark was quoting Ernest Hemingway, and Papa was right. This was the key to understanding it all.

Later I did have a look at Hemingway's *Death in the Afternoon*. The book isn't a novel. It's an extended essay on the bullfight for which Hemingway was an aficionado. "Bullfighting," he said, "is the only art in which the artist is in danger of death." The people still talk of the great matadors of the past. They talk of their bravery, their moves, their gory deaths.

Every move has a name and a history, Mark explained as we watched. When the matador swept his cape over the back of the bull, several thousand voices shouted "¡Ole!"

"You see," Mark said, "that was a veronica."

"A veronica?"

"Yes. Listen, are you Catholic?"

"No."

"Well, then when Christ carried his cross from the trial to the place of his crucifixion, all the little events that happened to him were detailed. They're called the Stations of the Cross."

I remembered that, of course, from the Via Dolorosa in Jerusalem. I recalled the pilgrims weeping and carrying their rented crosses across the cobblestones.

"The sixth station," Mark said, "is where a woman, Veronica, came out of the crowd to mop Christ's forehead."

Okay, I was starting to get it. The cape of the matador became the cloth of Veronica wiping the brow of the condemned prisoner. She mopped the brow of the one who was about to die. An interesting analogy. So there was a lot more to this than met a tourist's eyes.

It was, I realized, another one of those symbolic systems, as full and as subtle as any other. Once you understood what the symbols stood for, once you understood that it was a metaphor, well ... you were almost there.

But I still didn't get it.

Ω

Down even farther into Spain, into Andalusia, I came to Seville and Granada, the ancient Moorish capitals. The Moors were Muslims who had come up from Africa in the ninth century. This Moorish paradise lasted for more than five hundred years. It was a time of great scientific advance, an era of religious tolerance and true enlightenment.

In 1469 Ferdinand, king of Aragon, married Isabella, queen of Castile. With their combined military might they expelled the Moors from Spain in what was to be the final battle ever fought by armoured knights on horseback. Granada was the last of the Moorish strongholds to tumble. The palace fell in 1492, the same year Christopher Columbus sailed to America for Ferdinand and Isabella, a strange but true convergence of history. It was the end of one world and the beginning of the next, a massive sea change in human history. For a while Spain would become the most powerful nation on the planet.

Also in 1492 a linguist named Antonio de Nebrija put together the first book of Spanish grammar. When he presented it to Queen Isabella, she was confused. "What is this for?" she asked.

"Your Majesty," he replied. "Language is the perfect tool for building empires."

In the Alcázar palace in Seville a wide tapestry hangs on a wall. It shows the first Native brought back by Columbus from the New World. He has fallen to his knees in the massive cathedral of Seville, humbled before the altar. To me, though, he isn't prostrate before the power of the Catholic Church; he's collapsed in the face of the absurdity of everything. From the distant thatch huts of the Caribbean Sea to a stone edifice as big as a mountain was more than his fragile heart could believe.

Φ

In Granada I lined up to see the Alhambra, the fabled Moorish palace. In its heyday it was a place of sunlit rooms and gardens, a magnificent edifice that shamed the grim Dark Age castles of the Europeans.

The queue snaked around a garden. Even early in the morning the line was hundreds of metres long. For two hours I stood there by myself. Everyone around me was speaking Spanish, so I sort of withdrew into myself. After an interminable time, the young man behind me, who had been speaking Spanish to his girlfriend, suddenly said in perfect English, "Listen, if you want to take a break, we can hold your place."

I can't begin to tell you how surprised I was. I went to the washroom, and when I returned, we started talking. His name was Carlos, and he had studied for a year in the United States. Carlos, I'd noticed earlier, was from the New World. Judging by the features of his face, it was plain he had an indigenous ancestry. As it turned out, Carlos was from Colombia.

Spain's empire once covered half the world. It's gone now, but the language remains so that even in the deepest jungles, even in the most inaccessible mountains of South America, the indigenous peoples speak the tongue of a faraway land.

"Colombia," Carlos said, "is a beautiful country, but no one thinks of it that way."

"What do you mean?"

"Well, what do you think of Colombia?"

The answer was plain. "Cocaine, drug lords, guerrillas ... lots of bad stuff."

"That's right. I'm an economics student, but everywhere I go, as soon as I pull out my passport ..." He paused for a moment, then continued. "Flying here, I was held at the airport in Madrid for ten hours."

"Why?"

"Because," he said, "I'm a rock climber. I'm climbing here in the north and also in France. There's some of the best climbing in the world in both places — a Mecca for climbers. Well, you know, climbers use a kind of talcum powder for their hands. You have to keep them dry." An impish grin appeared on his face. "Whenever I show my passport, they take me aside and tear my bags apart. In one bag they found my talcum powder and, of course, they thought ..."

He laughed and so did I. We hooted until the other people in the line regarded us strangely.

"They had to get it tested, they told me," Carlos said between wheezes. "I tried to explain things to them, but —" He exploded in laughter again. "Dumb fucks! They really pissed me off." Old Carlos had learned his English well.

He told me, too, that he was cutting his trip short. The new

71

government in Colombia had called for an all-out war against the guerrillas. The last government had promoted a policy of appeasement, a leave-us-alone-and-we'll-leave-you-alone sort of thinking. That didn't work. Carlos told me he felt he should be home when things started happening.

"It's sad," he said. "Colombia really is a beautiful country. For example, have you ever heard of the pink dolphins?"

"No."

"Well, they live in the tributaries of the Amazon. They're the only freshwater dolphins in the world. They're pink and quite rare. In Colombia we have a legend about them. The male of the species can change into a human form at will. Often they'll come into the towns when they know there's going to be a big party. They're very handsome, it's said, and so they seduce young girls and sleep with them. Always, though, they wear hats to hide the blowholes high on their foreheads. It's the only way to know they're not human."

It was then that I realized Carlos was wearing a ball cap. I pointed at it. "So what's under *your* hat, Carlos?"

$$\Psi$$

When I got as far south in Spain as I could go, I signed up for a sailing course. Although I was still in Europe, I was no longer in Spain. I was in Gibraltar, a very odd place and the remnant of yet another great empire.

Like Spain before it, Britain cast its net over the world, and Gibraltar was one of its catches. The colony is as English as Trafalgar Square. You can buy fish and chips there and pay for it in British pounds. If you walk a thousand steps to your right, however, you find yourself back in Spain.

Very odd. And, of course, rearing above everything is the Rock. It's quite a slab of stone, knifing out of the dark ocean. Across the straits a similar mountain looms out of the water near Africa. Together they're called the Pillars of Hercules, the doorway to the Mediterranean.

If you control this point, you dominate the Mediterranean. And that's why Gibraltar is still British. Up on the Rock, kilometres and kilometres of secret tunnels bore into the cliffs. No one knows quite what's in there, but I walked up and discovered razor wire marked with forbidding signs from the Ministry of Defence.

I had come here for sailing lessons. During the first days, we went into the harbour to sail. I learned to tie the required knots and crank on the necessary winches. Phil was the skipper of our ship. He had lived in Gibraltar all his life and was quite certain the tunnels above us were filled with British military surveillance technology — stuff beyond the wildest dreams of the civilian world. He spoke in hushed tones with, oddly, a bit of a lisp, as well. Perhaps it was something in the air.

Anyway, Gibraltar remains resolutely British. Unlike Hong Kong, the United Kingdom will never let it go. It won it fair and square, and anyone who says otherwise can step right up for a very proper thrashing.

ع

The end of the sailing lesson was to be a crossing from Gibraltar to Africa. We would sail under our own power, but what I didn't realize is that we would be heading into a war zone. Just as I got there, a small war broke out. The previous week Morocco had invaded tiny Isla del Perejil, quite literally Parsley Island.

It was the first invasion of European soil since the Second World War — a turf battle, to be sure. Territory was being marked again. I admit, though, I'm using the words *war* and *battle* pretty loosely. About a dozen poorly armed Moroccan frontier guards landed on the island, equipped with a radio, two flags, and a couple of tents. No one was there to see them

73

raise the flag except some lizards, bugs, and possibly a very confused goat.

Spain, however, was incensed. The island historically belonged to it. It was protected by the North Atlantic Treaty Organization, so the Spanish immediately sent a warship to straighten things out.

Phil, our sailing instructor, laughed off the danger. Despite the fact that we would be sailing right by Isla del Perejil, he insisted the war had nothing to do with us.

Tell that to a bullet.

I noticed that Phil had a strange accent. His *th* sound was always an *f*. "Fank you," he'd say politely when I handed him one of the charts. "I fink today I'll get you to raise the sails by yourself."

We spent a few days tacking and gybing in Gibraltar's harbour beneath the massive Rock. From the top of Gibraltar, on a clear day, Mount Acha on the coast of Africa is visible. Also up on the Rock are the famous Barbary apes, the only primates in Europe. Actually, they were brought over by British soldiers a couple of centuries ago. The troops kept the monkeys as pets not long before the Battle of Trafalgar, and a number of the apes went wild, perhaps when their owners didn't return from the battle. When I was on Gibraltar, they howled over the mountaintop, snapped at tourists' fingers, defecated on cars, and stole my goddamn water bottle!

At the other end of the Rock is St. Michael's Cave. It was here in 1855 that a strange thick-furrowed skull was unearthed. Two years later a similar skull was uncovered in a place called Neanderthal, Germany. The Neanderthal race was once as common on this planet as we are now. For some reason, though, they all disappeared about thirty thousand years ago.

Here were a people even older than the Basques, so old they weren't even quite human. It's not known, for example, if Neanderthals spoke any language. They had skulls and jaws significantly different from ours, but the existence of vocal cords can neither be proven nor disproven. Neanderthals did have a small hyoid bone, a technical necessity for having a larynx, and they possessed a gene, FOXP2, which is associated with human language. However, this gene is also found in songbirds so that it's difficult to say what sort of communication systems Neanderthals employed.

In fact, the lack of language might be one of the central reasons Neanderthals died out and we're still around. Somehow we found the ability to communicate abstract ideas to one another, to strategize and plan for the future. It is this aptitude that most surely marked the emergence and dominance of Cro-Magnon Man ... us. We developed the most complicated and intricate communication system yet seen and soon spread across the Earth, usurping Neanderthals, tackling all environments, and conquering even the vast seas that lay before us.

⫛

On the third day Phil announced we would attempt the crossing to Morocco, especially since a good wind was blowing. I was excited, despite the fact that I barely knew what I was doing. The straits we'd be crossing marked the entrance to the Mediterranean Sea. For Phoenicians who sailed through here three thousand years earlier it was the end of the world. For ancient Greeks it was a portal into the great unknown. Columbus tested his ships here, and so did Magellan. All of these explorers sailed through these fabled gates into the great unmapped Atlantic.

We had just made it out of the harbour when Phil glanced up at the sky. "I fink we better get our harnesses on."

I frowned. "Harnesses?"

"Yeah, you're going to need them."

He wasn't kidding. Out in the straits the wind whipped up to thirty-eight knots. All of a sudden we were skudding across the waves almost out of control. I pulled on the necessary ropes and winched when I could, though truthfully most of the time I held on to the railing for dear life while the roiling waves crashed over me. Phil stood in front of me, manning the wheel, laughing maniacally into the wind.

Halfway over to Africa, Phil pointed at the whitecaps as a pair of dolphins shot out of a cresting wave. They were like torpedoes, and soon a pod of them wove in and out of our wake. It was a magical moment.

"Carlos," I called, "is that you out there?"

After a few hours, the waters calmed a bit and the sandy red hills of Morocco appeared in the distance. Phil looked at his watch and began to yip. "We've made a record crossing. That's the fastest one I've ever done."

"Great, Phil, that's just great," I said.

Jutting from the shoreline was the little rock tumble of Isla del Perejil. I didn't see any goats, but the Moroccan flag was gone. The War of Parsley Island was finished, and Europe, apparently, had come through victorious again. The great continent of empires remained unscathed.

PART TWO

Into the East

Genghis Khan Rides Again

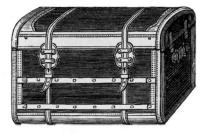

Coming into Istanbul by sea
is enchanting. The minarets of the Blue Mosque come into view
over crumbling medieval walls, and Topkapı Palace, ancient
home of sultans and harems, tips down to the water's edge. As
visitors proceed through the Golden Horn, they spy on a hillside
the dusty red dome of Hagia Sophia, the first great basilica of
Christendom. Everything is much as it would have been for the
Crusaders a thousand years before.

Istanbul is the crossroads of the world. At its back lies
Europe, to the south is Africa, and to the east, across the
Bosphorus, is a great slab of land jutting from Asia — Asia
Minor in the old books, the Ottoman Empire until the end of

the First World War, and now simply Turkey.

It's quite fair to say there's no other country on Earth quite like Turkey: Muslim but not Arabic, an ally of both Europe and its Islamic neighbours, a secular democracy tucked between the flashpoints of the Balkans and the Middle East, unsure which way it should turn.

The Turkish language, too, is an anomaly. It's a member of the Altaic family of languages, but like the country itself it snakes its roots through both the West and the East. The written text, for example, is now produced in the Latin alphabet. This momentous change occurred in 1928 when Mustafa Kemal Atatürk, the father of modern Turkey, declared that his country would adopt a Western script. The language had previously been written in Arabic, but many of its written conventions didn't seem to suit Turkish.

Atatürk was warned by his advisers that changing the written language would take several years of consultations and at least five more years to implement. But Atatürk declared that the changeover would be done in three months, and such was his leadership that the shift was accomplished in only six weeks. The old writing system was forbidden by law, and it's said that Atatürk himself appeared in many parks with a slate and chalk to teach the new script to his people.

That's the story, and despite the abundance of umlauts and little squiggles over and under letters, I could at least make out the words. Our ship pulled up under the Galata Bridge, and nosing my way through the crowds, I followed the signs to Sultanahmet, the heart of old Istanbul. Istanbul was once known as Byzantium, a Greek city. In the Roman era it became Constantinople — the city of Constantine the Great.

I eventually found a little hotel not four hundred metres from Hagia Sophia. In 537 A.D. this grand domed church rose above the city, centuries before the great Gothic cathedrals of Europe were even contemplated. It remained a Christian church for almost a thousand years and then it was a mosque for a further five hundred. Now it's a secular museum. Across from Hagia Sophia is the Blue Mosque. Both buildings have minarets, one at each corner, and both are capped with giant domes, but the Blue Mosque isn't blue at all. Its polished stones are more like silver, glimmering under the great azure sky. The Turks took Constantinople for their own in 1452, and shortly thereafter erected this mighty twin companion of Hagia Sophia.

Since then the city has been Istanbul, at the edge of two very different worlds. This, I thought, made it the perfect place to see where the strange brushes up against the familiar, to watch what happens when one understanding touches another.

Ω

In Turkey there's plenty to buy and lots of people willing to sell. Turks haggle most unmercifully. The shopkeepers call out greetings and invite you in for apple tea. If you accept, you're hooked.

"I want to buy a carpet" in Turkish is *Halı almak istiyorum.* The word order is pretty odd. "Carpet to buy I want" would be the literal translation. It's a sentence I would caution against saying too loudly. You'll be mobbed and you'll have enough carpets slapped in front of you to cover a small country.

Turkish also makes me think about Noam Chomsky again. Here is the sort of grammatical structure he talks about. There are rules to how things move around, Chomsky says. Just as in mathematics where a formula like $a^2 + 2ab + b^2$ very neatly transforms itself into $(a + b)^2$, *Halı almak istiyorum* becomes "Carpet — to buy — I want" and finally "I want to buy a carpet."

Yes, the underlying structures are the same. Chomsky is correct, at least about grammar. The thing is, though, a grammar is not a language. It's the clockwork of a language, the gears and cogs that spin it into being, but it's not the language itself. What good ol' Chomsky misses is the most important element of all. He neglects to talk about the words. He forgets to specify exactly what the a^2 or the b^2 stand for, and that's where things start to get interesting.

The word *halı*, for example, is translated as *carpet*, but does that mean it corresponds exactly to our word *carpet*? I'm not sure. What we call a carpet is the thing we order from a store that sells rugs. We choose the colour, say, rose or a simple beige weave, and that's it. Or we might purchase a throw rug at Ikea because it's on sale or because it looks as if it might match our wallpaper.

In Turkey a *halım* (the full root) is an ancient art form. I saw women working on looms, painstakingly weaving intricate patterns one line at a time so that a single carpet might take months to finish. I'd seen the sheep's wool and the silk cocoons — little beads, smooth and shiny — that rattled with the remains of the insects still inside. I'd seen the great vats for dying colours: real indigo, saffron and the milk of daisies, chestnuts for brown. I felt the heat beneath the vats, and I'd grown dizzy with their vapours.

All this magnificent feast of the senses is wrapped up in *halım*. It's not there in *carpet*.

The same could be said for the verb *to buy*, which in Turkish, *almak*, involves much more than the slapping down of a credit card. For any self-respecting Turk there's the interminable game of haggling to be undertaken — with counter-offer after counter-offer slowly being whittling to a middle ground. After and only after these long negotiations does the shopkeeper pause and slowly nod, graciously accepting a final deal.

And so, no, the two languages — English and Turkish — aren't merely reversed grammars of the same thing. The individual words are place holders for our concepts, our whole way of thinking about a thing or an action. It's quite simple: by words our thoughts are given wings.

Φ

I did, however, want to sample one thing while I was in Istanbul
— a Turkish bath. It is, or at least was, something central to
the culture. So, just up from Sultanahmet, I found Cağaloğlu
Hamamı, a three-hundred-year-old bathhouse. From the very
beginning I didn't have the slightest idea what I was doing.
Apparently, some pretty famous people had been there in the
past — Kaiser Wilhelm II, Franz Liszt, and even Edward VII,
king of England. So what were these guys up to exactly?

I confess I had visions of a harem. I'd seen the one true
Harem just that morning over at Topkapı Palace. It was the name
of a certain part of the palace where the sultan's girls actually
lived. So at the bathhouse my suspicions were confirmed when I
was shown into a little room and told to take off all my clothes.
This was going to be good, I thought. I had visions of the dance
of the seven veils, ill-begotten dreams of nubile young Turkish
maidens feeding me grapes.

The door opened, and a large hairy man stood there. He
looked like Joseph Stalin in a tight white T-shirt. "*Çabuk*," he
growled. Later I learned that this meant "Quickly."

I stood up, radiant in my nakedness. With hairy arms, the
man wrapped a towel around my midsection. "*Çabuk Çabuk*,"
he said. That meant "C'mon, you lard-assed white man, get a
move on." In Turkish there isn't really a word for "very much."
To emphasize something you say it twice. You might call a pretty
girl (of which there are a surprising number in Turkey) *güzel* or
beautiful. Whereas a real humdinger of a supermodel would be
"*Güzel güzel*."

My bath attendant, the ever-faithful Stalin look-alike,
nodded his swarthy head down the hallway. Suddenly, I felt as if
I were in prison. What had I gotten myself into?

He led me to another door and all but pushed me in. I
was alone in an ancient domed room. Water plopped from
somewhere. I started sweating profusely, but then realized this
huge area was a steam room. High above in the domed ceiling

83

were little holes covered inexplicably with coloured glass so that the place reminded me of a cathedral. The coloured beams of light angled through the steam, and I found a piece of rock to sit on. It wasn't overly hot, and after ten minutes or so, sitting alone in the dreadful echoing silence, I figured I would at least wash my hair. It needed it, and though I hadn't brought shampoo, I had smuggled in a bar of soap. There were rock sinks built into the walls and taps above them, so I lathered up my hair. That was a mistake. The sinks had no drains. They were just big bowls really, and surely, I could see now, only meant for splashing cold water onto your face. I left a floating scum of soap bubbles and stray hair, committing a diplomatic gaffe and an insult to all of Turkey.

What about Stalin? What would he do to me when he saw what I'd done? Carefully, I snuck out through the massive wooden door on the large clackety wooden clogs I had to wear on my feet. So I didn't even make it halfway down the hallway before Stalin appeared again, tipped off by the footwear. I'd thought about kicking the clogs off, but the floors had several centuries of green mildew on them, and I figured I'd take my chances.

Stalin beckoned, a ham-hock palm waving me toward him. He grabbed me by the arm, and in a swift movement removed my modest towel. Then he led me into a proper shower room, sat me in a wooden chair by the wall, and watched as I went through the motions of washing.

I smiled at him once or twice, but he only grunted. When I finished my absurd pantomime, he moved toward me again, and in as neat a move as I've ever seen, folded a towel over my head and another around my midsection. They were neat folds, the kind a waiter in a fancy restaurant achieves with napkins. I felt like a walking piece of origami.

He took me back to the room where my clothes were, and I sat in silence for a while, then dressed and strolled out. There was no one to see me out, and I wondered if this was the same treatment kings once received. Or what about Kaiser Wilhelm — surely, that brusque Teutonic emperor had required something more?

Later I learned that Stalin would have given me a massage if I'd paid him more money. I talked with other travellers who had gone for this treatment and been soundly thrashed like a slab of meat in a packing plant. Perhaps I'd missed the richness of the cultural experience, but I was happy Stalin had kept his oven mitts off me.

Ψ

Turkish is a fascinating language. It's an agglutinating tongue, which means it piles suffixes onto the ends of root words in an almost endless train of syllables. The verb *to break* is, for example, *kırmak* (the undotted *ı* is a particular feature of Turkish, giving an *i* sound such as in the English word *sir*). From this root you can get agglutinized constructions like *kırılmadılar mı*, meaning "Were they not broken?"

Turkish, moreover, is related to most of the languages of central Asia — to Uzbek and Azerbaijani, even to Mongolian. Recent scholarship has collected substantial evidence that Korean and even Japanese might also be members of this same wide-ranging family. There are even scholars who see a link between Turkish and the Uralic agglutinating languages — Hungarian and Finnish, for instance.

So how was Turkish peppered across half the world? The answer lies in the fabled Silk Road.

It was from the shores of Constantinople that Marco Polo began his journeys. He came up to Constantinople from Venice but didn't bother to write about that part of the trip, since the route was well-known to European travellers. Constantinople, after all, was then the seat of the Byzantine Empire. There wasn't much left of the Byzantines' magnificence, but their territory had served as a base for the Crusades of the past few centuries and they were still Christian.

85

From Constantinople, Polo crossed the Bosphorus and began his famous journals. He accompanied his father and uncle along the Silk Road, east across Afghanistan and into the western deserts of China. In time he came to the pleasure palaces at Ta-tu, court of the great and wise Kublai Khan.

Ta-tu is now Beijing, and the pleasure palaces are buried directly beneath the Forbidden City and Tiananmen Square. In all probability Polo learned to speak the tongues of his day. There are many passages in his journal that indicate he spoke directly with the great Khan. What they spoke wasn't Chinese. They conversed in a kind of Old Turkish.

And that's the clue. Turkish, on one side related to Hungarian and on the other to distant Korean, trailed along with the Mongol hordes. Kublai Khan's grandfather was none other than Genghis Khan, who led his armies across Asia right to the gates of Vienna, leaving his language in his wake, the tongue that eventually became Turkish.

ξ

I, too, set out across the Bosphorus, heading for the central plains of Turkey into a fairy-tale landscape known as Cappadocia. The name comes from an Old Persian word, *katspatuka*, which means "Land of the Beautiful Horses."

Here again was evidence of the old Silk Road, though for me the trek meant many more bloody hours on a Turkish bus. Right from the start the people at the *otogar* or bus station had booked too many people onto the vehicle. At first they wouldn't even let me on. Then it was decided that some people would probably get off at the first few stops, so I was allowed to sit in the aisle. After twelve hours, however, no one got off. In the end I spread out a slab of foam in the aisle and slept comfortably.

At seven in the morning, bleary-eyed, we got off the bus and found ourselves in the small town of Göreme, home to the famous rock churches. The place is crazy. Bizarre earthen cones rear out of the ground, huge and dotted with caves. This region is volcanic. Much of the original soil has eroded, and the cones and vents of lava are all that's left. They're called "fairy chimneys" and resemble giant stalagmites that soar fifteen to twenty metres into the air.

What's more, the material the cones are made of is known as tufa. It has the peculiar property of turning rock-hard when it's exposed to air and moisture, though it's as soft as Styrofoam inside. Over several millennia people living here have tunnelled into these formations and built dwellings.

In this town Fred Flintstone's Bedrock, albeit inhabited with strict Muslims, comes to life. The women are wrapped up modestly, and the men sport pajama pants and long, swarthy moustaches. There are goats, donkeys, and chickens, not to mention the region's fabulous ruined church caves. They are called *kilise* in Turkish, and I set off immediately to see them.

Thinking myself wise and adventurous, I rented a mountain bike from a pajama-clad entrepreneur. The landscape was dazzling, and I imagined myself scooting between the hoodoos and finding dinosaur bones and ancient pottery shards. The land was dotted with cacti, though, and my tires soon bled away their air. I fixed three flats before I gave up and threw the bike into the back of a passing truck for a lift to town. Then I set off again on foot.

At first everything was absolutely magical. A valley near the town contains the Open Air Museum. Numerous caves are found among the conical formations, but the ones here are special. They're the ancient churches that date from the eighth century at a time when Christianity was desperately clinging on in the face of Muslim armies from the east. In some of the caves there are still the remains of frescoes. In the Karanlık Kilise, or Dark Church, they're well preserved because there were no windows. In the Yilanlı Kilise, or Church of the Dragon, there are murals of St. George spearing a serpent.

Walking back to town, I got lost as usual. I followed a little stream that wasn't much more than a path. Up ahead, I encountered an old man tending his fields. I had already read in my guidebook that tourists were welcome to see the churches, but they better stay off the farmers' lands. It was a something of a sore point. I debated strategically turning around, since he hadn't seen me yet, then changed my mind and called out to him. I figured it would be better to announce my presence and apologize rather than risk being sprayed in the backside with buckshot.

The farmer turned and grinned toothlessly and warmheartedly, waving for me to join him. The old man didn't speak a word of English. He motioned for me to wait and then got his jacket, which was hanging in a nearby tree. The trees were thick with nectarines. The volcanic soil there, though it looks dry and chalky, is actually quite fertile. He returned, snatched down a nectarine, and handed it to me, then fumbled in the pocket of his jacket to withdraw a little book.

The old man had withered hands, the nails caked in the dirt of toil, but he opened the book reverentially and flipped to the first pages. There on the paper were the names and addresses of all those travellers who, like me, had stumbled across his fields. The entries went back almost twenty-five years. He handed me the stump of a pencil and turned to a bright new page. With a nod he indicated I should add my name to the list, which I did. I also took a picture of him, promising to send it to him later.

Then the farmer took me around his lands. I remember there were butterflies everywhere and strange fruit that resembled kiwis. The ones on the tree were sweet, but those that had dropped to the ground were like big raisins. As we strode down a narrow valley, he made drinking motions with his hand, intoning over and over the word *sodah*. I already knew from buying bottled water in Istanbul that the Turkish word for *water* was *su*, but when we came to a small pool squirting out of the ground, he bent to drink from it, cupping his hands. Then he pointed to me.

I thought of E.coli and giardia and all the terrible fevers one can get from contaminated water. At first I shook my head, but he insisted. When I finally dipped my hands into the water, raising it to my lips, I was surprised. It was bubbly, like champagne, and fizzed across my lips. It was indeed natural soda water.

After apple tea at the farmer's house, we said goodbye. In Turkish *goodbye* is *güle güle*. It's only said by the one left behind, not the one leaving, and it means, charmingly enough, "Go smiling."

I hiked back to the main road with the farmer's wife, who was carting a load of apples on a donkey. She didn't say a word to me, but when we reached the road, she pointed me in the direction of Göreme while she continued on without a backward glance the other way.

I did send the photographs to the farmer when I finally arrived home. He had scribbled down his own address, which I still have, smudged by his earth-worn hands. I picture him now smiling at the photo, thinking of the far-off travellers who had stumbled onto his lands.

89

 ⁊

Near Göreme is a caravanserai, an ancient stopover on the Silk Road. I took a bus to it one day and was surprised at how big it was. There were places to water camels and a cavernous area of shade where merchants whiled away the time playing simple board games and speaking about the road ahead.

Marco Polo almost certainly would have stopped there. It was only a week's journey out of Istanbul and the last vestiges of civilization. Polo was travelling into the truly unknown, just like me, and I wondered if he had sat by the fountain in the courtyard and watched the crescent moon rise in the east.

The Silk Road was actually a whole thread of trails, but they did lead all the way to ancient Beijing. What we label Turkey is properly called Türkiye by its inhabitants. The name is actually believed to derive from an old Chinese word, *Tu-küe*, meaning simply "People of the Earth" or "People of the Soil." Almost certainly the term was first used to describe the Mongols who rode west along the trails with the armies of Genghis Khan.

Languages can reveal their scatterings. We can track them back to their sources, their very beginnings. What we're really tracing, however, are semiotic systems, ways of being, and that's not so easy. Meaning is often wrapped in metaphors and layers of connotation. It expresses relationships and traditions in ways that might be unique to that people, that place in the world. And those meanings, those ways of being, are born, flourish, and die just as we do.

⋺

I was attacked again by dogs in Turkey. This time I was really scared. Never had I been so heart-thumpingly sure I was in the presence of Death surrounding me, eyeing me, waiting for its chance. I kept walking, trying to make my movements seem nonchalant, but I knew that one wrong step would cause Death to hurtle toward me in a single terrible last moment.

The dogs were German shepherds, and they were all around me, growling, snarling, and snapping at the air. And there I stood, fifteen thousand kilometres from home, alone and defenceless, waiting for them to rip into me.

I've had animals attack me before. A shark came after me in the crystal-clear waters off Belize, but it was blind, old, or something, and more or less bumped into me, then continued on its way. In Spain, as mentioned earlier, a German shepherd also assaulted me.

This time, though, the threat was far more unnerving. Cappadocia is a spooky place, a backwater in time where villagers tend orchards in tiny plots of land between eerie hoodoos. They scrape the soil with wooden hoes and pile their produce into carts drawn by donkeys. Outside the hostel where I stayed just such a donkey stood in the shade, so I took a photo of the poor beast and thought it quintessential Turkey, something not seen in staged and artificial tourist postcards. And that's where the problem with the German shepherds began.

On my third day in Göreme, having explored the magnificent Open Air Museum and Underground City, I entered a winding alleyway where a donkey was being hitched to a wagon. An old woman sat up front, and two young boys were in the back.

One of the boys waved to me and called out a greeting in English. He looked about nine, though he later told me he was twelve. Small and impish, he gestured me over. "You see *kiliselar?*" he asked.

"Yes, I've seen them all. They're beautiful."

"No, no ... you come ... you see."

There were ruins all over the Göreme region, and evidently Mehmet, as he introduced himself, had some on his family's land. He told me to hop into the cart with him and his little brother. The woman driving, their mother likely, whipped a stick across the donkey's back and set the cart in motion with hardly a glance at the stranger sitting with her children.

91

Here was an adventure, I thought, a story I could write about. The cart lurched forward. A cloudless sky arched above us. I chatted with Mehmet behind the clip-clopping donkey. The boy's English was broken and garbled, but he asked eagerly after my age, my nationality, and why I didn't have a wife.

We trundled across the rutted paths, out of the village, and into the weird valleys. The landscape was magical, and the boys chattered like happy squirrels. Finally, we pulled up at a little triangle of land, and the mother, still without a word to me, pulled a hoe from the cart and set off into a melon patch.

Mehmet took his little brother by the hand and told me to follow. We strode down a dusty trail that led into the volcanic spires. This was the path that would bring me to the first kernel of fright. It was a small thing in retrospect and nothing certainly that warranted fear, but it threw me off, disturbing me perhaps more than it should have.

I had known from the beginning that I would have to give the boy *bahşiş*, a tip for his services, and I didn't begrudge him that. We climbed into a cave church, literally spelunking through a series of tunnels that led into the tufa. The church itself was unremarkable. No murals remained, and only the vague outline of benches stuck out around the sides of the cross-shaped room. Still, it was something not seen by many eyes, and I owed Mehmet that much.

When we exited, the imp straightened pugnaciously and insisted on a completely exorbitant sum, equalling about $50. I think I laughed and offered him the equivalent of $3 in Turkish lira. I was prepared to haggle, but I was met with an odd defiance.

Mehmet restated his original price and placed his hands on his hips, eyeing me with a face that was suddenly combative. His lips tightened in anger, and I could see he was serious.

"Okay, here." I withdrew another bill and dangled it in front of him. I was growing impatient. It had taken me a while to learn how to haggle. I'd been taken in by quite a few shopkeepers before I learned to do the haggle dance properly. I would cut a shopkeeper's price by half, then he would try to edge me back up. Finally, I'd walk right out of the store, and inevitably he'd cheerfully chase me down the street, fully accepting my last offer.

Now such is the power of words that what happened next truly shocked me. Little Mehmet glared at me with utter hatred and pronounced the words no one ever wants to hear. *"Fuck off!"* He spat out the words with such vehemence that I took a step backward as if he'd physically hit me.

At most his stance should have irritated me — he was, after all, only a boy — but his words caught me so completely by surprise that I dropped the lira bills at his feet, threw my hands up in disgust, and turned to leave. It was the first sign that things were going terribly wrong.

Now swearing is a strange concept in any language. I remember Chantal from Quebec saying *"Sacrement!"* all the time. Swearing consists of the words that hit the hardest and the deepest. For the French they're religious terms. Most of the world, though, seems to swear in reference to bodily parts and functions.

Swear words also need to be filled with hard consonants — something that will crack off the tongue. *Fuck* in Turkish, for example, is *sik*. In the case of *fuck* we seem to have lost the original meaning (I've heard it said that it's based on an Old Germanic word applying to the act of a farmer planting a seed). But that doesn't really matter. *Fuck* is now used with relative ease as a noun, a verb, or an adjective pretty much anywhere.

I once thought about writing an article on swearing but didn't get very far. However, I did come across the interesting fact that a true curse, such as when you hit your thumb with a hammer, doesn't come from the language centre of the brain. That's strange because all language is thought to emerge from this little language centre, a marble-size pinch of brain cells behind our left ear — all our poetry, essays, and conversation, all the brilliant repartee that makes us human. Only our harshest curses actually emanate from elsewhere. They come from what is sometimes called the reptilian brain way below the cortex, a lump of basic tissue at the stem of the spinal cord. Wordless yells of pain also originate there.

Anyway, young Mehmet told me to fuck off quite convincingly. I thought he might heave a rock at me, such was his inexplicable hatred, but I turned my back and hustled off quickly into the hills.

The problem was that I really had no idea where I was going. The bizarre pinnacles towered around me, and the valleys and crevices between them revealed no trails. I circled one and then another, conscious of keeping my direction constant. I scrambled for fifteen minutes or so, then stopped, knowing the whole situation had become ridiculous. I felt a little embarrassed that

I was fleeing from the wrath of a twelve-year-old boy. Maybe I should have swatted him. Perhaps he would have happily accepted a much larger amount, something plainly out of line with what anything else was costing me in this area of Turkey. But there was nothing I could do at that point to amend the matter. The road lay somewhere south, and I was certain that if I maintained my general movement in that direction, I'd eventually arrive at the road and be able to follow it back to the village.

I walked a bit farther and then, to be careful, decided to climb to the top of one of the volcanic spires. Here they were fat cones, maybe three storeys tall, and from the crown of one I thought I might be able to spy a road. I was calming down now and began to think that the boy had had no idea of the power of the word he'd uttered. For him it might have been something meaningless to toss out when impatient. For a native speaker of English, though, it forms the most powerful of our curses, a cracking of ugly consonants thrown up from the most primordial part of the brain.

Puffing a bit, I tried to scuttle up a sharp slope of tufa. It was gritty like sandstone, and nothing much grew on it, so there were no roots for a foothold or branches to grasp. I was near the top when I fell, probably ten metres above the ground. Actually, I didn't fall as much as slide, tobogganing down the slope, spread-eagled, with my hands desperately clawing for something to grab. I managed to keep myself upright, and when I smacked into the gully at the bottom, it was my feet that hit first.

It could have been worse. I stood for a moment, breathing deeply, then slowly I turned my hands over to look at them. The palms were shredded and were bleeding badly. None of the abrasions were deep enough for stitches, but I knew I had to get back to the hostel immediately. I had to rinse the wounds and apply some disinfectant. Then I would have to bandage my hands and would likely not be able to clutch anything hard for several days to come.

Frustrated, I shook my head and set off again, winding around the massive pillars of rock. Manoeuvring up, over, through, and around the endless gullies and chasms, I eventually came to a softening and gentling in the landscape. The pinnacles were more distantly spaced here, and between them a jumble of irregularly shaped plots of land fought for space.

These were farmed plots, and though no one was around, it was at least a sign of civilization, so I knew I must be nearing a road. I'd been warned to stay off the fields. The people who tilled the fertile soil didn't look kindly on tourists trooping across their crops.

I skirted the edge of one large patch and then, with no trail in sight, started to work my way around the edges toward the next heap of stones that would carry me south. And that was where it happened. A large German shepherd was lying in a shallow irrigation ditch ahead of me. I didn't see it until it sprang up. The fur bristled across the back of its neck, and it began to bark, fangs bared and snapping at the air.

Almost instantly five more German shepherds reared up. They pranced toward me, barking insanely, closing into a pack and forming a semicircle around me. I had nothing with which to protect myself, though it occurred to me I could whirl my camera on its strap like a sling. It was a heavy old single-lens-reflex camera, and I could at least wallop one of the dogs before I went under.

Still, that was cold comfort. Sure I'd get at least one of them, but the rest would then maul me. They'd also kill me if I tried to run. However, I figured they wouldn't attack if I didn't make any sudden aggressive movements. The dogs stood their ground, howling hot fury, but instinctively they wouldn't strike until I reacted. And I wouldn't flip that evolutionary switch for them. I didn't stop but kept walking at the same pace I'd been going when the first dog popped up. That beast was slightly off to the side now, and by keeping a steady pace, I moved between it and the others. I kept my eyes on the ground, held my breath, and continued on.

With my head lowered I strolled right through that snarling pack — an electric moment that but for the flicker of a finger could have set them ripping into me. I kept moving, conscious of them still growling at my back, but they didn't follow and I didn't turn. Even when I rounded the corner, I didn't run. After about ten minutes, I came to a road. My hands were now smarting and shaking at the same time, while my jaw was tight with tension.

It doesn't sound that bad in retrospect, but I know now that I had been closer to death than I'd ever been before, and that still spooks me. The incident in Turkey was much more terrifying than my adventure with the dogs that actually did bite me in northern Spain.

Perhaps time is needed to construct an edifice for fear, a racheting of tension is required, each moment slightly more unnerving than the last — capped, of course, with the perversely fascinating prospect of one's own death. *Is this really the way it will be?* we think. *Can it be ... in a place like this?*

The day after I was surrounded by German shepherds in Turkey, as I was leaving the village of Göreme, hands bandaged and heart stilled, I ambled past the building where Mehmet lived. The cart was there, and he was playing in the back of it. When he looked up at me, his face brightened into a smile. Then he lifted a hand and waved. "Hello, Canada!" he called merrily. And what could I do but wave back at him? I gave him an uncomfortable grin, then hoisted my backpack higher onto my shoulders.

A ten-hour bus journey brought me to the sparkling beaches of Ölüdeniz, and there the broad Aegean Sea washed away all my fears. Somewhere else my time of dying would come. Without violence, I hoped, without misfortune or pain. Like everyone else in the world, I want to slip away gently, old and grey, surrounded by the familiar clutter of a well-lived life.

Oh, and on that particular marathon bus journey, our driver, a jovial man from the far-off Black Sea region, bore a faintly familiar name — Genghis.

5

On the Roof of the World

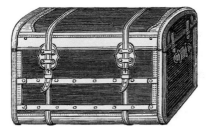

Nepal is one of the poorest countries in the world. I didn't know that when I first visited the place, though. My plane floated over the green-terraced fields, and I thought everything looked quite nice. The airport at Kathmandu was modern and clean, and even when we were mobbed by street kids wishing to carry our luggage the fifty metres or so to the bus, well, I'd seen that elsewhere many times.

It was only when we drove into the pockmarked back alleys of Kathmandu that I really began to see the extent of the city's wretchedness. There was a lot of garbage strewn about, a great deal of decaying concrete scattered everywhere, and far too many skeletal dogs wandering around. Most of all, though, there were the people: hundreds, thousands, millions of lost souls.

There are now five million people packed into Kathmandu. It didn't used to be that way. Amit, who was to be our Nepalese guide for the next two weeks of trekking, seemed almost apologetic. He was born in Kathmandu when it was no more than a village. Amit remembered the first television in town and how it was set up outside a butcher shop. Benches were put out, and everyone came to watch as the sky darkened into evening.

In the late 1960s, hippies discovered Kathmandu. Freak Street is still there, and it's hard to walk more than a few metres through the tourist district, Thamel, without a rickshaw driver hissing, "Hash? Hash? You want to buy hash?"

Thamel, in fact, is pretty cool. It's the base from which most tourists launch their treks along the Annapurna circuit or even up to Base Camp at Mount Everest. But I was going somewhere else. My plan was to hike up and over the mountains into legendary Tibet.

For many years I'd dreamed of going to Tibet. It's the ultimate destination for an adventure traveller — the roof of the world, Shangri-La in the remote Himalayas. Eight of the ten highest peaks in the world are in Tibet, including, of course, the dark northern flanks of Mount Everest itself.

I had arranged to go into Tibet through Nepal, and as fate would have it, I happened to arrive in Kathmandu on the fiftieth anniversary of the first successful climb of Everest by Sir Edmund Hillary and Tenzing Norgay, his Sherpa guide. Nepal was abuzz with the anniversary celebrations, or at least the climbing community was. The average Nepalese watched from afar, bound in an unbreakable chain of poverty.

Matters have gotten worse for most Nepalese over the past few years. The average income is about $300 a year, less than a dollar a day, and the government has been in chaos for almost a decade. The entire royal family was massacred in 2001. In the calm dawn hours of a bright June day, a nephew in the royal clan seemingly snapped. He wandered through the palace with an arsenal of semi-automatic weapons and systematically mowed down the king, the queen, the heir apparent, and three other princes and princesses. Some fairy-tale land!

On top of that, in 1996, much of the country was plunged into a civil war with the Communist Party of Nepal, a neo-Maoist group. They killed about three hundred policemen — mostly in the far-flung western provinces — and were occasionally responsible for bombings in Kathmandu itself. More than twelve thousand people were slaughtered. Eventually, in 2007, the monarchy was abolished, and under a peace deal a year later, elections were held in which the Communist Party won the most seats in the new parliament. A little later the communists were ousted, and today uncertainty still prevails in the troubled nation.

"We have a saying in Nepalese," Amit told me. *"Key gar ney."* This phrase is usually accompanied by a shoulder shrug and one of those wobbly head gestures often found in Hindu countries. It means, quite literally, "What to do? What to do?" But far from being a real cry of helplessness, there's somehow a touch of humour left in the phrase. Maybe that's a Hindu thing, an observation that life is often not under our control, and like it or not, that's the way it is.

Amit was a good sort. Actually, he was as Western as I was. He was engaged to a girl from London he'd met while leading a trek into India. She had been in the group, and as he told me, it only took a matter of days for them to fall head over heels in love with each other. Beth was her name, and she was moving to Kathmandu to live with Amit. I hoped she knew what she was getting into.

Still, Amit had it better than most Nepalese, since he worked for a British tour company. He often philosophized about his life. "When I was a young boy in Kathmandu," he told me, "I never imagined I could have a job like this, that I could be the equal of Westerners. But now the truth is that my life is very confusing. This job takes me away from reality. I go to fabulous places, but I'm not one of the tourists. And when I come home, I'm no longer Nepalese, either."

Nepal, he said, was once a great empire encompassing large chunks of Southeast Asia. Buddha, Amit told me, had been born in the time of this vast kingdom. But somehow everything had been frittered away during the past two hundred years. Now Nepal was a tiny remote kingdom — well, not even a kingdom anymore — a backwater of the great Ganges River.

"Bloody hell!" Amit cried, shaking his head. "Sometimes I can't stop thinking about what's happened to us."

The Thamel district in Kathmandu is an island removed from all the strife. It was built on the tourist trade. At one of the restaurants there, the Rum Doodle, you get a free meal if you summit Everest. There wasn't much chance of us doing that, but Amit introduced us, anyway, to his favourite Nepalese snack — momo. He scarfed down these little meat-filled dumplings as if there were no tomorrow, always asking for the "buff" momos. It took us a while to realize that the ground beef inside didn't come from cows. Since Nepal is a Hindu nation, cattle are sacred and are allowed to lumber down streets with impunity. But water buffalo are another matter.

The unlucky water buffalo would provide us with all the beef we could consume until we reached Tibet. Then it would be yaks. Yak momos aren't the greatest delicacy, but they would become a staple of our trip, sizzling over open flames at the top of the world.

During the next two days, our group arrived one by one at the hotel in Kathmandu. I had never participated in an organized group trek before, but a group visa was the only way I could get into Tibet. Groups also had to be accompanied by a designated government guide, which wouldn't be Amit. He would be the tour leader, but at the Chinese-held border we'd be met by another guide, something we were all a bit leery about. None of us were too happy at the thought of being saddled with a communist stooge, someone who would ensure that we received the proper party line.

That was later, though. Now we were in Kathmandu, and Amit was spelling everything out for us. There would be nine of us. Bryan was from Yorkshire and had just returned from skiing to the North Pole. A Norwegian couple, who had already been all over the world, was using this hard-core trek as an unlikely honeymoon. Even our Nepalese guide, Amit, born and raised in Kathmandu, was travelling into Tibet for the very first time.

Ω

The landslide had come hurtling off the mountain, sweeping away the road in front of us. A couple of boulders the size of Volkswagens had rolled onto the thoroughfare only twenty minutes before we arrived. No matter. It was our third landslide that day, and we were getting used to them.

Our party was in the foothills of the Himalayas, having driven north from Kathmandu. A solitary road comes up through the high passes here. There's just one way to get into Tibet, and it's the highest and possibly the most remote highway in the world.

The rainy season was drawing to a close, which meant water was literally gushing off the green hillsides in sheets. These waterfalls would go on to feed most of the rivers of southern Asia, but for now they were undermining the road and washing away entire hillsides.

We managed to drive over and around the first two landslides, but this third one was something else. *"Key gar ney,"* I said, shrugging.

Amit stared at me for a moment, surprised, then grinned. "You got it!"

There was nothing we could do except grab our backpacks and hike over the giant boulders. On the other side there was another stranded bus, so we simply swapped vehicles with the passengers there. Our new bus turned around and headed back toward the high passes and the border of Tibet.

Eventually, we came to a deep gorge. Over it was a narrow bridge from which all motor traffic was banned. On the opposite side was an archway with Chinese characters carved into it.

Amit grew serious. He had a sheaf of paperwork in his hands, and we followed him across the bridge to a small office. Amit spoke with some guards dressed in the peaked caps of the Chinese military, and out came a young man with a moon face.

This was Tashi, who would be our Tibetan guide. That's not his real name, for reasons I'll explain later. He shook hands with Amit, who wouldn't turn us over here but would continue as the representative of the last vestiges of Western civilization. In hushed tones they talked. Tashi spoke five languages — Chinese, Tibetan, Hindu, Nepali, and English, as well as a smattering of other dialects from all of the above.

I was encouraged to see that he was clearly of Tibetan ancestry rather than Chinese. However, we all knew he was the government-appointed guide, and he didn't seem very friendly, certainly nothing like the jovial Amit. Tashi didn't really speak to us at all. He sat at the front of the bus and conversed quietly with the driver, never smiling.

We drove into the green hills above the gorge to the border town of Zhang Mu. In Tibetan it's called Khasa, but it's primarily a Chinese border outpost now. That night we didn't get much sleep. Across the lane from us was a tavern, and deep into the evening the Chinese troops from the border post crooned sad, wailing karaoke tunes. They were young kids, really, who were far from home. The soldiers were posted here for a one-year hitch, or for two years, and they had a word for that — *jian*. In Mandarin *jian* means "a thing that's difficult to do." I got the idea that the Chinese didn't wish to be here any more than the Tibetans wanted them there.

Φ

As Buddhism travelled up through the mountain passes into Tibet, Mongolia, and eventually China, it brought with it an unexpected treasure: literacy. Sometime in the ninth century A.D. an Indian monk named Padmansambhava journeyed into Tibet riding on the back of a tiger, as legends say. He proceeded to bring the word of Buddha to these mountain people, transposing much of these new ideas onto an older and more animistic religion called Bön, which means "to invoke," an interesting shift from "to awake."

In Tibet, Padmansambhava composed a number of texts and buried them like hidden treasures deep in the Gampo Hills of central Tibet. They were eventually unearthed years later by the reincarnation of one of his disciples. Among these sacred texts was the *Bardo Thötröl*, better known in the West as *The Tibetan Book of the Dead*.

Actually, it's an instruction book to be read to a dying person, and to be continuously read — or chanted, really — over a corpse for the twenty-four hours following the actual death. The idea is to comfort and tell the soul what to expect, not only at the actual moment of death but in the period of latency following it, guiding the soul through to the eventual rebirth that will occur. The *Bardo Thötröl* is, in fact, one of the very first texts of written Tibetan. The word *Bardo*, for example, is Tibetan and not Sanskrit. Quite literally *bar* means "in between" and *do* is an island, referring to the "intermediate state" (or "in-between-ness," for lack of a better term) between one's death and the incarnation into the next life.

After a twenty-four-hour period, when the soul has left the body, the body itself is taken to a special designated area for what

103

is called a sky burial. The hair is cut off, not unlike a scalping, and then the body is systematically hacked apart with axes. The various bits, bloody pieces of flesh and bone, are strewn across the rocky ground. Tibetans see nothing disturbing about this. It's only a disposal, and in a weird way, quite beautiful, since the idea is that the birds of prey —falcons and eagles — fly off with the various bits and pieces, scattering them to the winds.

Sky burials are still undertaken today, though outsiders are no longer allowed to see them. I was told that tourists, even if accompanied by a Tibetan local, would have rocks thrown at them (quite rightly) if they tried to witness such a sight.

The reality now is that feral dogs take much of the spoils. Dogs can be particularly ferocious in Tibet. They're believed to be the reincarnations of failed monks, those poor boys who entered the monastery at the age of seven or eight and lasted only a few years before they couldn't take it anymore. These boys leave the monastery, and though there's no great shame in this, the old ways dictate that their next life, as a sort of penance, will be as a dog. The dogs are then allowed, even welcomed back, into the monastery compounds. They're thought to be returning to make amends.

Many of the monasteries are built over old sky burial sites. These are geographical points of significance from which souls depart, from which the *Bardo Thötröl* is invoked.

Ψ

I was thinking a lot about the *Bardo Thötröl*. It seemed the sort of unfamiliar way of thinking I was searching for. Tashi kept using the English word *soul* when he spoke about the *Bardo Thötröl*. I saw him talking it over with Amit. "It's not quite right," Amit said. "Tashi wants you to know that the English word *soul* isn't quite the right translation, but you don't have any other word, so it will have to do."

Words, contrary to what current political correctness might say, aren't always easily translated from one language into another. They don't always match up. The Tibetan canon is filled with complex philosophical ideas, and when we try to translate them into English, we're often at a loss. *Soul*, for example, is a word heavy with Judeo-Christian connotations. When Tibetans die, a kind of *energy* leaves their bodies. It isn't the individual's consciousness. I've heard it referred to instead as "clear light," and that's a better approximation. It's a "life force" that departs a body at death only to take up lodging in another creature a short time later.

So translations don't exactly correspond. *Suffering*, for example, comes up a lot in Western tracts on Buddhism. Buddha himself famously observed that to be born is to suffer. The exact word he used was *dukkha*. But *suffering* isn't quite it. *Dukkha* means "hard to bear," all right, but it also includes the ideas of dissatisfaction, a something-is-not-quite-right feeling, something frustrating and hollow. It's perhaps more closely aligned to Henry David Thoreau's observation that "the mass of men lead lives of quiet desperation." And we all know how true that is.

105

To my great surprise there isn't even a word in Tibetan for *Buddhist*. The term Tibetans use is *nangha*, which means "insider." Again this leads to misconceptions on the part of Westerners. *Nangha* doesn't refer to those who were born in Tibet. It's not a term of exclusion that makes the rest of us "outsiders." *Nangha* — "insider" — means "those who look inside themselves," or those who meditate, who have recognized that external things are only temporary and illusive.

The point, and it's an important one, is that in words of cultural significance, translations are dangerous things. We're usually okay with the denotations of a word (that is, a word's direct reference — this tree, that mountain), but a whirl of connotations also surround them, connotations that aren't usually apparent to those outside the language group. Such words carry weights and subtle shadings that aren't always obvious to foreigners, so the only way to understand them is to let go of everything that's familiar to us, to cut the moorings of our Western mindsets and sail into the unknown.

ξ

After Zhang Mu, we drove for almost an entire day into the highest mountains on Earth. We passed through the clouds. Waterfalls gushed down the hills, and for hours and hours there was no one else on this hairpin road. No towns, no signs, nothing but a dirt track winding up into the vast Himalayas.

In the late afternoon the landscape suddenly changed. We had reached the Nyalum Pass. *Nyalum* means something like "the path to hell." We had come out above the clouds into a moonscape where the only signs of life were the rock cairns strewn with long strings of Buddhist prayer flags.

At three thousand metres the Nyalum Pass is the true entrance to Tibet. In front of us was a desolate land, the Tibetan Plateau, the roof of the world, an area almost the size of India. Even the low valleys here are higher than the tops of the Canadian Rockies in my own backyard. And we weren't done. Our party continued up after that to the Lalung La Pass at more than five thousand metres. We inched over it and found that we had at last put the highest of the mountains behind us.

The dirt track we were travelling on ribboned between mountain passes for a thousand kilometres all the way to Lhasa. It's called the Friendship Highway, but that's a cruel euphemism. During the Cultural Revolution in the late 1960s, Mao Zedong's Red Guards ravaged this sad land, destroying more than sixty-five hundred monasteries. Here and there we could see the ruins on the tops of mountains. The monks from these monasteries, gentle old men who had spent much of their lives in quiet study and prayer, were forced to work on the road we were now travelling along. Many of them died during its construction.

On the second day, thumping along the so-called Friendship Highway, our guide Tashi finally spoke to me. We had stopped beside some nameless expanse to take photographs when he crept quietly up to me.

"Excuse me," he said. "You are Canadian?"

I'd walked off to stand beside a gurgling stream, and he'd followed. The others were taking snapshots of the mountains behind us. "Yes," I said.

"Then I will tell you something. A friend of mine is now in jail ... for three years."

"Why?"

"He was the same as me. He was guiding a group like this across to Lhasa. All of them were Canadian." He looked at me hard. "My friend began to tell them of the troubles. He spoke about things he should not have. And then ..."

"What?"

"At the end, when they came to Lhasa, one of the Canadians ..."

"Yes?"

"One of the Canadians was not Canadian. The man had a false passport. He was a spy. He turned in the guide, and now my friend is in jail for three years. Do you understand? I see you writing and I must talk to you. I must warn you to be careful."

Tashi stared at me for a few moments. "I must ask that you do not use my name in your writing. There are only a few Tibetan guides left. I am afraid for my job. Now they bring three hundred Chinese guides down. They are on a salary, but we are only paid for each trip, and there are fewer and fewer trips assigned to us. I think I will not be able to work much longer."

So Tashi isn't his real name. He also asked that I not use any photographs of him. It was too dangerous, and I began to see my own ridiculous fears for what they really were. I had

107

been afraid he was a Chinese Communist Party official. He, in turn, had been gravely afraid of us. It had taken a few days, but Tashi was finally assured that none of us were spies. When we got back on our bus, he made his first full speech to all of us. "Inside the bus," he instructed us, "you can ask me anything. I will tell you the truth. When we are stopped, though, and especially when we are in the monasteries, please, you are not to speak of politics."

That night we pulled into Tingri, the first real town since the border. The place where we stayed had a number of tiny rooms built around a gravel courtyard. There were squat toilets around the side — hideous, smelly things where it was best to pinch your nose, close your eyes, and get your business over with as quickly as possible.

After sorting our things, we gathered in the little inn. At the low tables inside I tried, for the first and last time, the famous yak butter tea. It's called *solja* or *föcha*, depending on the dialect (the *ja* or *cha* root coming from the Sanskrit *chai* for "tea"). My God, it was terrible stuff — like warm, salty liquid lard.

"It's bearable," one of our group members insisted, "as long as you don't think of it as tea. Think soup ... and it's not that bad."

There had been no rain since the day we left — we were up too high for that now — but the clouds filled the sky like a flat grey slate.

"When the skies are blue," Tashi said, "you can see the full range of the Himalayas from here."

We were lucky enough to see one of the great mountains — Cho Oyu, the Turquoise Goddess. I'd never heard of it before, but at 8,200 metres it's the sixth highest peak on the planet.

"Just behind that hill," Tashi said, waving across the long plain, "is Mount Everest."

Unfortunately, there was nothing behind the hill except clouds, and I had already acquired the beginning of a fierce headache. Everyone felt terrible. It was the first sign of altitude sickness. I went to my room to lie down. At about seven in the evening I happened to glance up from the book I was reading and spotted a high, snowy peak dancing above the clouds outside the window. It was just behind the little hill.

"Mount Everest!" I cried. Jumping up, I ran outside and knocked on the doors of the other rooms. "The clouds have broken! You can see it!"

Everyone poured out. We all went back up to the dirt road and watched as the mountain unveiled itself. Some Tibetan children descended from the village. *"Chomolungma,"* I said to them, but of course they saw it almost every day of their lives. They smiled at me, amused at my excitement. In Tibetan, *Chomolungma* means "Goddess Mother Earth" — a better name, by far, than ours.

I was looking at the little-seen North Face. In 1924 Englishman George Mallory attempted to climb the mountain from this side. Mallory was the one who, when asked why he wanted to climb Everest, famously quipped, "Because it's there." He died on the northeast shoulder of the mountain, the first of many Westerners, and it wasn't until 1999 that his mummified body was discovered in the ice at eight thousand metres. No one knows for sure if he was on his way up or whether he had, in fact, reached the summit and was on his way down to the safety of his base camp.

The top of Everest, or Chomolungma, is actually in the jet stream. Fierce winds rage off its summit, and we were lucky to see it at all. Tibetans, though, don't consider Chomolungma to be particularly sacred. Their most hallowed peak, and the goal of many pilgrimages, is Mount Kailash far to the west. Kailash is thought by Tibetans to be the source of the four major rivers of Asia, one going north, one south, one east, and one west. The

109

one that drops to the south is the legendary Ganges, the most holy of Hindu rivers.

$$\Omega$$

When we came to the next high pass, Gyatso La at 5,252 metres, I saw more strings of prayer flags. In Tibetan they're called *lungta* or "wind horses." In Tibetan Buddhism the mind is often likened to a horse. In the beginning it's a wild thing, bucking, fearful, and skittish. It needs to be subdued, trained, and focused. These wind horses are yet another metaphor to be opened up, another door into the understanding of the language and the people.

Tibet and Mongolia, of course, are well-known for their horses. Tibetans are thought to have migrated a couple of thousand years ago from Mongolia, and the two languages are definitely related. Nomadic herders probably brought these short, stocky horses with them. It is believed that these animals can race forever, and thus the idea of the wind horse arose.

Set on the high passes these prayer flags gallop on the winds to the far corners of the world. They're blessings, each pertaining to one of the five elements.

"Five elements?" I asked Tashi. The wind was blowing hard, and I had to lean into him to hear his answer.

"Yes." His voice rose above the screaming wind. "In the West you have four elements."

"Earth, air, water, and fire."

"Yes."

"But you have five?"

"The fifth element is …" Tashi hesitated. We'd had problems with this word before. "The fifth element is the soul."

And there it was again. The flags were fluttering behind us in strings of five repeating colours. The white flags were for the soul, clear light, the life energy that's neither born nor dies, the thing that's all around us and is as central to the Tibetan universe as water and fire.

Tashi later told me the story of an ancient king who chopped down too many trees for firewood. The king himself became sick, as all things are connected, and the only solution was to hang green flags (that colour representing earth) to put things back into balance. It worked. The king recovered, and the trees began to grow again.

I once heard a man on the radio say that these prayer flags were set out on high mountain passes so that their prayers could easily reach heaven. That's a twisting of the real idea to conform to our Western religious beliefs. The flags instead are more like compassion wishes. They don't ask for anything. They're simply hopes that little sparkles of compassion will fly out on the winds to reach all living things everywhere.

Φ

111

Two days later we came to Shigatse and the famous monastery at Tashilhunpo. Tashi seemed agitated. "This," he explained, "is the monastery of the Panchen Lama, the second highest lama to his holiness, the Dalai Lama. Please," Tashi warned us again. "Do not talk of politics here."

Tashilhunpo once held several thousand monks. Now there is only a handful. It's a dark, low-beamed place with the smell of a thousand years of yak butter candles.

As we entered, a man emerged and suddenly waved us back, almost pushing us out the door.

"What's happening?" I asked Tashi.

"He says the monastery is temporarily closed," Tashi said. Then he suddenly lowered his voice. "High party officials are arriving. We must wait. We can go in only after they leave."

Sure enough, a Land Rover pulled up, surrounded by police vehicles. I had a video camera and flicked it on. Tashi nudged me.

"Not a good idea," he hissed. As I started to shut off the camera, I felt a presence behind me. I turned and there was the largest Chinese man I'd ever seen. He wore dark sunglasses, and though there was no earphone wire dangling into his collar, I could tell immediately that he was a security agent. I didn't have to be told twice. I turned off the camera.

An hour or so later, when the coast was clear, we entered the monastery. Tashi pointed out a large photo of the tenth Panchen Lama. "He died in 1989," Tashi said. Beneath it was a photo of a boy. "And that is the reincarnation, the eleventh Panchen Lama." He swept us on abruptly into the next room.

It was only when we got back out onto the road, thumping along in our bus, that Tashi stood to speak. He was upset. "I wish to say now that the boy in the picture is not the true Panchen Lama." Tashi's words emerged with difficulty. "Let me tell you the full story." He took a deep breath and said that in 1959 when the Dalai Lama fled from Tibet the Panchen Lama had remained. Choekyi Gyaltsen, the tenth incarnation of the Panchen, believed it was better to try to work with the Chinese government.

During the Cultural Revolution, however, the Chinese threw the Panchen Lama in jail. And even when he was finally released many years later, he was only allowed to make brief trips back to Tashilhunpo. On a cold January day in 1989 the Panchen Lama was visiting Tashilhunpo. He complained of feeling ill and went to bed early. The Panchen Lama was fifty years old at the time, and all reports suggest he wasn't in the best of shape. A few hours later a monk was sent up to bring him an extra blanket against the cold. The monk was surprised to find the room surrounded by Chinese security agents. They wouldn't let anybody in. In the morning they announced that the Panchen Lama had died during the night.

Tashi paused and looked at us one by one. "It is possible that he died in his sleep of natural causes, but we Tibetans do not believe that. They would not allow anyone to see the body, so we believe he was poisoned. You must understand this. It is the job of the Dalai Lama to find the reincarnation of the Panchen Lama. Only he can do that. In the same way it is the job of the Panchen Lama to find the reincarnation of the Dalai Lama. That is how it works. And now this boy, our true Panchen Lama, is missing."

"Who is the boy in the photo then?" I asked.

"The Chinese named their own Panchen Lama. Both of his parents are members of the Communist Party, and now everyone must worship this new boy, but he is not the Panchen Lama."

It was a brilliant and terrible stroke. The present Dalai Lama is over seventy years old. He is in good health, but the day will come when he will die, and when he does, there will only be the Chinese-controlled Panchen Lama to find his reincarnation — and then the old way will be finished. An ancient line will be severed forever.

A brutal blow had been delivered to the very heart of Tibet, and I thought again of the *Bardo Thötröl*, *The Tibetan Book of the Dead*. It seemed to me as if the first chants were beginning. Here was a culture being killed. Here was slow death, a gradual strangulation.

Φ

It took us almost ten days to drive from Kathmandu to Lhasa, and we passed few real towns. The people here are scattered, and many continue to lead nomadic lives, moving across the plains with their goats and yaks.

When we did encounter towns, the people were suddenly different. In every major settlement the population was more than half Han Chinese. Chinese shops lined streets that were strung with red banners proclaiming Communist Party slogans. There were soldiers, guards, and spies almost everywhere.

The Chinese call Tibet *Xizang*. *Xi* is "west"; *zang* is often translated as "treasure box." It's a Chinese character homonym.

113

The character is sounded out *zang*, but also represents *tsang*, the word for the ancient Tibetan region for which Tashilhunpo is the capital.

The Tibetan Plateau is a treasure box rich in minerals. It boasts gold and silver, but it also has significant reserves of uranium. David, one of the Norwegians in our group, claimed that the Chinese weren't only harvesting this uranium but also using Tibet's vast plains for nuclear waste dumps. And then there was the hydroelectric power. If the force of the rivers that careened off the high mountains could be harnessed, they could easily provide power for much of western China. Indeed, almost the last thing the tenth Panchen Lama spoke out against was the building of a dam on the road between Tashilhunpo and Lhasa. We passed by it, and in the stone-cold waters of the lake that had now been formed, the ruins of a monastery rose on an island. It was sad and beautiful and dreadfully lonely out there in the backwash of the dam.

There are no exact numbers, but the population of indigenous Tibetan people is thought to be fewer than six million. They're spread, as I've said, over an area almost as large as India, a region a full sixth of the total Chinese land mass. In fact, Tibetans aren't a unified people at all. In the west reside the Khampa, fiercely nomadic and famous horse riders. We saw many Khampa on pilgrimages, hair braided with bright red wool, faces darkened and chiselled by the sun and wind. In the north are the Amdo. The current Dalai Lama was born in this region, and the dialect he spoke as a child, indeed the tongue his mother employed throughout her life, couldn't be understood in Lhasa.

Tibetan isn't really a single language but a collection of sometimes quite strikingly different dialects (as is the case with many "languages" around the world). The word *hair*, for example, becomes *škya* in the Amdo dialect and *štra* in the Kham dialect, while in the south, in Bhutan, they say *kya*. Similarly, a Ladakhi (from Ladakh in the far west) says *sa*, while an upper-class resident of Lhasa says *tsa*.

Furthermore, if any of these people are literate and are asked to write the word for *hair* down, they'll all produce the same written form (properly something like *skra*), which is really the ninth-century pronunciation — a form crystallized at a time when the Sanskrit writing system was first introduced.

Unfortunately, the outlying dialects are quickly disappearing, which is the first sign that the language as a whole is in trouble. In the far-flung regions of Tibet the people might still speak their own dialects at home, but increasingly, because they haven't learned the dialect of Lhasa, they conduct their business in Chinese or even English. Their children might not need to speak the dialect at all so that in a generation or two that dialect will most likely be dead. The dialect of Lhasa will hang on longer, but it, too, is being systematically dismantled and has been rendered useless and without value.

As we drove over the last high pass to Lhasa, Tashi told us his story. When he was a child, he had fled over the passes and into India. The Chinese built new schools, Tashi told us, but they weren't for people like him. From grades one to six, Tibetan is taught, but after that the language of instruction is Chinese. Before you say that's oppressive, however, consider that English is also widely taught in place of the native Tibetan. What's more, education is expensive at about 800 yuan (or $100) for three months, far outside what the average Tibetan can afford. Accordingly, most Tibetan children don't go to school. As a boy of only twelve, Tashi fled by himself over the mountains and down into India, solely to get an education.

"Where did you go?" I asked.

"To Dharamsala."

"That's where the Dalai Lama is," I said.

"Yes." Tashi smiled. "I was there for three years. I heard him speak many times."

"But then ... why are you back here?"

"The authorities in Lhasa took my father. They took him to the security building and asked him where I was." Tashi paused; I was beginning to learn what his pauses prefaced. "Of course, they already knew where I was. It was no good for my father to try to lie. It would just be worse for him. As it was, they told him that his pay would be cut off until I returned. What could I do? I had to come back."

Tashi told me later that if and when the guide job ended for him, he would return to India. There was no life and no future for him in Tibet otherwise. "The Tibetan language," Tashi said, "is useless." What he meant was that it wouldn't get him a job. It wouldn't get him anywhere in this world. And that's how a language is murdered.

What we need to remember is that when a language such as Tibetan dies it's not only its denotations — the literal dictionary meanings — that are lost. Denotations are relatively easily translated from one language into another — *bird, chair, hand*. What's much more important, as I've already said, are the connotations, the baggage a word carries with it, the metaphors it sails on. Like the wind horses on the high passes, the connotations are the ideas that lie at the heart of a language and culture. When these connotations are lost, the whole feel of that world, the way of being, disappears. For Tibet, on the roof of the world, *The Tibetan Book of the Dead* is already being chanted.

Ψ

When at last we came to the fabled city of Lhasa, we pressed our faces against the bus's windows, searching for the Tibetan capital's most famous landmark. However, we discovered something quite shocking. The fabulous Potala Palace is now almost completely obscured by block after block of squat grey apartment flats and department stores. A telecommunications tower stands on the hill where the ancient medical school used to sit. The little district of Shol, which had lain at the foot of the Potala, is gone, replaced by a wide plaza blaring with Chinese music. It was as if we had arrived in a thoroughly Chinese city. And, sadly, we had.

A majority of the population of Lhasa is now Han Chinese. Individually, they're not to blame. Many of them are small shopkeepers who have come to make a better life for themselves, just like everyone else. The one-child-per-family regulations of China are relaxed in Tibet, and there's extra money for working at high altitude so that the incentives are pretty tempting to many young Chinese. Most of all, though, there's the simple fact that China has well over a billion people. In Tibet there are a few million. It's easy to see what the Chinese government is thinking.

Lhasa itself lies in the Tsangpo Valley where barley, wheat, rapeseed, turnips, carrots, apples, pears, potatoes, onions, and cabbage are grown. It's the capital of the old region of Ü. Lhasa's name means Ground (*sa*) of the Gods (*lha*), the place where the gods dwell. It's no coincidence that the high passes are also called *la*, especially since they're all places of great spiritual force.

Until 1950 Lhasa had twenty thousand monks, but to become a monk today you need permission from the government. That's usually denied, of course, and while previously perhaps 25 percent of the population consisted of monks, now there are fewer and fewer young men entering the monasteries.

The final blow came when the first rail line into Tibet was completed. It links Beijing with Lhasa, coming up over the northern reaches of the Tibetan Plateau. And with the railway came a flood of mining operations, a swamp of cheap goods, and an unstoppable flood of people.

The project is one of the four main initiatives of the most recent Five Year Plan in China (one of the others being the infamous Three Gorges Dam on the Yangtze River). Unfortunately, this project likely spells the end of the fabled civilization of Tibet. As more and more ethnic Chinese populate Tibet, the traditional culture of the country withers. There's a saying in Tibet: "Under the communists man exploits man; under capitalism it's the other way around."

ξ

The Potala Palace rises like a fortress over the Tibetan Plateau. For almost four hundred years it was the seat of the Dalai Lama, but as I stood on its doorstep waiting to enter, Tashi gripped my arm. "Don't say anything inside. There are microphones everywhere." Then he took me into the whispering darkness of a lost world.

There are a thousand rooms in the Potala, but only thirty-five were open to us. I wasn't allowed to take photographs. At various points down the hallways monks sat on cushions, scrutinizing us in a way that made me think they weren't monks at all. This is Tibet today, a place of spies and surveillance.

Within moments of entering I was lost. Dark passageways twisted and turned like tunnels. Somewhere in the lower levels we came to the Stupa Thom of the fifth Dalai Lama, perhaps the greatest of the fourteen people who have held that title. The stupa had five levels, one again for each of the five elements, like the prayer flags. This one, however, was a couple of storeys high, was made of 3,721 kilograms of solid gold, and was studded with more than ten thousand pearls and gems. I wondered how this edifice could have possibly survived the Cultural Revolution. But it did, and even in the dark shadows it radiated a special beauty.

As we moved up through the various levels, I realized that the Potala was as large and intricate as any of the royal castles of Europe. Toward the end of our "tour" we were taken through the tiny apartments that had belonged to the current Dalai Lama as a child. I was surprised that we were allowed to see them at all, and I suspect they were left pretty much as they had been when he fled in 1959. The rooms looked comfortable, with cushions on the floor and draperies on the walls. Candles flickered in the polished wood, but nothing could erase the sense of emptiness.

A thick silence embraced the rooms, and I could almost see the ghost of a small boy there, prisoner to his fate, writing out his lessons in the quiet shadows of history.

ৰ

That night Tashi took us to a Chinese disco. We had all felt the need to let loose a little. So when the Lhasa beer arrived by the dozen, we chugged them down with abandon. My head started to swim. Tashi raised his glass again. *"Shepta!"* he called.

"Shepta!" we returned.

All over the world there are such words: *skål, sláinte, salud, prost, l'chaim*. They all mean "cheers" or "to your health," preferably with a drink in hand.

Amit joined in. *"Boomshunkar!"* he said, "Cheers!" in Nepali. This toast was a particularly good one, we thought, so we all *boomshunkar-ed* him at the top of our lungs. Soon enough a kind of floor show began. I had never seen anything quite like it. A dancing papier mâché yak tottered out, and the young female dancers who, beer notwithstanding, were looking pretty good, proceeded to milk it. Then there were more songs, karaoke really, crooned by the pretty Tibetans.

"What are they singing about?" I asked Tashi.

He listened for a moment. "Agricultural production. They are saying that the agricultural production is very good this year."

So to the sweet strains of a Chinese version of "Moon River" the young ladies belted their hearts out to the simple statistics of barley yields.

I had already seen a few quirky things in Lhasa. We had all gotten a good laugh at many of the Chinese shopkeepers' signs. SUPER EXCELLENT SNACK OF CHONG KING, one had read. Another was: THE STORE OF GREAT BENEFIT. When we went in to check that one out, Amit had pulled a little box off a shelf. "Look at this," he had said, laughing. Beside the Chinese characters was the English translation — INSURANCE GLOVES, it read — and when Amit opened the package, the insurance gloves had turned out to be condoms.

Outside the disco, at about two in the morning, we came across a barbershop set up on the sidewalk. Who knew what the barber was thinking — unless he was clever enough to know that drunken tourists stumbling onto the forbidden streets would instantly desire a haircut. So we all lined up for this old man and got trimmed.

I approached the mirror a bit tentatively the next morning, but found to my delight that the barber had actually done a good job. When I joined the rest of our group downstairs for a hungover breakfast, all the guys were preening a bit and admiring one another's brand-new hairdos.

Ω

120

We were lucky enough to be staying in the Barkhor area of Lhasa. Barkhor is the ancient marketplace, and at the centre of it is a temple called Jokhang. We had arrived, after ten days of hard travelling, to find the Potala Palace surrounded by a very Chinese city. Many of the earliest buildings had been bulldozed, so it was with some relief that we found ourselves in the old section of the city.

We put down our backpacks and sat on a stoop that overlooked Jokhang, none of us talking, everyone a bit tired and depressed and almost ready to go home. In front of us, though, an amazing procession was taking place. It went on all day, from the first rays of dawn to the setting of the sun over the distant hills. The pilgrims had come.

From across Tibet these people had arrived, many elderly, having walked several thousand kilometres to get here. Jokhang is the single most holy place in Tibet, and our little inn was directly across the street from it.

The pilgrims had come to do their final *kora*, a circumnavigation of the temple in which they walked three times around the sacred building before entering. Many of them twirled hand-held prayer wheels. As we sat there dejected, watching an era of history seemingly coming to a close in front of us, it was Bryan from Yorkshire who got up first.

Bryan was in his late fifties but was a hard-core traveller. Only two months earlier this usually quiet man had skied to the North Pole from a Russian whaling station at the edge of the Arctic ice sheet. Suddenly, he got up and joined the pilgrims. I sat for a moment longer, then got to my feet, as well. Hundreds of pilgrims were milling around the temple now, and I strolled among them, unsure what their reaction would be. But I needn't have worried. I was quickly enveloped by weathered, aged faces lighting up in smiles. Curiously, old people here often have near-perfect teeth. Either it's something to do with the plain diet, or as Tashi told me later, we were literally too high for most forms of bacteria to live. As I walked with the pilgrims, I was greeted with more flashing smiles and was touched warmly on the shoulder.

Like them, I proceeded around Jokhang three times in a moment of true transcendence. That's what I recall most about Tibet — being carried along in a crowd of smiling, rag-tattered pilgrims. Near the doors the most pious prostrated themselves over and over. Some, I later learned, had actually come across the entire country on hands and knees, springing up to pray, taking a step forward, then down again. It must have taken months to get here like that.

Φ

On my last day in Lhasa I asked Tashi what would happen next. Did he think there was any chance the Dalai Lama would be allowed to return to Tibet?

"Listen," he said, "you know when Mao Zedong died in 1982, that's when the Panchen Lama began to speak out. Then Deng Xiaoping took over as paramount leader."

"Tiananmen Square," I said.

"Yes, Deng was the Chinese leader during the massacre. But we waited, and in the 1990s Deng was succeeded by Jiang Zemin, who became the president of the People's Republic of China. But he, too, has now stepped down, and our worst fears have come true. In March 2003, Hu Jintao became president."

Hu Jintao, I found out later, is now general secretary of the Chinese Communist Party, president of the country, and chairman of the Central Military Commission. Currently, he's the most powerful man in China.

"The West," Tashi continued, "is waiting to see what Hu Jintao will do. But we in Tibet already know."

"Know what?"

"In 1989, when our Panchen Lama died, Hu Jintao was in charge of Tibet. He was the head of the Party Committee here. So most likely it was he who gave the orders to poison the Panchen Lama."

"If he was poisoned," I said.

"Yes, but in our minds there is no 'if.' So when you ask me, do I think the Dalai Lama will be allowed to return ..." Tashi didn't need to finish that sentence. I knew the answer.

6

The Heart of Darkness

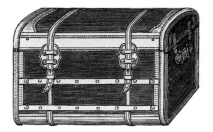

The airport at Siem Reap was small. Our plane careered out of the night sky and skidded across the tarmac. When we finally rolled to a stop, there was only silence and darkness. We stepped onto the landing field and were herded toward the customs house by a row of grim soldiers. In their hands were machine guns.

We lined up solemnly to pay for our visas. I handed an American $20 bill to an "official" behind the desk and saw him slip the note into his pocket before I'd even fully turned my back.

Outside, the air was hot and thick with the musk of tropical vegetation. No birds sang; there was only the swish of palm fronds in the evening breeze. A scurry of taxi drivers besieged us, and we chose one randomly to bump across the dusty yellow road into Siem Reap. I was with an older New Zealand couple I'd met in the line, and they'd heard of a place called Sweet Dreams. That was good enough for me. The taxi driver pretended he'd never heard of Sweet Dreams. Of course, he wanted to take us to another place he knew that was "very fine, very good." Undoubtedly, it belonged to a friend or relative, but we insisted on Sweet Dreams, so he grudgingly turned down an alley and dropped us off at a high concrete wall.

Immediately, everything changed for the better. We were met by the family that ran Sweet Dreams. They were all smiles and good cheer. A frog hopped happily across the pavement at our feet, the first relief in a tense night. Soon I found myself in a clean room for $6 a night, and I even had a whirling fan overhead. I stopped and breathed deeply. I was in Cambodia and was about to see a place I'd dreamed about for half my life.

Only a few kilometres north of Siem Reap are the temples of Angkor. Eight hundred years have come and gone since Angkor shone with magnificence. Some say Angkor was the first city on Earth to reach a population of one million. It was the capital of the ancient Khmer civilization, a kingdom that once stretched across the length of Southeast Asia. Most of it is now gone, eaten up by the jungle. The old houses and the shops were made of wood. Even the palaces of the kings were constructed of mahogany and teak, and only the temples were built of stone because of an ancient Khmer belief. The gods, it was thought, were solely worthy of such permanence, and just their dwellings could be made of stone. So today all that remains of Angkor are these temples, dotted like islands in a jungle landscape of three hundred square kilometres.

The temples, in turn, are intricately carved with inscriptions in ancient Khmer and Sanskrit. Along the bases of many temples are bas reliefs, statues embedded in the walls as if they're emerging from the stone, and these bas reliefs recount both the great Hindu epics and the rise and fall of the civilization at Angkor, a place far removed in both time and geography from anything I had ever seen. I was looking forward to unlocking some of their secrets, if indeed I was able to understand them at all.

Ψ

In the morning the birds were singing. I went down for breakfast and was quickly introduced to the young man who would be my driver. I hadn't asked for a driver, and a guide wasn't strictly necessary here, but at a dollar a day it was a luxury worth indulging in. Vana was twenty-three years old. He wore an old green baseball cap and smiled at me shyly. It was then that I realized nobody here was much older than twenty-five. The old people were missing. They were all dead. The Killing Fields had taken care of them.

Eighty percent of the Cambodian population was born after 1979. That's the year the Khmer Rouge was finally ousted from Phnom Penh, the country's capital, and when the true extent of its crimes against humanity started to become apparent. Well over two and a half million people perished out of a total population of about seven million. All the intellectuals — teachers, professionals, anyone wearing glasses — were rounded up, as was everybody who had anything to do with the West. They were tortured and murdered, and their bodies were dumped in anonymous fields. To make matters worse, the Khmer Rouge forcibly removed Cambodians from the nation's cities and towns. These people were shunted onto farms and expected to eke out a living from the soil, though they were shopkeepers and simple businessman who had never planted seeds in their lives. Many of these relocated Cambodians starved to death. Others suffered greatly or perished when the Khmer Rouge cleared out of Phnom Penh and continued to fight a civil war against the invading Vietnamese and their Cambodian allies throughout the 1980s and early 1990s.

125

The Khmer Rouge was a neo-Maoist organization that took its cue from the devastating Cultural Revolution in China. It wanted to purify Cambodia of all outside influences in a misguided attempt to turn the clock back to the great age of Angkor. The Khmer Rouge attempted to create something akin to a second Khmer empire. In the end that wasn't possible — no more so than trying to turn Europe back into the weave of absolute monarchies it had once been, or re-creating the Confederate States of America.

Vana was born in the dying days of the Khmer Rouge terror. He was a gentle soul who spoke English quite well. So for the next few days I rode behind him on his little motor scooter in the hot tropical wind.

ξ

The word *khmer* means "slave," an ethnonym adopted later by Cambodia's Thai and Vietnamese conquerors. What a telling epithet. The history of Cambodia is a story like no other right up to the present day. It's such a long, sad tale, a saga of kings, snakes, rivers, and gods. But like any good saga, one has to start at the beginning, in this case with the fabulous city of Angkor.

Vana and I zipped up a vaguely paved road. Astride the scooter, I squinted through the dust and sunlight. There was no indication that we were about to come upon one of the wonders of the world. A snake wiggled across the road, while a monkey sat in the shade of a tree. We buzzed past them and approached a moat running beside the road. The water in it flashed sharply in the sun. And then, just on the other side, the outer walls of Angkor Wat appeared.

Angkor Wat is a temple that was built in the early years of the twelfth century. It is said to be the most perfect piece of architecture in the world. We rounded a corner and went up onto a dirt trail between some trees. Vana halted the scooter, and I hopped off. Before us was the Rainbow Bridge. It crossed the moat and went in through the outer gates. I walked under the archway and found myself in darkness for a moment. Then I emerged into a world I couldn't believe and got my first good look at Angkor Wat. Suddenly, I was faced with one of humanity's great accomplishments. It was gorgeous, breathtaking, an edifice that no amount of adjectives could fully capture.

Vana stood behind me, silent, allowing me to take in the view. When I finally turned, he came up beside me. "Do you see the lotus towers?" he asked. I saw them, one in each corner of the great building, and a fifth, the most massive, rising from the centre of the temple, intricately carved, soaring darkly and majestically into the sky.

The ancient Khmer people adopted an old Hindu belief that a temple must be built to exact mathematical proportions. If the measurements of the temple were perfect, they thought, then there would also be perfection in the universe.

I was looking at perfection.

Angkor Wat is huge. It's actually the largest religious monument in the world and is even larger in area than St. Peter's in Rome. This temple took more than thirty years to erect and is only one of hundreds throughout the jungle in northern Cambodia. It's a Hindu temple dedicated especially to the god Vishnu.

Three immense terraces rise above a wide plain. The Rainbow Bridge sweeps in toward them. The balustrades are long carved snakes. These are called *nagas* — "snake" in Sanskrit — and they're an especially prominent symbol here. This was the stuff I was searching for — how these ancient minds thought, how they encoded their world.

Between the outer walls and the temple itself were wide fields where a few dozen villagers swung scythes. I couldn't figure out if they were actually harvesting something or whether they were cutting the long grass around the temple. But I knew Angkor Wat was built by such people once upon a time. The scene I was witnessing wasn't so different from what it would have been eight hundred years earlier.

I entered the temple and had it almost to myself. A few villagers were gathered around their morning meals, but there were very few tourists. Slowly, I climbed from level to level, and at the top, the third terrace, up a steep set of rock steps, I came into the inner sanctum. Only the king and his high priests were allowed here in ancient times. From this vantage point I could survey the whole complex. The lotus towers represent the five peaks of holy Mount Meru. Vana told me all this, though I had no idea what Mount Meru was supposed to be. Pointing out across the fields, he said that the outer walls represent the mountain ranges that hem in the Earth, and outside that, the deep and tranquil moat suggests the infinite seas that surround the world. So, in effect, Angkor Wat is the world, the entire universe.

This metaphor was one of the first of many I needed to understand. *The temple is the world.* I thought about that, remembering my studies in linguistics. Metaphors are much more than literary devices, far more than poetic tricks. A proper metaphor stands in for a whole field of meaning.

In fact, the human mind is uncannily good at constructing these metaphorical systems. Languages are infused with such metaphors, and they're often so subtle that we have no idea we're working under conceptual umbrellas. For example, *love* in English is "madness" so that we are "crazy for someone." They drive us "out of our minds." To u*nderstand* in English is "to see." We talk about it with such phrases as "Am I making myself clear?", "Do you get the picture?", and "Let me point it out to you." Happiness is up ("I'm on top of the world," "Things are looking up," "That boosted my spirits"), and sadness is down ("I'm feeling down," "My spirits sank," "I fell into a depression").

Metaphors pervade language. They lie beneath the surface but form the context by which we systematize our thinking. Each language has them, though they vary from language to language so much that cross-cultural misunderstanding often arises from a misreading of the underlying metaphors. Whole structures of meaning, entire ways of seeing the world, are embedded in the phrases we utter. And these are truly the foundations of our Palace of Words.

ζ

Vana led me up to the second terrace. There were Buddhist monks there, the young males in saffron robes, the old women in white. They were burning incense, and on a kind of patio, an old man I had assumed was a monk had doffed his robes. He was bare-chested and sinewy. With an old broom he swept the stones where a puddle of water had gathered from the last rainstorm. It was hard to tell how old he was, perhaps sixty or even seventy, but I stopped and watched him for a while. His thin arms pumped the broom, and the whisking of its stalks echoed throughout the stone architecture. Strangely entranced, I followed his movements until he glanced up at me. This was the first truly old person I'd seen here, and there was something powerful in that. Even Vana seemed profoundly respectful of this peasant monk, and after a few moments, he pulled me away and out onto the first terrace.

Around the outside of the lower terrace ran the legendary bas reliefs of Angkor Wat. They go on for eight hundred metres along the side of the massive building, then around a corner and onward for a total of almost three and a half kilometres of carvings. Along the western walls, aligned as they are with the blood-red sunsets, are scenes of violence, destruction, and death. Here I found battle scenes from the history of Angkor — curving and swirling armies locked in frozen stone. The soldiers of the great enemy, the Cham troops of ancient Vietnam, march across the walls, glaring out across the centuries.

In the other direction, on the eastern walls, the rising of the morning sun illuminates a set of very different carvings. These are the Hindu creation myths, and one, a set of carvings that runs almost four hundred metres, has become more famous than all the rest. It tells the story of the Churning of the Sea of Milk.

I had come here specifically to see this lengthy saga in stone as a sort of personal test, as a way to plunge myself into an utterly alien world. The Churning of the Sea of Milk is a central story in the Hindu epics. To understand it one must comprehend something about the god Vishnu. Hinduism, I must admit, is among the most confusing of religions for me. Hundreds and even thousands of gods attend the world. Some of my bewilderment rests in the fact that gods such as Vishnu can appear in different incarnations. After all, I still have problems figuring out the Holy Trinity in Catholicism, so what luck would I have with a god who appears in at least nine different forms?

Vishnu, the Preserver, descends to the rescue of the world whenever it's threatened by catastrophe. Nine times it has happened. A tenth is still to come. Vishnu appears as different avatars, sometimes as a human (as in his incarnation as the man, Krishna), sometimes as an animal. Always, though, he guides the world to ultimate triumph over chaos.

So this set of carvings represents one of Vishnu's nine incarnations, in this case as a turtle. What happened was that before the world existed as we know it the gods and demons battled with one another. The fighting went on for so long and grew into such violence that the very emergence of the universe was lost in a swell of anarchy.

Here, I admit, I'm already unclear about the details. I keep, of course, trying to wedge the story into my own Western conceptions, but it simply won't fit. At any rate, Vishnu appeared to these feuding gods and demons and gave them a task in which they would seemingly work against one another but in reality would act together. Confused? Don't worry. I was, too, until I saw the line of carvings at Angkor Wat. The task was a tug-of-war, very much like the game we know in the West.

The gods would pull on one side and the demons on the other. The rope itself was really a snake — the *naga* symbol again. The only difference between this cosmic match and a simple tug-of-war game was that the rope, or in this case the snake, had wrapped itself around a mountain between the two pulling sides — Mount Meru, of course, the same peak that Angkor Wat represents.

So with the gods tugging on one side and the demons on the other, they slowly began to churn this mountain, like the agitator in the centre of a washing machine. Back and forth they went until the mountain swung around one way and then the other so that it churned the cosmos. Vishnu, now in the form of a turtle, held the mountain on his back, and together the gods and demons spun the universe into being.

A strange story indeed, but it was exactly what I was looking for — something so different, so loaded with alien metaphors that I would have to struggle mightily to make any real sense of it. I wanted to find something so profoundly outside my own experience that I could see just how far the elastic band of human thought snapped.

What do these long lines of carved figures mean? They tug on a giant snake, turning a mountain, churning the Sea of Milk. I can only reach for a Western metaphor: The Sea of Milk is our own Milky Way, the deep stars of night. That made sense to me — the gods spinning the universe into existence. And with the spiral galaxies left as confirmation of this swirling and churning, the metaphor seemed appropriate.

Of course it's not. I was nowhere near the mark.

It's a difficult exercise, teasing out metaphors. According to the Hindu epic, the churning cast off magical elephants and exotic dancing girls called *apsaras* (whose beautiful images are all over Angkor). They have nothing to do with our modern Western conceptions of the universe. I'd done the best I could to figure everything out, but I was no Carl Jung, Northrop Frye, or Joseph Campbell. I couldn't identify the archetypes that matched

131

up with any of the myths I was familiar with. I couldn't sort out the metaphors of this odd story. They were simply not available to my ways of thinking.

꒳

Later Vana told me there was more to the story. He explained it carefully, watching me nod when I understood, going back over it when he noticed I wasn't getting it. The snake, the *naga*, was named Vasuki. This snake, being looped around the mountain and tugged back and forth by the gods and demons … well, he gradually became sick. Finally, he started to throw up. He vomited out a terrible blue poison, just as the universe was being churned into existence. Vishnu, already holding up the mountain, could do little but witness the blue vomit spreading like a mushroom cloud. Another of the great Hindu gods, Shiva, appeared and swallowed the poison even as it threatened to destroy the new world. Shiva drank down the dangerous venom, which burned him so badly that it left his throat a frightful blue. But in his sacrifice he saved the world.

Now there was something vaguely familiar. A god and a sacrifice. It fitted in with another story I'd heard.

A couple of hundred years ago, when the first real contacts were made between Cambodia and the West, a young missionary appeared in the jungle eager to preach the gospel of Christ. The man tried to introduce the idea of Jesus to the villagers. He attempted to impress upon them the importance of Christ's sacrifice upon the cross, showing the local people his wooden crucifix and explaining everything. But they were profoundly uninterested.

An old villager, taking pity on the missionary, told the visitor about the Churning of the Sea of Milk, about the snake Vasuki and the spinning and the spewing out of his venom. The missionary, who apparently was a clever young chap, thought about everything for a long time and then painted his own little figure of Jesus a deep shade of blue. He brought it out again, and this time, slowly, comprehension lit the eyes of the villagers. The missionary held up the blue crucifix for all to see. It was the sacrifice of the god, he explained. He sacrificed himself in order to save the world. The stories were the same.

So metaphors can, with difficulty, be unfolded. Jesus, in this case, needed to be blue. That was the Khmer — actually, the Hindu — symbol for sacrifice. The villagers understood that, and so, too, did I.

$$\Omega$$

Over the next few days Vana took me to temple after temple on his puttering scooter. At one temple I was followed for an hour or so by a bright young boy who must have been about seven years old. I'd seen many children put to work here. I called this little guy Cowboy because of the print of a cartoon cowpuncher on his ragged T-shirt. He told me he would be my guide, but for the most part I showed him around the place, explaining as best I could what my guidebook was telling me about the history and architecture of this particular temple. At the end I bought him a Coca-Cola, and he seemed delighted with the deal. So Cowboy, probably much as Vana had done before him, was learning English.

133

It's dangerous, though. The kids can make a decent living learning a foreign tongue, but there's a cost. Another small slice of the world becomes generic, a part of the all-consuming face of the West. Should I be feeding the children Coca-Cola? Will it turn their young throats blue?

Vana and I developed a strange relationship, as well. After spending each day tramping around Angkor, we returned in the evenings to Sweet Dreams. Usually, he would ask if I was hungry and then disappear around the back to the kitchen.

One night Vana came out with a dish of food. He insisted that I sit and be served by him, as if he were a waiter or even a servant. I tried to get him to sit, too, and finally, uncomfortably, he slid beside me, unsure of his role. This action went against everything he knew. That we could be equals, that we could be friends, was alien to him.

We talked some more, and he seemed to lighten up a bit. Finally, he leaned into me and said, "Tomorrow I can take you to the Linga River. This is something you must see."

"All right."

"It's far," he warned.

"That's okay."

"So we go early?"

"All right." I braced myself to get up in the dark hours before dawn.

Φ

Vana took me farther north than most people go — to the outlying ruins of the old city of Angkor. In the distance, as we scootered over the potholed road past water buffalo and rice paddies, were the sacred mountains, the Phnom, and along the way we witnessed people harvesting the land as they had for centuries. We stopped once while Vana got his bearings. We had already been travelling for more than an hour and our destination was drawing near.

Finally, we arrived at a nondescript trail, and Vana asked me if I was really up for the walk that lay ahead. It was four or five kilometres to the top, he said, and the day was scorching. I told him I did lots of hiking in Alberta in the mountains near where I lived. Of course, I knew this would be different. Here I would be slogging through the jungle. I talked of bears, Vana spoke of snakes, and we each tried to scare the other all the way up the hot, winding trail.

After a while, we came to a river and followed a red-earth path along its banks. Here and there we saw signs that the ancients had preceded us. Faces were carved into the rocks in the river, and water splashed over them eerily. Eventually, the river opened into a pool with a cascading waterfall. We scampered across the rocks like children, and I noticed that my skin had grown browner. For the first time I felt as if we were friends, as if I were justified being here.

We sat at the top of the waterfall, and Vana told me another story. Cambodia has always been famous for its folktales. They might even be older than the Hindu epics and are certainly at the heart of what it means to be Cambodian. The Hindu books came to Cambodia with the omnipresent Sanskrit. Modern Khmer is now written in this same swirling text, but ancient Khmer survives on its own, untempered by outside influences, and is most purely heard in folktales. Like Aesop's fables, the Cambodian tales are often allegories. They have morals to be learned and are frequently thinly veiled references to real situations and human folly.

135

When the world was still young, Vana told me, and the palaces of Angkor were newly constructed, there was a young king on the throne. He was, of course, delighted with his magnificent new city. In fact, he thought it was the distilled essence of beauty.

Convinced that the city's loveliness lay in its newness, the king decreed that nothing old should ever appear within its precincts. Nothing should stain the city's beauty. So all old things were removed or hidden, and in time even old people were banned from its streets and ramparts.

There was one old man who had lived in a simple hut for as long as anyone could remember. But he, too, was forced to leave the city that had been built around him. He took up his things and fled, coming after a time to an old cave that lay on the banks of a roiling river.

The years went by, but of course all things change, all things are impermanent, and the day came when the armies of the great enemy, the Cham from far-off Vietnam, arrived at the gates of the city. They arrived with elephants and war chariots and were clearly the superior force. The young king of Angkor, in desperation, sought to negotiate with the king of the Cham before his city was laid waste.

The king cowered before the Great Cham, and the conqueror laughed and mocked him. This Great Cham was a lover of riddles and saw a chance for some fun. "You can keep your kingdom," he told the Angkor king, "if you can answer this."

He held out a piece of wood. It was as long as a thigh bone and just a little wider, cut as it was from a young tree not far from the palace. "Tell me," the Great Cham said, "which way this branch has grown. Which is the bottom and which is the top? Give me the right answer, and I shall spare your city. You have one day to decide."

Frantically, the young king went down to the swirling river to think. He sat on its bank and stared at the riddle stick the Cham had given him. Which was the bottom? It was impossible to tell.

Eventually, the old man emerged from his cave. He saw the distress on the young king's features. Moved by the monarch's weeping, he asked if he could help. When the king showed the branch to the old man and explained the riddle, the old man snatched it and heaved it into the water.

Near the shore was a small whirlpool, and as the piece of wood approached it, the old man told the king to watch the branch carefully. It would, he said, be pulled down on the side that was the heaviest — its bottom. That was where it had grown from. The top would bob up, and the river would tug at the bottom.

And so that was what happened. The king pulled the branch from the whirlpool and ran with the answer back to the mighty Cham. When all was done and the armies of the Cham had departed, the young king realized the truth. He saw at last that beauty was fleeting and that the wisdom that came with age was infinitely more important. The old man had saved the kingdom, so the king fell on bended knee and asked for forgiveness. The elderly, he decided, were the wise ones of the land, and thereafter at Angkor the old ones became the most honoured. It was the old ones whose souls inhabited the stones in the river. It was the old ones who remembered everything most clearly.

Ψ

There is a famous saying in Khmer: *Ngoey skát àon dák króap.* It translates as: "The immature rice stalk stands erect, while the mature stalk, heavy with grain, bends over." What it's really about is bowing, humbling oneself before one's elders. Khmer parents teach that to their children. They must show respect toward their elders by bowing to them. In Khmer the word *àon* is used to describe this show of respect, though it's also used to describe the bending over of the mature rice stalk. Seen in a rice plant, it's an indication of the bounty, richness, and maturity of the grain. In a person it indicates good character and respect and, of course, wisdom.

137

The Mon-Khmer language is spoken by more than seven million people in Cambodia. It belongs to a family of languages called Austro-Asiatic. Most of the other tongues in this group are quite small. They're spoken in pockets from northeastern India all the way to Sumatra in the Indonesian archipelago. The two largest languages in the family are Khmer and Vietnamese. But unlike Vietnamese (with six tones) or Chinese (with four tones) or even Thai (with five tones), Khmer is somewhat unusual in Asia because it isn't tonal.

Even so, I confess that I didn't learn very much Khmer. Vana spoke English well enough to converse on almost any subject, and even when I asked him some difficult questions about Buddhism, he looked up the English words he didn't know —

he must have had a dictionary in his hut — and then gave me a better answer in the morning.

On my last day in Angkor, Vana and I visited a section of palaces and terraces called Angkor Thom in the very heart of the city, a site encircled by a massive twelve-kilometre wall. In each of the cardinal directions there were gates, and guarding the gates and lining the roads that entered them, were long columns of carved stone figures. When we puttered through the southern gate on Vana's scooter, I saw something quite remarkable. Between the statues, strung from one stone figure to the next, was a long balustrade. Vana told me to peer closer, and when I did, I spotted a snake. It was Vasuki, the *naga*, and these were the gods and demons from the Churning of the Sea of Milk. The story was obvious, but this time Angkor was being spun into existence from the very fabric of the universe. The Khmer had taken the ancient Hindu epic and made it their own.

Above the gates I noticed a large carved Bodhisattva face. Many believe that this is the face of the last and greatest of the kings of Angkor, gazing down upon all who enter his city. In 1181, Jayavarman VII came to power, and it was he who built Angkor Thom.

Vana squinted at the sun and told me that Jayavarman's royal palace was inside these walls. Little is known of this king, though one thing is certain: he broke with the Hinduism that had come before him and became a devout Buddhist. Since that time, Cambodia has been a Buddhist country.

In the centre of Angkor Thom sits an ancient Buddhist temple called Bayon. At its entrance are fortune tellers and sellers of incense, though saffron-robed monks still glide through the galleries of Bayon. Buddhism, of course, has a particular relevance here. A release from the suffering of the world is available through Buddhism, and no one can argue that Cambodians haven't had their share of misery.

Among the Buddha's last words to his disciples were: "If a snake lives in your room, and you wish to have a peaceful sleep, you must first chase it out. And so it is you must break the bonds of worldly passions and drive them away as you would a snake." Here again is a transcendental idea. The snake that churned Angkor into being must now be chased away. The symbols were changing, and it was time for dissolution, time for the great collapse.

Around the lower galleries of Bayon there are more bas reliefs. As they do at Angkor Wat, the carvings encircle the temple, but here the stone gives way to something wholly different. Perhaps it's the Buddhist influence, but for once there are no scenes of kings and their epics. Here instead are carvings of everyday people, the lives of Khmer peasants from eight hundred years ago.

The reliefs show the women of the city gathering at the market, potters producing cups and plates, and a group of wine drinkers watching a distant performance of royal dancers from a window. There are seeming legions of shopkeepers touting their wares. Farther on there are fishermen on nearby Tonlé Sap Lake. One man has mysteriously fallen overboard and a crocodile rises to meet him. The reliefs blend together so that in the next scene there are gamblers betting on a cockfight. Another huddle of men trues a wheel. It's a kingdom of the people under the wise and gentle rule of Jayavarman the Buddhist.

After Jayavarman died in 1221, there were no more temples built at Angkor. The city began its long, inevitable decay. It was almost as if, in only a generation or two, the people left behind their desire for worldly things and all ideas of grandeur. Year after year the jungle encroached on the great city. The wooden buildings rotted and collapsed, and at last the temples themselves were lost in the undergrowth. It was the end of Angkor. The churning had been completed.

I said goodbye to Vana that night. I would be leaving early in the morning and wouldn't see him again.

ξ

At dawn I clambered into the long boat that would take me across Tonlé Sap Lake and eventually to Phnom Penh. There had been a mighty crack of thunder the night before, heralding the advent of the rains. Tonlé Sap, the largest lake in Southeast Asia, swells wildly in the rainy season, and the river at its other end might be one of only a handful on Earth to actually reverse direction from season to season. In the dry season it flows south toward Phnom Penh, emptying into the Mekong River. In the rainy season it flows north into the lake. Bizarre.

I rode on the roof of the boat for a while, gazing at the fishing villages tucked among the reeds of the shore, but then the sun came out of the clouds and I fled into the cool shadows below the deck. For many hours we chugged along the river until finally we came to the docks at Phnom Penh.

Suddenly, things were quite different. In this sad, dusty city, not only did I see no old people, I also noticed a frightening amount of younger ones missing legs and shuffling about on makeshift crutches. Cambodia is still one of the most heavily land-mined countries in the world. Many are leftovers from the Vietnam War, and a great deal are American. The Americans bombed Cambodia heavily in the early 1970s in an attempt to break up Vietcong supply lines. These supply lines took no notice of the official borders, of course, so they penetrated deep into Cambodia.

One type of land mine is made entirely of plastic explosives and can't be located with traditional metal detectors. The big problem is that, during the rainy season, these plastic land mines often float off. They're now dispersed across the country and can be found almost anywhere. Sadly, it seems as if every tenth person in Cambodia has had an appendage blown off by a land mine.

Phnom Penh is a nasty, windblown hellhole. The taxis are mostly motor scooters, and when I hopped onto one, the driver first addressed me in French. He was probably thirty-five years old, one of the few people of that age around. I wondered what he had done during the Khmer Rouge years. He scowled a lot, and I imagined he might once have been a child soldier of the Khmer Rouge. His French was quite fluent, but he switched to broken English when he realized I wasn't European.

"You want to shoot gun?" he asked.

"Excuse me?"

"Kalashnikov, M-16, you choose."

I had heard of this sort of thing. You were taken out to a place where you did indeed have a choice of weapon at a dollar a round. "I'm not really interested."

"You want to throw hand grenade?" The city whizzed by us. He tipped his head back slightly so I could hear over the wind.

"What?"

"Is okay," he said. "You throw grenade into water."

Apparently, this was the best idea they'd come up with for tourism. Someone else had told me that for $50 I could shoot a rocket launcher at a water buffalo and watch it explode.

"Okay, okay ..." My driver paused for a moment. "So you want girl?"

"Look, just take me to the market."

The Russian market in Phnom Penh was on Ho Chi Minh Boulevard. I got a kick out of that. The market was so wide open a place that you could not only buy almost any pirated music CD or DVD movie, you could pretty much purchase any computer software you wanted, as well. Ho Chi Minh would have loved that.

It was hard to make light of Phnom Penh, though I was trying my best. One hot, dusty afternoon when I was walking back to my hotel, I saw a familiar sign — the red-and-white logo of Pizza Hut. I had a real yen for pizza, so I went in and had one. I was the only one there. Actually, it didn't taste that great, and when I went back out to the street, I studied the sign more closely. It mimicked the Pizza Hut logo exactly, but instead of saying Pizza Hut what it really said was Pizza Hat.

ㄹ

Off on a side street of Phnom Penh is the city's dirtiest little secret — the building known as S-21. Even the name sounded ominous to me. Once, in fact, it was simply a school, an L-shaped building filled with classrooms set on a small wooded hill near the centre of town. The Khmer Rouge took it over, though, and it became the most imfamous prison in Cambodia.

It's known to the locals as Tuol Sleng. The name is a play on words. *Tuol* is simply the name of the small hill. *Sleng*, though, has a double meaning, actually, a triple one now. It's the name of one of the indigenous trees of Cambodia. The fruit of these trees, however, is highly poisonous, and in the Khmer tongue, *sleng* has also become an adjective that signifies "bearing poison."

There was that *naga* thing once again — the poisonous vomit of Vasuki. But in Khmer slang *sleng* also means "to have guilt." Bearing poison … and guilt.

That's pretty apt. S-21 became the very gates of hell. When the city was being cleared of people, the intellectuals were taken here. Even knowing a language besides Khmer was enough to warrant the death penalty. Individual classrooms were walled into smaller cells and fitted with bars. In effect, the former school became a torture chamber.

Even more alarming, the real shock troops of the Khmer Rouge were the orphaned children, roving gangs of heavily armed ten- and twelve-year-olds, completely brainwashed, as vicious as any mercenary. They seemed to have no consciences. Like packs of dogs, they bit and snapped and did the dirty work of the new regime.

S-21 is now a sort of museum. Much of it has been left as it was during those grim days. There are burn marks on the floors and rusty patches that might be blood.

What I found hardest to take were the photographs. After being arrested, each prisoner had his or her Polaroid picture taken. These have now been collected and are displayed on the walls in a macabre gallery of faces. Some faces stare blankly, puzzled, but a good number flinch at the camera flash. There's clearly fear in their eyes, and their mouths are tight with anxiety.

Of the 10,499 prisoners who were brought to S-21, it's believed that only seven survived. I was reminded of the concentration camps in Europe. Here is another black mark on humanity that will take many generations to erase.

Ω

In a squat little building in Phnom Penh is the Cambodian Institute for Human Rights. Its director is Kassie Neou. He's responsible for the day-to-day operations of the institute, which is a thankless, almost overwhelming task. Neou is bent with age now, but he's no ordinary person.

143

He was a teacher before the darkness set in, and when the Khmer Rouge came, he was imprisoned. His only crime was that he was suspected of speaking English. Neou, though, is a survivor. He was tortured and sentenced to be executed, but his guards were mostly children. The wise Neou escaped death night after night by telling stories to his keepers, by appealing to the scraps of childhood remaining in these ravaging mobs of child warriors.

Neou recounted the old Hindu myths and what he could remember of Aesop's fables, and they sat at his feet, gazed up at him, and listened. And he told them the Cambodian folktales, as well.

Perhaps he narrated the one about the old man and the river, about the king and the stick and the riddle. It's astonishing really. Like the old man of legend cast out of Angkor, Neou, too, was banished from his city. He also lived in hiding for months, though it wasn't in a cave. Finally, however, he was discovered and taken away to what he thought would be certain death.

Like Scheherazade in *One Thousand and One Nights*, Neou prevailed by spinning tales. Our stories are everything, of course. Built from the bricks and mortar of meaning, the stories we tell ourselves over and over become our worlds. We have come from them and we return to them.

There's still a lot of work for Neou to do. Cambodia isn't out of the darkness yet. There are remnants of the blue poison everywhere.

From the glory and beauty of Angkor to the very depths of hell, Cambodia has seen it all — the very best and worst humanity can muster. Slowly, the tourists are dribbling back. Neou will continue his work, though there are few others like him. The old ones are mostly gone, and the villages in Cambodia belong to children. But the country's youth herald what will come. Slowly, like the endless cycle of lives in both Hinduism and Buddhism, the soul of this country is re-emerging, churning itself into a new and better world.

7

One Thousand Words for Rice

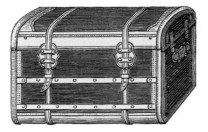

The capital of Thailand is Bangkok, but that's not what Thais call the city. Bangkok was the original site of the capital more than two hundred years ago, but King Rama I decided to move the seat of power across the river to another place called Krung Thep. Today Krung Thep is what we mistakenly call Bangkok.

Actually, Krung Thep is the city's shortened name. The real moniker is slightly longer. It's Krung Thep Mahanakhon Amon Rattanakosin Mahinthara Ayuthaya Mahadilok Phop Noppharat Ratchathani Burirom Udomratchaniwet Mahasathan Amon Piman Awatan Sathit Sakkathattiya Witsanukam Prasit, which translates into "The city of angels, the great city, the residence of the Emerald Buddha, the impregnable city of Ayutthaya, of God Indra, the grand capital of the world endowed with nine precious gems, the happy city, abounding in an enormous royal palace that resembles the heavenly abode where reigns the reincarnated god, a city given by Indra and built by Vishnukarn."

That's a mouthful, so in English we call the place Bangkok. And it's no city of angels. It might not be the most dreadful town I've been to, but it's big and ugly and more than a little squalid. Ten million people are spread over the mud flats. Sluggish brown canals worm through Bangkok's centre, their fetid water lapping against building stilts and supports. Every spare stretch of sidewalk is lined with street vendors' carts, noodles simmering in oil, sun-darkened hands busy in endless toil.

In spite of everything, though, Thais are a friendly bunch. Smiles come easily, and the poverty isn't quite as grinding as it is in other places. This is simply life in Asia — crowded, dusty, and noisy. Rusty bicycles clank down rutted streets, and *songthaews* — covered pickup trucks with bench seats — putter along with engines no more powerful than lawn mowers. The antique taxis spew black exhaust and bleat tinny horns every few metres.

The angels must wear earplugs.

I stayed at a little guest house near the river where the floors were polished and clean and girls cooked, cleaned, and played pranks. They'd sneak up with cups of water and pour them over one another's heads, then squeal with laughter.

There's a Thai word for this sort of nutty behaviour: *sanook.* All elements of life are suffused with it. *Sanook* roughly translates as "the fun factor." Few enterprises are undertaken without first asking how much *sanook* will be involved, how much fun will that be? And if there won't be fun, is it really worth doing?

Those are all good questions. Thailand, unlike the other nations of Southeast Asia, was never under the thumb of a foreign power, a fact that has given Thais a confidence that doesn't exist among the citizens of its neighbours. Despite Thailand's penchant

146

for sponging up Western culture, everything here retains an essence of the Thai way of doing things.

Φ

There are exactly five first-person pronouns in English. Unfortunately, this is the kind of linguistic fact that bores most people, but bear with me. I have a point to make. The first-person pronouns are *me*, *myself*, and *I*, as well as two more, *my* and *mine*, the possessive first-person pronouns. Five. Count 'em. Exactly five.

In Thai there are seventeen of these pronouns. I won't pretend to understand the deeper intricacies of the language, but apparently these pronouns vary according to who's speaking, whom they're speaking to, and the relationship between the two. What I'm getting at is that language marks, very carefully, the social situation in which it takes place. It describes the amount of respect given by the one who's talking, and the degree of respect for the one being spoken to. It's another way of defining territory, I suppose, or at least making clear who wields the most power. In linguistic circles that's known as pragmatics. For my money that's one of the most interesting and subtle fields in the whole science of human relations.

147

We tend to be a bit oblivious of social stratification in English because that language is one of the few tongues in the world that doesn't directly mark it. Most Indo-European languages have familiar and formal pronouns. In French someone is addressed as *tu* or *vous*, depending on whether the situation is friendly or formal. English once had *thou* as opposed to *you*, but except in school studies of Elizabethan poetry, one doesn't come across that distinction anymore. Sometime over the past four hundred years the familiar *thou* vanished and everyone in English became a little more equal — at least in everyday speech.

Don't get cocky, though. English doesn't entirely lack such quirky pragmatic structures. We tend to define our relationships in a more underhanded and sneaky manner. Take a simple sentence such as "Open the window." In real life we would rarely say something so bluntly. "Open the window" sounds like a command. In fact, it is a command, and we would only use this direct form in, say, yelling at a particularly out-of-control child, as in "Go to your room." By itself these forms are almost rude in their directness, so we soften them with a politeness marker: "Open the window, please."

But that's not really a whole lot better. What would really be heard in a true conversation is probably: "Would you mind opening the window?" or "Do you think you could open the window a smidgen?" Those sentences are already two levels of directness away from the simple request, "Open the window," and that's only the beginning of pragmatic complexity. A person could say, for example, "Do you find it hot in here?" which sounds suspiciously like a question. There's no reference at all to a window or the opening of it, and yet to a native speaker of English (or a native speaker with some sensitivity), the meaning would be fairly clear: "Open the damn window." That's linguistic pragmatics at its finest.

So what does all that have to do with Thailand? Actually, quite a lot. Thai is at the extreme other end of the spectrum. The pragmatic structures in Thai are overtly marked. The seventeen first-person pronoun markers I mentioned earlier are all about defining, very exactly, the relationships between people.

$$\Psi$$

In Thailand I'm a *farang*, a "foreigner." It's not a derogatory term. It's just like calling the sky blue or water wet. That's what I am — a pasty-faced foreigner. I'd left Bangkok behind and come down to Koh Samui in the Gulf of Siam. It's one of a string of islands off the southeast coast of Thailand.

In 1981 an airport runway was laid down through the palm trees here, and the little island has never been the same. Tourism took off. I wasn't at all surprised to see a McDonald's. But Starbucks? And yet there it was two hundred metres from the beach. Step right up and get your half-caf soy macchiato. Weird.

Thailand is a country that's never been occupied, except briefly by Japan in the Second World War, so its people don't have a bad taste in their mouths about other cultures and ways of being. They seem to soak everything up and even delight in it.

Out in front of the Starbucks was an old man with a dark, weathered face. He'd been a fisherman, I guess, once upon a time. When he turned, though, I noticed that he had English printing on the front of his T-shirt: LAUGH WHILE YOU CAN, MONKEY BOY. I had no idea what that meant, but it became a sort of motto for the rest of my trip. It was *sanook* again — laughing like a Monkey Boy.

ε

I was looking for something a little less touristy than Koh Samui. Thailand has a legendary *farang* beach culture. Remember the movie *The Beach*? Leonardo DiCaprio's character sets off to find a beach untouched by commercialism — a hidden shore where a small community of travellers have set up camp, leaving the world behind. I wanted to discover something like that. Something pure. Something that matched the picture I had in my head of a perfect tropical paradise.

So I took a long-tailed boat, in a rather jaw-clenching passage, over the open ocean, up to the next island of Koh Phangan. People had told me Koh Phangan was what Koh Samui had been thirty years ago, but with one big difference. Koh Phagnan has become world-famous for its full moon party. Every month, a few days before a full moon, thousands of young backpackers descend on Haat Riin Beach, turning it into a madhouse.

Once upon a time the scene on Koh Phagnan was probably pretty cool — a big bonfire, some guitars, a lot of intoxicants under the starry dome — but now it was just crazy. The long white beach was transformed into a sea of bobbing human flesh. Ten thousand people raved all night long, spilling into the water under the greatest disco ball of them all — a tropical moon.

It was already dark when I arrived at Haat Riin by boat, though the moon had yet to rise above the hills. No matter. Coming into shore was like a scene out of *Apocalypse Now*. Strings of lights were draped across the buildings that fronted the beach, and already the music was thumping so hard that I could hear it far out to sea over the rolling waves.

The throngs were mostly the young über-cool from around the world, sporting uniforms of tattoos and coloured hair. They danced until daylight, roaming from bar to bar, buzzing on whatever they could find.

The Dutch couple I'd come over with got themselves revved up with diet pills and Red Bull. It sounded a bit dodgy to me, so I stuck with green-brown bottles of Singha beer. I lost the Dutch couple for a while but found them again later, faces laughing through the crowds until eventually everything became a tremendous blur of limbs, grins, and bass lines. Here and there girls whirled balls of fire on long strings. The fire drew looping lines though the darkness around them — an effect I'm sure the diet pills enhanced.

By the time the sky lightened, announcing morning, I was wet and tired and caked in sand. I'd had enough and made my way to the boats bobbing just out from shore. Soon I was skipping across the waves in the pink dawn, wishing only for a warm shower and a soft bed.

ㄱ

Way up on the northeast coast of Koh Phangan I found a terrific beach in a double bay called Thong Nai Pan. I rented a thatch hut on the sand for $6. A plate of pad thai, a full meal in itself, cost fifty cents. I figured that if I sold everything I had back home, I could live on the beach for another twenty or thirty years.

There was a neo-hippy air to the place. Cushions and low tables on bamboo platforms created little chilled-out cafés where, as in Amsterdam, you could get almost anything. One afternoon I glanced at my bare feet and realized I hadn't seen my shoes for a couple of days. Later I found them outside a restaurant where I'd left them several days earlier.

On one of my last days in Thailand I was walking on a distant stretch of beach, completely by myself, when I heard a crash in the nearby foliage. Right in front of me an elephant lumbered out of the palms, thundered onto the beach, and waded almost delicately into the surf. When the beast was about knee-high in the surf, it knelt and wallowed in the water.

Then a man, the elephant's handler as it turned out, came out of the trees. He stood beside me and watched the magnificent grey colossus gambol in the water. The handler had a long barbed stick to steer elephants. The hook would snag the beasts' ears and turn them in the desired direction. I figured the elephant frolicking in the sea was employed to move the trees cleared for more hut enclosures. Still, as I drank in the spectacle before me, I realized how strange and surprising this world was — as unpredictable as a giggling Thai girl dumping cold water on a smug foreign head, or an elephant thumping out of the bush to take a bath.

151

Ω

The pilot's voice crackled over the intercom. "If you look out the left side windows, you'll see Gunung Agung." He paused for a moment, then added, "Boy, I never get tired of that."

I peered across the aisle. Framed in the airplane window was the largest volcano I'd ever seen. I had left Thailand, flying south, and was now somewhere over Indonesia, a chain of ancient volcanic islands. The most famous Indonesian volcano is Krakatoa between Java and Sumatra. It blew apart in 1883, causing the Earth's weather patterns to change for several years.

Gunung Agung was on the next island over. It shone in the morning sun, standing head and shoulders above the intricately terraced rice paddies of the incredible little island of Bali. "I fly over this all the time," the pilot continued. "But I never get used to it. Look at that. It's beautiful."

And it was.

Our plane touched down at Denpassar Airport in the south of Bali. We were mobbed by touts as soon as we got out of the terminal. Most of them wanted to take us to Kuta Beach. That was where most of the tourists went; the place was a sprawl of partying Australians, drinking and surfing and then drinking some more.

I'd had enough of beach life at the Full Moon Party in Thailand. To me Kuta isn't what Bali is all about. If you get beyond the ravages of tourism, Bali is a tiny jewel and houses one of the world's most remarkable cultures. So I managed to ward off the insistent young men tugging at my sleeves and boarded a minivan inland to Ubud, the centre of cultural life on the island and home to artists, dancers, and woodcarvers working at the very peak of human inventiveness.

Most of Ubud gathers around a central street. At the top of it is the highway leading south or north, while at the bottom is the Monkey Forest Sanctuary. There's not really much of a forest left, but there certainly are monkeys — nasty brutes that snap at your fingers. A roadside stand outside the sanctuary sells bananas to feed the simian brigands.

I saw one girl hide a few bananas under her shirt, thinking the monkeys wouldn't notice. She figured she could hand them out gradually. Big mistake. They were all over her. My method was to chuck all the bananas I had and take a quick step back. It was like witnessing a shark feeding, or mauling. The greedy little creatures stole from one another, bared their fangs, and exhibited the most appalling manners.

A little deeper into the sanctuary is the first of three Hindu temples. Out in front are statues of lions and wild boars. Ganesh, the elephant-headed Hindu god, is there, too, as well as unfamiliar dog-faced demons and fat little gods. Around each of the midsections of these stone gods the villagers have draped black-and-white-checkered cloths representing the duality of good and evil. Red hibiscus flowers are tucked behind their stone ears, and offerings are placed in front of them: fruit and more flowers generally, but sometimes, inexplicably, full bottles of Coca-Cola or Sprite. Thirsty business, this being a god.

Of course, the monkeys clamber all over the temples. We watched as one smart little thing bashed a coconut on the stone walls in a vain attempt to get it opened. Beside the temple, workers were mending a fence, and one of them had to halt work frequently and yell at the monkeys. He had parked his bicycle beside the trees, and the monkeys, one in particular, kept climbing up to chew on his bicycle seat, taking great chunks out with relish, chewing the foam, and running off when the poor man desperately attempted to stop him.

153

Where, I thought, was the god of bicycle seats and why couldn't he fight off these almost human-faced little devils?

Φ

Indonesia is one of the great land bridges of the world. More than seventeen thousand islands are strung like a necklace in the sapphire waters on either side of the equator between Malaysia and Papua New Guinea. When Krakatoa exploded, an intense interest was focused on Indonesia and something quite unexpected was discovered. An ancient skull cap was unearthed on nearby Java in 1891. Tests showed it to be seven hundred thousand years old, and it captivated the scientific world. Was this the missing link? The flat plate of bone (and a femur that turned up later) is still hotly debated in the anthropological community.

Creationists cry out that it's only the skull of a gibbon, though most serious scientists have now classified the remains in the rather nebulous category of *Homo erectus*. This was a stage that preceded us — *Homo sapiens* — so it seems "people" have been wandering across the Indonesian archipelago for a very long time, since we first stood on our own feet.

The indigenous people of Australia are believed by many to have migrated to their current location about seventy thousand years ago when the water levels of the world's oceans were lower and they followed game across a land bridge connecting New Guinea and Australia. Still later, Indonesia was likely the launching pad of Polynesians sailing into the vast stretches of the Pacific Ocean.

The Indonesian archipelago has always been a great crossroads, a bridge across worlds, and Bali sits in the middle of everything. The earliest writing in Bali is carved into a stone pillar near the village of Sanur on the east coast. It's Sanskrit and dates to the ninth century A.D. The pillar was left by traders from India making their way across the islands, and it must have been these first merchants from the subcontinent who brought the first glimmers of Hinduism, a religion that took root a thousand years ago to form a great Hindu empire known as the Majappahit Kingdom.

Eventually, however, a tidal wave of Islam swept into Indonesia from Malaysia. The Hindu dynasty faltered, and the last Majappahit king, with an entourage of scholars, artists, and intelligentsia, quietly slipped away to little Bali. There they set up the odd mix of religion and customs that is Balinese Hinduism. Agama Hine Dharma, as it's properly known, focuses primarily on balancing the good and evil spirits of the world. It's a tremendously complex system that addresses itself especially to the calendars and rituals involved in the planting and harvesting of rice.

Rice cultivation is crucial to the Balinese way of life and has shaped the island both geographically and socially. Where it was once thick jungle, the quintessential Balinese landscape is now terraced with rice paddies. Each community has a *subak* or rice-growing organization that manages work, allocates the use of water, and plans irrigation schedules. What's more is that all these schedules are arranged around a highly developed set of rituals based on the whims and acts of Hindu gods and goddesses.

Everything is calculated from the various transportation systems of these deities (some fly on birds, others hitchhike on snakes) to their emotional colours and even to their associated compass directions. It's tremendously elaborate, obtuse even, and it's just the sort of menial job for which humans, always fiddling with numbers and schedules, are perfectly suited to undertake.

Ψ

I suppose that here I could come up with another bizarre linguistic fact, such as that the Balinese have one hundred and twenty different words for rice. That sounds plausible. In truth, though, it's blatantly false.

155

I have a problem with this idea of counting words. It's said that Arabic has five hundred words for sand, and of course everyone knows the story about the Inuit and their many words for snow. That's all wrong, of course. And even if a particular language has an overabundance of words for a specific thing, it doesn't necessarily mean anything. In English there are a considerable number of words to describe the properties of light, far more than other languages. We have *shine, sparkle,* and *twinkle*. We have unbelievably subtle distinctions such as *glimmer* and *glitter* but, really, it doesn't mean we see light better than other people. It doesn't mean we're the world's authorities on the properties of light.

So, no, the Balinese don't have an especially large number of words for rice (and I doubt they have a word for snow at all). Practically speaking, there are only three categories referring to rice: *padi*, from which English gets the term *paddy*, as in rice (though the word here actually only refers to a growing rice plant); *nasi*, which is cooked rice; and *beras*, which refers to the harvested but not yet cooked rice.

The real story of language is, as always, far more interesting. In Bali the people actually have a number of completely different languages to talk about rice. Remember that stuff about Thai pronouns and English indirectness? Well, that's peanuts compared to what goes on in Bali.

We're into the territory of pragmatics again, and the languages of Indonesia contain some of the most interesting structures I've ever come across. In Bali there are five almost completely different forms of the language, depending on who's speaking to whom and what the given situation is. To provide a simple example: on Java, the next island over, they speak in two forms:

High Javanese: *Menapa pandjenengan badé dahar sekul kalijan kaspé samenika?*
Low Javanese: *Apa kowé arep mangan sega lan kaspé saiki?*

Both of the above sentences mean: "Are you going to eat rice and cassava now?" Notice that the only word identical in both sentences is the one for cassava (*kaspé*). Everything else is so different that they could almost be considered separate languages. Imagine if you had to speak English to your social inferiors (say, children and maybe lawyers) and French to your superiors (such as your boss). That's something like the linguistic situation on Java. Now imagine if you had to speak English to children, French to your boss, Spanish to your friends at work, Italian to your neighbours, and Portuguese to strangers. That describes the social and linguistic situation on Bali.

So saying that the Balinese have umpteen dozen words for rice really misses the point. It's not the rice they're naming.

They're indicating the relationships between themselves. They're identifying one another.

ξ

One hot tropical evening, with the thin slice of a crescent moon hanging inexplicably upside down in the sky, I travelled to the outskirts of town to see the famous *legong* dance. In Bali, dance is an incredibly sacred affair. A combination of movement and storytelling, it's an infinitely subtle and refined orchestra of gestures seen nowhere else on the planet.

The central dancers in *legong* are two girls, usually no more than eight years old. The girls start training for the dance as soon as their feet touch the ground, literally, and the stretched fingers and darting eyes, the strange cock of the head, and delicate side steps are a choreography handed down through the centuries. Even at eight years of age, these girls are masters and a joy to watch.

157

The story of the dance derives from a Javanese tale dating to the twelfth century. On a journey a king finds a maiden lost in the forest. He takes her and locks her into a prison. When the maiden's brother, a prince in his own right, learns of this, he threatens war. The king is warned by a bird — a black raven — that this fight will end in his death. Foolishly, he pursues the war and is indeed killed. The maiden, in her captivity, holds two fans, and it's these fans, come to life, that are the *legong*. Magically, the young girls appear and dance, dressed in gold brocade to symbolize the fans. Without question they're the stars of the show.

Underscoring the intricate dance is the gamelan orchestra, which uses a series of instruments that look like upturned metal pots. The instruments are struck with tiny mallets so that gamelan music plinks and plonks quite delicately, reminding one of the sounds of a child's toy piano. However, the plunking is steady and hypnotic and becomes almost trance-like. Four or five men sit on one side, with the omnipresent checkered cloths about their midsections, playing wooden flutes, while a single drummer stands behind them. On the other side of the stage are the gamelan players proper, seven or eight men with an assortment of different-sized pots clustered about, all within reach of their tiny dulcimer hammers.

Spellbound, I listened and watched. This was no Kodak moment, carefully crafted for the entertainment of tourists. The story really did unfold like a fan and was sheer magic.

ᴢ⟩

The next day the sun dangled directly overhead so that there were no shadows anywhere. It sat on my head and shoulders, heavily, tangibly, like the meaty hand of a belligerent god. On a fence in front of me was a poster. CREMATION TODAY, it read. TOURISTS WELCOME.

It seemed strange that someone would put up posters to announce such an event, expressly inviting tourists, and for a moment I suspected a catch, a scam, one more way of separating the naive traveller from his sweaty dollars. But then I didn't know Bali.

I really did want to see what happened at a cremation, though, so I went to the designated meeting place where they squeezed eight or nine of us into a minivan. I had no idea where we were going, and after an hour or so of driving, we were delivered to a village lane and the bus sped off. This was to be the first of many confused moments. Carefully crafted confusion, I might add.

We knew we were in the right place because lying in the dust was one of the large papier mâché statues used to transport bodies to the cremation site. It formed a pretty good semblance of a lion, and I found out later that this was the animal representing the caste of the deceased.

To get out of the sun we walked up the street to a pavilion that had been set up. In the pavilion were more gamelan players. The musical pots and pans were attached to large wooden frames so the musicians could carry everything and play as they marched. Soon we were all marching. As the procession started, we galloped ahead to snap photos. In front of the procession trundled a truck with a large water tank. A man stood in the rear of the truck with a high-pressure hose and swept it back and forth over the dusty road. Sometimes he aimed it up to shower water over the mourners. Far from being insulted, they good-naturedly smiled and laughed at the shower.

The native marchers couldn't really be called mourners. The entire village seemed to have come out — several hundred people, most of them dressed in black, and they weren't acting that mournful. In fact, they giggled openly, sang, and even danced. This was a scene of real celebration distinctly in opposition to our sombre Western funerals.

In fairness to Westerners and to human empathy in general, the bodies to be cremated in this ceremony aren't recently deceased. It's the custom in Bali to bury corpses immediately following death so that the earth will clean the bones, which means only the bones are actually cremated. There's also a practical aspect to the ritual, since the passage of time after burial allows the family of the deceased to save up for the cremation ceremony. The entire village is invited to these extravaganzas so that they cost a pretty penny to put together. For that reason, too, several people are often cremated at once in a sort of funeral by bulk. A prestigious day is divined and only then do the old bones rise from the earth. They're wrapped in white shrouds, gingerly, and placed on a bier usually shaped into the animal that represents their caste.

On the day we went, the villagers sang and chanted, with three papier mâché towers, like parade floats, tottering above them, shouldered into the air by dozens of men. Every few metres the

159

villagers would stop and turn the giant statues, spinning them awkwardly three times before continuing the procession.

As I mentioned earlier, the ritual is all about confusion. The Balinese Hindu belief is that a spirit separated from its body by death will be confused and will desperately try to cling to what it's known for a lifetime. It will try to return to its body so it can stay in the village, which means it has to be coaxed away, fooled a little bit. The loud noise, the jingling and clanking, the singing and dancing, are all done to confuse the lonely spirit.

The spirit is literally spun around, mixing it up further so that it can't find its way back. Lastly, the mourners dress in black so the spirit can't see them. The idea is that it won't recognize anyone and will be forced to conclude that it must go elsewhere. The day I attended the ritual the locals, of course, were dressed in black. We tourists, I later found out, were invited on purpose. Like all good tourists everywhere, we wore an assortment of badly fitting colourful hats and an unflattering rainbow of shorts. What we didn't wear was black, especially in the tropical heat. So the first people the spirits saw were us. No doubt that scared them immensely.

The cremation ceremony is quite brilliant. Bali is a place that has soaked in the sauces of many different cultures. From each it's taken a little something. At a performance of another sacred dance I watched a scene unfold in which the god Rama was surrounded by hideous demons. They bubbled around him and spoke in distinct English. That was a poke at us — a highly traditional dance with white-faced demons from the wicked West.

Ω

From birth to death and everything in between the Balinese have an approach to life that's radically different from that in the West. The culture is rich and the language is almost insurmountably difficult. It has an internal sense, though, largely based on the old Hindu caste system.

The indigenous language of Bali, as a whole, is called Bahasa Bali. As I said, it marks social structure exactly, so much so that, depending on who's talking (and who is being talked to), any one of five completely different forms might be employed. Each has its own vocabulary, and to some degree its own grammar. According to the particular caste of the speaker and specific caste of the individual being spoken to, up to five completely different sentences might be uttered — all meaning the same thing.

This is linguistic pragmatics gone ballistic. Initially, two Balinese strangers, not knowing the other's caste, start a conversation in what's called Basa Alus, the high language. Basa Alus came directly from the Hindu-Javanese court languages of the tenth century. It was the language of the original Majappahit Kingdom, the tongue of the scholars and artists who arrived on Bali with the exiled royal court of Java.

At some point in our hypothetical conversation the caste level of one speaker would be asked (or surmised) and the levels would be adjusted accordingly. The Balinese language uses very few greetings or politeness markers otherwise. There are no equivalents for *please* or *thank you*, for example, nor is there anything that translates into "good morning" or "good evening." All these things are marked in the form that's used.

A second form is called Basa Lumrah and is applied when talking to people of the same caste, and between family and friends. A third is called Basa Sor and is employed when speaking to people of a lower caste or to people who are non-caste. Basa Madia is a fourth form and is a polite language utilized for conversing with strangers or with people to whom one wishes to show respect.

Basa Singgih, the fifth form, is the most distinct of all. Its grammar and vocabulary are completely unlike the others. It's used to address persons of high caste, usually in formal and religious contexts. Even the Balinese aren't always fluent in this language. Written Basa Singgih, oddly enough, is the language seen on the signs of welcome and farewell found in most Balinese villages.

Between the five forms there are separate vocabularies that encompass about a thousand basic words. Most of these relate to descriptions of people and their actions. More recently, the five forms have become blended and simplified so that it's now common to speak of three forms: a low or informal Balinese (essentially Basa Lumrah), a polite Balinese (mostly Basa Madia), and a high Balinese (a mixture of Basa Alus and Basa Singgih).

For example, the word for *yes* in low Balinese would be *nggih* or sometimes *saja*. In polite Balinese *yes* would be *inggih* or *patut*, and in high Balinese *yes* could only be *patut*. On the other hand, the word for *no* in low Balinese is *sing* or *tuara*, while in polite Balinese it's *tan* and in high Balinese it's *nenten* or *tan wenten*. Bewildering, isn't it?

162

Φ

Languages are relative things. They describe a particular manner of existence in the world, a way of being that's somehow different from that of the speaker of a different language. The Balinese languages are a good example of that. It's almost impossible for us to untangle the complexities involved in their social stratification. It's enough perhaps to understand how very different the whole system is from English. But, and here's the crux of the matter, the truth is that it's merely a different set of rules, a different game, for getting at much the same things done with English.

Actually, English takes as many different forms as Balinese does. There is, for starters, no single language that can unequivocally be called Standard English. We speak in a variety of ways, and like the Balinese, what we say is largely a product of the social situations we find ourselves in.

There are, of course, many different accents and grammars in English, each quite accurately marking our social and geographical status. For instance, there's the Cockney English of a character like Eliza Doolittle in George Bernard Shaw's play *Pygmalion* (here, even the name is telling) who speaks like this: "I ain't done nothing wrong. I'm a good girl, I am, and I won't pick up no free and easy ways." Such speech is replete with double negatives, archaic contractions, and slang that locates her specifically to the poorest neighbourhoods of London at the end of the nineteenth century. Contrast that with the proper Oxford English of Professor Henry Higgins or, for that matter, the queen of England. And yes, all these accents and dialects are most certainly English.

We have Irish and Scottish and idiolects such as those found in African-American hip hop lyrics. We have the baffling jargon of legalese (its sole purpose is to baffle, one might say) and the Latin-based vocabularies of medicine and science. We have the slang of teenagers and the soliloquies of Hamlet.

But all of the above are grandly, profoundly English.

Even a single individual, in the course of a normal day, speaks in a number of completely different forms. Think about it. Among friends we might well swear more freely, especially over a beer or two, watching, say, a hockey game. But at work, or in a job interview, or meeting in-laws for the first time, we speak quite differently, since we're acutely aware of the different contexts and change our language accordingly.

All peoples, in every language, adjust their words to the social situations at hand. The Balinese system is almost absurdly overt about it, while English marks things more subtly, but everything comes down to much the same thing. We have different systems, sometimes unimaginably dissimilar, but we're all aware of the social context and how much obsequiousness or straightforwardness is needed. That's a fundamental component of our communication with one another, and many of our mistakes

163

— our miscommunications — in understanding people from different language backgrounds can often be traced to a difference in how the relationship between the speakers is marked.

Ψ

Sometimes whole oceans of misunderstanding lie between people. Sometimes words do fail us. I flew home by way of Osaka, Japan. Actually, we touched down there for a couple of hours. I was continuing on, flying into the broad Pacific, but even as we were descending over the great inland sea called Seto Naikai, something about the date tweaked my memory.

It was August 6, and it didn't take me long to remember that this was the exact date, back in 1945, that a plane ducked out of the clouds, just as we were now doing, not too far from where we were, to drop an atomic bomb on Hiroshima.

Everyone knows the story, but few are aware of what happened in the days leading up to the bombing. It's actually one of my favourite linguistic stories, a case study in pragmatics and an excellent example of miscommunication.

On July 26, 1945, a final ultimatum was issued to the Japanese prime minister. It was called the Potsdam Declaration, and it came from the Chinese provisional government, Prime Minister Winston Churchill of Great Britain, and President Harry S. Truman of the United States.

Truman, desperate with the moral consequences of unleashing the terrible weapon now available to him, offered a last way out to the unsuspecting Japanese. I can imagine him well. He wasn't the sort of politician we have today. Harry was a simple farmer and had worked on the railways in younger days, even sleeping in hobo camps — a true man of the people. I can picture him wracked with guilt, sitting slouched at the big desk in the Oval Office, head lowered with the crushing weight of what might soon happen.

So, knowing what the others didn't, he spent a little longer on the paragraphs intended for the Japanese prime minister. "The might that now converges on Japan is immeasurably greater than that which [was] applied to the Nazis," he wrote. "The full application of our military power, backed by our resolve, all mean the inevitable and complete destruction of the Japanese armed forces and, just as inevitably, the utter devastation of the Japanese homeland."

Of course, Truman couldn't tell the Japanese exactly what was going to happen. The atomic bomb and the Manhattan Project were still carefully guarded secrets and would be for another ten days, but he meant precisely what he said about "utter devastation." He wasn't mincing words, and he fervently hoped his message would be taken to heart.

I guess the U.S. president didn't really expect a reply, but it's in the reply that the story gets interesting. On Saturday, July 28, Prime Minister Suzuki agreed to hold a press conference at four o'clock at which time he would answer the Allied declaration. To the all-important expected question "What will you do?" Suzuki replied suddenly and simply, *"Mokusatsu."*

Mokusatsu is an intriguing word. *Moku* means "silence," whereas the word *satsu* means "to kill." The literal interpretation then is "to kill with silence." As with many words, however, there are different shades of meaning. *Mokusatsu*, under some circumstances, can refer to the withholding of opinion. We can understand it in the context of the way in which politicians often respond by saying "No comment." It's a sort of ducking of the question, maybe leaving it for later, perhaps hoping the whole issue will go away. Or, a little more aggressively, *mokusatsu* can signify a conspicuous ignoring of something, as perhaps one might disregard a troublesome uncle who's had too much to drink at a wedding. Of course, in extreme cases the word can be translated as a "fuck-you" silence.

However, the silence of a "No comment" and the silence of a "Fuck you" are quite different, and Truman's translators had a real job on their hands. As it turned out, the translation was as predictable as it was tragic. Truman remembered it like this: "They gave us a very snotty answer. They told me to go to hell, words to that effect."

Nine days later the United States obliterated Hiroshima and sixty-four thousand innocent souls. The silence kept up for another day and then Nagasaki, too, was annihilated.

So here's the point: what did the Japanese prime minister really mean? To the end of his life in 1948, Suzuki refused to say. Saving face is incredibly important in Japanese culture, and who's kidding anyone — it's important in every culture. If Suzuki had truly meant for the Americans to wait a few days, if he had meant to say he needed more time to answer the proposal fully, then apparently he hadn't made himself clear and the bombing could be seen as the result of his ineptitude.

On the other hand, if he had truly meant to tell the Americans to go to hell, then by doing so he brought hell itself down on two of his cities. In either case he would have lost face for his decision. So perhaps it was best to say nothing.

Sometimes words carry the weight of a bomb.

PART THREE

Under the Southern Cross

8

Islands of the Many-Coloured Waters

Our plane landed in Tahiti at about three in the morning, and despite the ungodly hour, a little ukulele band was there to greet us. Three rather large women plinked their way through a song of welcome. The air was warm and thick with orange blossoms, and overhead, stars were scattered across the sky like sugar on a black countertop. The women swayed in their muumuus, singing along to the ukuleles, and I thought, *Hey, this is going to be great. Classic South Pacific.*

I planned on camping in Tahiti. I'd brought my tent and all my gear and now struggled with it, lugging it through customs and into the airport arrivals hall. *Now what?* I thought. I didn't really know where I was going, and it was still the middle of the night.

It didn't turn out to be much of a problem. A young woman stood near the doors holding a sign that read HITI MAHANA CAMPING, and soon I found myself bouncing along a road in the open back of a truck with three or four other travellers. Trucks take the places of buses here. They're simply called *le truck*, and I sat in the back of this particular one while the strange stars of the southern hemisphere whipped by above me. I gazed at them and tried to pick out the Southern Cross, the great crucifix of stars that can only be seen south of the equator. Scouring the sky, I scanned from one horizon to the other, but I couldn't spot it.

The campground was an old coconut plantation, and it was pretty much dawn by the time I started to erect my tent. An old Polynesian villager came down to watch me. "*Ia orana*," he said, which is the Tahitian greeting. I nodded back at him, and he watched me as I set up the tent.

I fumbled with the ropes and pegs, and when I finally finished, the old man shook his head slowly. I couldn't figure out why until his eyes strayed upward and I followed his gaze. I'd put my tent beneath a coconut tree. It had seemed like the right thing to do in the South Pacific, but by the time his eyes returned to mine, I understood him. Coconuts fall out of trees, and my tent was directly beneath them. The villager laughed and walked off as I swore and began to tear down the tent.

It's actually a fact that one of the leading causes of death in the South Pacific is being killed by falling coconuts. But I didn't know that then. For me it was perfectly reasonable to set up a tent under a tree. It afforded shade and some protection from the elements, and where I was from things hardly ever fell out of trees.

The word for *tree* in Tahitian is *auteraa*. That's important, because a tree in Tahitian and a tree in English aren't really the same things. Words can stand in for all sorts of information. They represent a whole range of things — in this case, not just a tree but what a tree looks like, what it feels like, even what can be made out of it. For Polynesians, *auteraa* is mental shorthand for the way a tree's bark is used for the skin of an ocean-going outrigger, for the way its palm fronds dance in the wind like waves, and for the way those fronds can be woven together for roofing. And yes, even for the fact that it might drop coconuts on the unwary.

ξ

Tahiti is one of a constellation of islands called the Society Islands. They include several hundred reefs and atolls spread over an area roughly the size of Europe. Tahiti is in the middle and is the biggest island. Many of the islands have volcanic peaks, like shards of broken green glass slicing into the hot blue sky. White sailboats bob gently inside the coral reefs that encircle the old volcanoes, and the lagoons are a neon shade of turquoise.

The ancient name of Tahiti is Tahiti-nui-I-te-vai-uri-rau, all one big fat word that translates as "Great Tahiti of the Many-Coloured Waters." They're fond of long words in Tahiti. Tahitian is an agglutinating language, one of those boring linguistic terms I remember only by imagining that it refers to glue. It means that, like Turkish or Hungarian or many of the aboriginal American languages, Tahitian works by "gluing" prefixes and suffixes onto root words so that a single word can encompass an entire thought.

171

The language is part of the Polynesian group of languages, which in turn belongs to the larger Austronesian family that includes Malay and Indonesian. In fact, Polynesians are believed to have sailed from Indonesia several thousand years ago. They likely crossed vast stretches of water in nothing more than outrigger canoes, travelling from island to island in what was probably the world's most remarkable migration. Surveying only by stars, and certainly the Southern Cross, they managed to find their way to all the far-flung islands of the largest ocean on Earth.

It's thought that these Polynesian explorers reached Tahiti about a thousand years ago. The people of Tahiti call themselves *Maohi*, and that's a clue in itself. It's only a slight hardening of the final consonant to the word *Maori*, and there you have it. These people came to Tahiti from Samoa via the Cook Islands and then some mysteriously circled back to wind up in New Zealand as the indigenous people there — the fierce Maori. All of them are Polynesians.

On the north shore of Tahiti there was a small clapboard village on a black sand beach not far from our campground. I was sitting at the edge of the beach with a plump couple from northern England watching the sunset when one of the young men from the village strolled up and sat beside us to talk.

His name was Tavita, the Tahitian equivalent of David, and like all Polynesians, he was quick to smile and make conversation. He spoke three languages: Tahitian, of course, and French for dealing with officials and the police, and lately he'd taught himself English, good for nothing except speaking to backpackers who occasionally ambled down to his beach.

His olive skin, tattooed with turtles and geometric patterns, rippled with muscles, and his face, handsome and hardened, set him off from pasty-faced tourists like us. Tavita was slightly drunk and carried a large water container filled with beer. After greeting us and introducing himself, he leaned into us a little aggressively. "I am like the wind," he hissed. "I can brush against your cheek gently." Here he swept an opened palm across his cheek. "Or I can sting and cut you."

That frightened the British couple, so they moved off and cowered together in whispered conversation, leaving Tavita and me alone. For some reason I was more curious than intimidated and launched into a conversation with the towering Polynesian.

He was poor, but he seemed to possess a tremendous intelligence, and I soon warmed to him.

We talked about the French government that still rules Tahiti as a colony and how it tested, until recently, nuclear weapons on the tiny atolls far out to sea.

"Do you wish the French gone?" I asked.

"It is not for me to say. It is not a choice for me."

"No, but if you could, would you have them leave?"

He regarded me wistfully, patting his chest and the multitude of tattoos there. "It is not a choice."

"Okay," I said, determined to get an answer, something that would satisfy my Western thinking. "But the French are a problem."

"No ... no problem."

"But ..."

"It is only a problem if you choose to see it as a problem."

I let the wisdom of those words sink in and began to understand him. Tavita was like the multicoloured fish that flitted and sparkled through the coral reefs. He was like the birds that swooped among the palm fronds. Tavita belonged here — beyond governments, rules, and borders. This was Tavita's place, his beach.

I asked him about one of his tattoos — an elegant turtle. "Very sacred," he told me, but he wouldn't say more.

Tattoo comes from the Polynesian word *tatau*. The root *tata* refers to an act performed by the hands, while the suffix *u* means something of colour. People here get their first tattoos at about the age of twelve, marking the division between child and adult. Girls receive their first tattoos on their right hands. After that they're allowed to prepare meals, and more important, take part in the ritual of washing a deceased's body with anointed oils. For men, historically at least, the more tattoos they had, the more prestige they were accorded in the community. When the first European sailors appeared, they seemed to like them, too. They

173

brought the practice with them back to their home ports, and tattoos became marks of the sea.

Tattoos, like words, are symbols. Polynesians never had a writing system, but they most certainly had a complex language of symbols. Symbols are prevalent in all cultures whether there's a writing system or not. This manipulation of signs or symbols seems to be an essential human trait. With a squiggle or two we manage to indicate complex ideas. Whether something is carved into stone, marked on paper, spoken into the air, or cut into the body, it's all the same. These marks, or symbols, say where we've come from and what we believe in. We construct them carefully to say exactly who we are.

$$\Omega$$

After a few days on Tahiti, I decided to make a run to the legendary island of Bora Bora. Bracing myself on the deck of the heaving, chugging rust bucket of a ferry, I desperately clutched my guidebook to the South Pacific despite the fact that it had already failed me badly. There was nothing in it to warn me about the stomach-churning, seventeen-hour marathon I was enduring. In fact, for a good part of the voyage the book lost all relationship with reading and metamorphosed into a hard but necessary pillow.

A cyclone, apparently, had blown up from the Antarctic. It had kicked up the sea and wind, and the waves around the ferry were easily eight or ten metres high, like black hills rolling, frothing, and tossing.

In order to escape seasickness, I gobbled a pill given to me by a girl I'd met on Tahiti. I didn't know what kind of horse tranquilizer it was, but it worked. All through the night I faded in and out of a coma. I felt the ferry rise on waves as high as a house, then drop like an elevator on the other side. But I didn't get sick, and in the early morning at last we inched through a break in the coral reef that had been dynamited by American GIs in 1942 and entered the emerald lagoon of Bora Bora.

My guidebook opens its section on Bora Bora with a quote from James Mitchener, declaring the island to be the most beautiful on the planet. It might have been then, but it was hard to see that now through the driving rain. The book, of course, also insisted that this was the dry season, "somewhat cooler and more comfortable."

In the comfort of the somewhat cooler howling maelstrom, I disembarked from the ferry. Palms swayed in the wind like dancers, and I was again told not to stand under the trees. For one thing they offered almost no protection from the rain, and for another they were dropping coconuts like drunken jugglers — cannonballs that thudded into the sand with lethal force.

I hoisted my bags and tottered to a tiny campground called Chez Pauline. It was set between a Club Med and a second, even more extravagant resort. Either of them were available for about fifty-two thousand South Pacific francs a night or $500. My little spot cost me $10.

The only other camper was Irene, a fellow Canadian, a pharmacist from Toronto who looked like Queen Victoria in the prime of her reign. To call her portly would be to wrap her in the kindest of descriptions. She bore her great bulk regally and solemnly, keeping much to herself and the affairs of her personal royal court, which she kept in a bag in her tent.

On the next day, when the rain stopped but the winds still raged at almost cyclone force, Queen Victoria and I rented bicycles to take in the sights of the island. The bicycles were a sight themselves — ancient rusted things with metal baskets in front that rattled and clanked over the palm fronds and the occasional unexploded coconut littering the road.

It's only about twenty kilometres around the whole island, and when we turned the very first corner, we were humbled by our initial sight of Mount Otemanu. A green felt covering rises in the centre of the island, but then from the very heart of it a colossal bare black slab of granite thrusts a further thousand metres into the sky. This is picture-postcard stuff, but as we wheeled a little farther we realized the photographers were conveniently cropping out the clapboard village of Vaitape that lies beneath the mountain.

Polynesians are like any other first peoples. They've been swindled and gouged by the French, though it could really have been any other "enlightened" superpower. The South Pacific, like the Caribbean, was neatly divided among all the formerly great powers of Europe. Funny thing is, though, the people here seem really happy. Everyone says hello, and if you answer back in Tahitian, you receive the largest and most heartfelt of smiles.

Perhaps they're happy because, unlike other first peoples, their culture is thriving. All the signs are in French, but everyone generally ignores them and speaks Tahitian. The little shirtless children are everywhere, roving in chuckling, tumbling packs across the streets and fields. And everywhere there's singing, accompanied by ukuleles and sometimes terrific drumming.

The highlight of the bicycle trip was the discovery of a *marae*. I say "discovery" because, though my guidebook mentions it, we had to double back up and down the road several times before we spotted it. A *marae* is an ancient ceremonial site, usually a walled platform of rocks. This one was half tumbled into the sea, but on the rocks that still clung to land there were petrographs — paintings on the stone.

I bent to peer at one of them. It was a sea turtle. The simple lines were almost identical to the one Tavita had tattooed on his shoulder. The symbol was the same.

$$\Phi$$

I remember long ago going through the ordeal of writing my master's thesis in linguistics. At the end of the process, with a three-hundred-page manuscript in my hands, I still had to undergo the defence. That entailed sitting at a long table with four professors facing me. It was a bit like a job interview. The professors hammered me with objections to my thesis, and I had to defend it.

Everything went very well. Most of the process was polite. One professor, I think, told me I should use more commas in my writing. Another thanked me for my analysis of the Sapir-Whorf hypothesis. But there's always someone who plays the devil's advocate.

For me it was Dr. Hirabayashi. He was of Japanese descent and therefore had quite an interest in words like *mokusatsu* and the whole idea of cross-linguistic misunderstanding. He sat quietly through most of the second round of my thesis defence and then, just as things seemed to be concluding nicely, stabbed me with a question.

"Where, precisely, does culture fall in all of this?" he asked, staring me down.

I had talked of nothing but language and grammar, and I was a bit taken aback. My work wasn't about culture. I was researching languages.

"How can you separate the two things?" he pressed.

"I ... ah ... ah ..."

Another professor jumped in to save me, but I've never forgotten that question about culture. Not that I bear any grudge against Dr. Hirabayashi. In fact, he probably pushed me to think harder than the other professors did, especially since I didn't need more commas, just more common sense.

It's taken me ten years to come up with my answer, but I'm ready for you now, Dr. Hirabayashi. A decade of travelling through the countries, cultures, and languages of the world has finally given me some understanding.

A language is made up of symbols that we call words. It's what we term a semiotic system, a method for creating meanings. The basis of semiotic theory has its roots in the work of the Swiss

177

linguist Ferdinand de Saussure, who noted that languages consist of a vast array of what he called "signs." Such signs are made up of two parts: the signifier, that is, the symbol; and the signified, the thing that's being represented. What makes Saussure's theory different is that symbols don't necessarily stand in for real things in the real world. Symbols stand in for meanings.

The thing is, though, symbols are found in a wide array of things, not only languages. A culture is made up of many symbolic, or semiotic, systems. Tattoos, for example. The tattoo of a turtle, to expand on Saussure, doesn't represent a real turtle. Instead it signifies a meaning — in effect, what turtles mean to Polynesians.

All the trappings of what we might call culture — clothing styles, food, dance, art, architecture — are kinds of semiotic systems. And all of them have their various symbols.

Language is merely one of these systems. Whether individual words are spoken or written, they are, in plain terms, a random group of sounds, or a random group of lines, standing in for meanings. It's like what I said earlier about trees. In English we use the symbol *tree* to represent a whole lot of information about the thing that's growing in our backyard. Tahitians use the word *auteraa*, and though some of the meanings are going to be the same between the two languages (both have roots and leaves, both need water and sunshine to live), there's also a whole lot of other things that differ, such as the fact that an *auteraa* can bonk the unwary with its coconuts.

So words can't always be translated easily from one culture into another. A turtle is clearly a turtle no matter where one goes in the world, but the symbol for a turtle, whether it's a tattoo, a word, or a pattern on a dress, doesn't necessarily refer to the same thing at all.

And that, Dr. Hirabayashi, is precisely where the rough edges and sharp corners of language bump solidly against the bigger picture that is culture. Just like recipes, architecture, clothes, dances, or hairstyles, words are symbols, the building blocks of cultures. Certainly, languages aren't the only way we create our worlds, but they're the most intricate, the most nuanced. Languages are the most efficient and versatile means we've come up with so far for defining our worlds.

Ψ

I boarded the ferry back to Tahiti with Queen Victoria the next day. She threw up once on the trip back but wasn't amused. On Tahiti-nui-I-te-vai-uri-rau I set up my tent on the beach again, nowhere near a coconut tree this time. The beach I stayed on was beside a spit of land called Point Venus. There's a story to that. It got its name from a voyage in 1769 by another of my many patron saints of travelling: Captain James Cook. Cook sailed to Tahiti in his ship the *Endeavour* to document a transit of Venus — that and discover Australia and New Zealand.

The *Endeavour* sailed into this very same bay, and the sailors must have seen immediately that they had entered paradise. The stories of bare-breasted women paddling out in canoes to meet the gob-smacked sailors are all true.

But while his men were enjoying themselves, Cook and one of his navigators, a certain William Bligh, were working on charts. The Royal Astronomical Society had partly funded Cook's trip, sending him here specifically to observe the transit of Venus. A transit occurs when a planet moves in front of the sun. It appears as a small black dot moving from right to left across the solar plane, and with the right instruments it can be timed and measured quite accurately. So, as a true child of the Enlightenment, Cook measured the angle of the sun at the first sign of the transit, while at precisely the same time on the other side of the world, in Greenwich, England, a royal astronomer measured a second set of angles. All this then produced an exact triangulation whereby the exact distance between the Earth and the sun was, for the first time, revealed.

I'm a little lost on the exact mathematics here, but somehow this measurement was used to determine longitude on Earth (the lines running north to south) with considerable accuracy. Navigators had long been able to determine latitude (the lines running east and west), but until Cook's measurements there was no real accurate method to determine longitude. So this was a major breakthrough. The mapping and measurement of the entire planet's surface could now be completed.

Venus, actually, pops up all the time in the study of the world's cultures. It's called, alternatively, "the morning star" or "the evening star." Even in English we've hung on to those terms because they make sense. That's how we see them in the night sky, and it takes some fairly complex math to show that the two stars are actually just one, a planet, in fact, seen in different places in the sky at different times of the year.

So the word *star* (*te fetia* in Tahitian) is a pretty complicated little ball of meaning. Stars mark time as well as place and were surely the signposts by which ancient Tahitians navigated their way across the ocean. Like trees, they're real things in the real world, but humans manage to infuse them with meanings far beyond their simple existence.

ξ

Let me tell you now that I made a very foolish decision on this trip. I bought myself what's called an Island Pass. That means that one ticket allowed me to stop at any five islands I liked, any islands at all in the broad Pacific.

There are a number of reputable companies that offer this kind of a pass, but I opted for the cheapest one. Big mistake. I ended up buying a ticket on what might be the worst airline in the world.

I first had problems with this airline way back in California. When I arrived in Los Angeles, ready to fly to Tahiti, I wandered around the airport for some time searching for the airline's ticket desk. I couldn't find it anywhere. Then, finally, I shuffled over and asked a security guard where it might be. He spoke into his walkie-talkie, looked concerned, then said, "I'm sorry, sir. That airline's no longer allowed to fly in U.S. airspace. The FAA has banned it."

That should have been my first clue.

Well, all right, what happens in this sort of circumstance is that, under international law, I'm able to get on another carrier to take me to the first place my airline *is* allowed to fly into. And they have to pay for it. So I spent a few hours kicking around the L.A. terminal and eventually got onto an Air New Zealand flight that took me to Tahiti. Not bad, I thought. I felt as if I'd been bumped up onto a better airline, anyway.

So now I'd had a few weeks in Tahiti, and it was time to try out this little airline again. I hefted my bags and headed for the airport with my trusty little Island Pass in hand.

The flight left Tahiti at around two in the morning. This was the usual time for arrivals and departures in the South Pacific. The planes come in from Los Angeles or Vancouver, West Coast cities, and jump across the wide Pacific, making stops at all the major islands along the way. These planes eventually head for Taipei or Singapore, and in this case, Auckland, New Zealand. With my Island Pass, though, I was bouncing over to the next group of islands — the Cooks — a thousand kilometres farther west.

I got on the plane, and we took off without any problems. The flight was only a couple of hours, and I must have nodded off because the next thing I recall was the runway at Rarotonga coming up fast beneath us. Rarotonga is the biggest of the Cook Islands. It's where the international airport is.

Our jetliner had its landing gear down already, but something wasn't right. Out of the small window I could see the ground rising to meet us, but we were coming into it too hard. The pilot must have realized that because all of a sudden he threw the plane into full throttle. We were thrown against our seats, sucked back with the G-force of the plane's emergency acceleration.

We zoomed back into the sky, and for a few moments no one reacted. Everyone glanced at one another politely as strangers in strange situations usually do. *What the hell was that all about?* I wondered.

After a few minutes, the pilot spoke to us over the intercom. His voice sounded professional and reassuring. "Ladies and gentlemen," he began, "we're experiencing some tailwinds so, uh, we're just going to go up and come in on the runway from the other way."

That sounded reasonable. What I and the other hundred passengers in the plane didn't know was that the next time would bring us all as close to sudden death as we'd probably ever get.

Now, admittedly, the runway at Rarotonga is short, ending with a pebbled beach and thundering surf. And the typhoon winds were real enough. Still, a bigger carrier would have allowed for that. It would have known. It would have at least told us we should probably fasten our seat belts.

We were above the clouds again. The plane banked widely through the early-morning sky, and we felt ourselves descend. I dared to peer out the window and saw the black runway rise beneath us again. Fifty metres, forty metres … and then *thump*. The plane's engines throttled into full acceleration. Now this wasn't the swell of power in a plane taking off. This was a sudden, mighty blast so that we were thrown back into our seats and a few loose bags and purses were swept down the aisle. At this point there were no longer any polite smiles. This time there was raw fear.

Rarotonga disappeared beneath us as we rose to cruising altitude once more. It was a good hour before the pilot spoke over the intercom this time. "Uh … ladies and gentlemen, this is your pilot speaking. We have, uh, had some problems and we've decided to turn around and head back, uh, for Tahiti."

There were groans around the cabin and nervous, excited chatter. What the hell was going on? It was another two hours back to Tahiti. Why were we going all that way? What was wrong?

When we finally landed in Tahiti, we hurried down the steps that had been wheeled up to the plane. Out on the tarmac an uncomfortable-looking airline official came out to meet us. He tried to speak, but the crowd was too noisy. A lot of people were quite angry.

Eventually, his message was passed along by those in the front of the mob who managed to hear him. Again, by law, the airline had to put us up for the night in Tahiti — at the carrier's expense. Or, as the official tried to explain, there was another possibility for those who wished to take advantage of it. This plane was needed in Auckland. That was the way things worked. These were glorified bus routes so that if a plane didn't arrive at its final destination, then the next flight after that wasn't going to happen, either. So the airline had decided to send our plane directly on to Auckland. Anyone who wanted to ride along was welcome, and the airline would then try to arrange a flight from there back to the Cook Islands.

183

Well, I'd already been in Tahiti for a few weeks, not that it was a bad place to spend a few extra days, but I'd never been to New Zealand, and here I was being offered a free trip. I put up my hand. "I'll go," I said. Surely, I figured, the plane wouldn't have a problem a third time.

$$\mathcal{A}$$

The end of this particular story is that I spent only five or six hours in Auckland. The airline did indeed arrange for a much smaller plane to take us the six hours back to the Cook Islands. The weather had settled down by then, and after some twenty or so hours of back and forth over the whole Pacific, I eventually made it to Rarotonga.

The next morning, still a bit of a zombie from lack of sleep, I was walking along the beach, surveying the new place, when a guy sitting on a beach towel began to wave at me. "Hey!" he called. "Hey, you! Yes … you!"

I pointed at myself, and he nodded, waving at me to come over. "Listen," he said when I got a bit closer, "you were on that plane yesterday, right?" He didn't have to explain which plane he meant. I didn't recognize him, though obviously he'd been on the plane, as well.

"Look at this," he said, holding up the *Cook Island Times*. On the front page in bold type was: NEAR DISASTER AT AIRPORT. There was also a large photograph of our plane angling over the airport terminal. One of the wings, clearly, had just missed the edge of the roof by mere metres. Fire trucks and a couple of ambulances had been assembled on the runway, as well.

Shit! I thought.

Ω

The next morning I woke up to the singing of angels. It took me a minute to realize I was still alive and lying safe and cozy in a bed in Rarotonga. Drifting in through the window was the sound of several hundred voices raised in song. I got up and glanced out the window. A little church stood just up from the beach. It was Sunday morning, and the service had begun.

Now I'm not a religious man, but I was drawn to the church like a cartoon character floating on the waft of an alluring scent. Most of the townspeople had gathered there, and from infant to elderly they were singing in five-part harmonies, a rich swell of chords accompanied faintly by the breaking surf two hundred metres away.

I stood for a while on the doorstop, and when a few villagers turned to see who was arriving late, they smiled and waved me in. They were singing a hymn in Maori that had been translated a hundred years ago, and I closed my eyes and let the sound fill the air around me. The Cook Island Maori are closely related to the New Zealand Maori. In fact, the Cook Islands are a protectorate of New Zealand to this day. The Cook Islanders have been on their islands for more than a thousand years.

In July 1823, Reverend John Williams of the London Missionary Society stormed onto the beaches here. He claimed to have discovered the Cook Islands, though there's ample evidence that a number of ships had already been here. Captain William Bligh anchored briefly in 1789. His ship was named the *Bounty*, and his arrival here was only a few weeks before the famous mutiny.

All over the South Pacific the countries of Europe were grabbing territory, but Reverend Williams was interested in territory of a different kind. He was concerned about human souls. Lucky for him, the Maori already happened to have an ancient religion that spoke of a central power, an ultimate god who ruled over a litany of lesser deities. Williams simply started smashing the *tiki*, the statues of the lesser gods. He spoke forcefully of the singular importance of the ultimate god, and over time the Maori began to listen to him.

185

Now here's something I'd seen before, this mapping of new symbols onto older ones. It was the "Blue Jesus" idea again. Sometimes, if the situation and the symbols are right, you can graft a new symbol, a new way of thinking, onto an older one. Symbols, after all, are constructions. We use them, like tools, to do the things we need them to do.

Williams's new religion stuck, and most Cook Islanders today are largely Protestant, though at least a few of the old ways remain. In the central villages of Rarotonga, for example, it's still quite common to see burial vaults in the front yards of many of the houses. These concrete structures are usually the graves of female relatives. It's thought to be disrespectful to throw dirt on females, so they can't have regular Christian burials. So dearly departed females aren't tucked away in cemeteries. They're put in the front yard, with the family car parked beside them, surrounded by spare tires and lawn ornaments.

After Reverend Williams converted the Cook Islanders, he continued preaching westward and met a strange fate in the New Hebrides (what's now called Vanuatu). The people there are Melanesian and didn't quite identify with the new set of symbols the missionary was handing out. Moreover, they were cannibals. They bludgeoned Williams to death on the beach as he arrived and carried his corpse off to the cooking pot. It's even said that his flesh had a faintly bitter taste, a hint perhaps of Protestant sanctity.

Φ

Melanesia was my next destination. I was scheduled to leave in two days, and already I was scared. The back of the now dog-eared Island Pass instructed me to phone and confirm my flight forty-eight hours ahead of time. When I phoned, I was greeted with another catastrophe.

"Your plane is leaving tonight, sir."

"Are you kidding me? I'm supposed to have two more days here."

"No, sir. It leaves at ten, sir. Tonight."

"Shit."

"Excuse me?"

"Oh, never mind."

Springing into action, I packed my things and hurried my goodbyes. It was already eight o'clock, and the sun had long since set. I raced to the airport, but it didn't matter in the end since the flight was predictably delayed. We ended up taking off around midnight.

I was now headed for Fiji, and the flight was meant to be about six hours. But this was, as I've said, quite possibly the worst airline in the world, so when the plane began to descend at 2:00 a.m. — four hours early — there were quizzical glances but not much panic. We'd all become quite familiar with this carrier's questionable operations.

We touched down, and as the plane rolled to a stop on the tarmac, a few of the passengers began to ask out loud, "Where are we?"

"Samoa," someone said. "Western Samoa."

"Samoa ... Jesus. Where's that?"

We all sat in the darkened plane for an indeterminable time. No stairs were rolled up to the fuselage, no bags were unloaded. Time is a relative thing on Western Samoa, so it took about an hour for us to get off the plane. Once more a harried airline employee arrived in a taxi to meet us on the tarmac.

"Why aren't we going to Fiji?" we pressed him. "Where are we? Where are we supposed to stay?"

Word filtered through that we would be stuck in Western Samoa for a couple of days, though no real reason was given. Some sort of international law kicked into effect again, and it became the airline's responsibility to accommodate us. (This airline wasn't only one of the most dangerous in the world but a financial disaster, as well.) A couple of buses arrived, and as luck would have it, they took us to the Aggie Grey, a rather legendary four-star resort in the main town of Apia.

I'd been living out of a backpack and a tent for almost a month, so I almost cried with joy to see a warm shower, a clean bed, and a room set in a beautifully manicured garden. At last I had found a real paradise.

If you look at a map of the world, you'll see something interesting about Samoa. The International Date Line runs right through it, or should, because actually the date line makes a special zigzag around Samoa. This deviation was made so that half of the island wouldn't be in Monday while the other half was in Tuesday.

In fact, it's still true that if you swim out far enough from the beach, you'll find yourself swimming on a different day than the day you left on dry land. For this reason a number of my fellow passengers started to call Samoa "the island at the end of the world," and our hotel became "the hotel at the end of the world."

Besides that, I really only knew two other things about Samoa. One was that the two main island groups were Western Samoa (to the north, in reality, and not to the west) and below it American Samoa, whose name I imagine had something to do with the U.S. presence there during the Second World War. Second, these were the islands where the famous anthropologist Margaret Mead did her groundbreaking work in the late 1920s. Her book was entitled *Coming of Age in Samoa*, a classic in the field, and it included her well-known descriptions of Fa'a Samoa, or Samoan customs.

She wrote of a place where there was sexual freedom before marriage. The teenagers, boys and girls, were encouraged to enjoy as many partners as possible, and as a result, there was almost no incidence of rape or any real violence against women. Her book, quite frankly, shocked the world. The "inept lover is a laughingstock," she wrote. There is absolutely "no frigidity," and no one resorts to pornography of any kind. Masturbation "is a universal habit." Homosexual activity is "very prevalent" and is regarded as "simply play." In general, Mead concluded that on Samoa the passage from childhood to adulthood wasn't burdened with anything close to the kind of emotional distress and confusion found in Western culture.

Unfortunately, she got almost everything wrong. It's a dangerous thing to dabble in cultural matters. That's why Dr. Hirabayashi scared me so badly. Cultures are incredibly complex things, and it's pretty easy to mess things up.

Mead didn't exactly falsify her findings, but somehow her projections of what she wanted to see came out in her writing. Or it could have been that the villagers were telling her what they thought she wanted to hear.

Fa'a Samoa, as the island culture is known, might have sexual mores that are different from our own, but Mead wasn't even close when she tried to describe them. She was after some kind of sexual utopia that really didn't exist, at least not in the islands of Samoa.

Ψ

I spent a couple of more days on Western Samoa and saw the most traditional culture I'd seen yet in the South Pacific. Many of the homes are thatched huts called *fales*. They're a simple construction with walls made of what look like bamboo blinds. They can be rolled up in the heat of the day and rolled down again at night when either privacy is needed or the breezes blowing off the ocean are cool.

The morning star here is called Tapuitea, pretty close to the word *te fetia* in Tahitian. The Southern Cross, which I still hadn't seen, is called Koluse I Saute.

Most of the people still seem to wear the traditional *lavalava*, a brightly painted cloth that wraps around the midsection. And most inhabitants are large. Imagine sumo wrestlers and you get the idea. I don't mean to steal a page from Margaret Mead's notebooks, but someone told me that body weight has something to do with respect. A person's girth, apparently, is a direct indication of wealth and therefore the measure of respect one receives in the community.

So though I won't stand behind that statement, I'll say that Samoans are a large people. When I finally got on the plane to leave, I was one of the only foreigners and a skinny runt at that. Among the one hundred and fifty or so passengers, I was sure that only a handful weighed less than a hundred kilograms, with a vast majority clocking in at something nearer one hundred and fifty.

That made me think of the world's worst airline again. Had it allowed for this sort of weight? What was the load capacity of our plane? I didn't want to appear rude, but surely we were sagging at

189

the seams. Given all the trouble we'd had before, I wasn't feeling particularly safe. In the end, however, all was well, and we took off into the starry night quite safely, headed at last for Fiji.

ع

Fiji is a scatter of islands in the eastern South Pacific. The people are no longer Polynesian, but Melanesian. Melanesian is a politically incorrect word that basically means their skin colour is darker. It's clear they're a different people, perhaps more closely related to the indigenous people of Australia or the islanders of New Guinea, though the Fijian languages remain in the general sphere of Polynesian.

There are two main islands, Viti Levu and Vanua Levu, though most tourists wind up on the former. The last of my flights with the worst airline in the world arrived there safely, outside the city of Nadi.

190

I took a lumbering old school bus down the coast and got off in the middle of nowhere. I'd heard about an eco-lodge there and had phoned ahead to say I was coming. For a few moments I stood with all my stuff by the side of the road, just me, the palms, and the distant sound of surf. Then a jeep appeared on the horizon, rumbling in a cloud of dust up the dirt road behind me. A friendly woman was behind the wheel. *"Bula,"* she said. "You for the Tambua?"

"That's me."

"Well, hop on in then."

By the late afternoon, I was sitting on a wooden chair gazing out over a coconut-strewn beach when something dark broke the surface of the water inside the reef. Then, like the Creature from the Black Lagoon, a hulking shape rose and stood on two legs. He was wearing a black neoprene scuba suit, and in his right hand was a massive spear gun stuck through with a couple of fish. He tugged off his mask. "Hi," he said.

"Ah ... hello," I replied.

"I'm Barry." He flippered awkwardly onto the beach. "I think you met my wife already." Barry shook the wiggling fish at me. "Dinner. C'mon up in half an hour."

Later that night, after a delicious feast of fresh fish, Barry took me to the nearby Fijian village. "You have to see a *kava* circle," he told me.

"A what?"

"Do you know what *bula* means?"

"Well, I think it means hello."

Barry laughed. "That's right, but there's a whole lot more. You'll see."

Bula is a word that turns up a lot in Fiji. Literally, it means "health" or "life," and the one place you really hear it is at a *kava* circle. No one gets out of Fiji alive without trying *kava*. It's a mild narcotic served in a great wooden bowl and tastes something like dishwater, though it's tremendously rude to refuse it. *E dua na bilo?* roughly means "Would you like to try a cup?" And the only answer is to brace yourself and say, "Yes, please."

As the wooden cup is passed to you, social decorum requires that you clap and enthusiastically exclaim, *"Bula Bula!"* (something, I suppose, like "To your health"), and swallow it in one foul gulp. When I drank the concoction, I felt my tongue swell and loll around helplessly in my mouth. A strange bit of tingling crept up and down my arms, but it wasn't unpleasant, and the villagers seemed delighted with my attempt.

A *kava* circle can be a real gossip session. It can also be a fairly serious discussion or meeting, but always it's a social occasion, and I'm told that because of it the incidence of alcoholism on Fiji is actually relatively low. Samoans are much more interested in *kava*.

Later on I staggered to my feet, and one of the villagers led me outside. We sat for a while on the beach under a great dome of stars. The surf washed in, and I felt warm and happy.

191

For the moment the world seemed a very peaceful place.

"*Kalokalo,*" my new friend said, pointing at the heavens.

High overhead, I made out a pattern of stars. All of a sudden it came into focus, and I almost leaped in recognition. Maybe it was because of my near-death experience on the plane. Perhaps it was because the *kava* had loosened me up a bit, but there it was — the great Southern Cross, Koluse I Saute. It leaned a little to the right and was bigger than I'd thought, but there it was — four bright stars sparkling in the tropical night.

This time I created my own meaning for it. Seeing the Southern Cross was, I figured, a sign that I had survived the worst airline in the world. It was a sign that I was truly in paradise. Like Margaret Mead, I had learned that things are often not what you expect, that what you think, especially about other people, is often coloured by your own way of thinking. In other words, I only saw the Southern Cross when I wasn't looking for it.

9

See You at Machu Picchu

Mount Veronica rises almost six thousand metres above the central highlands of Peru. Its snowcapped peaks hover above the clouds, pushing at the cold blue sky. In the ancient language of the Inca, the mountain is called Waka Wilkay, which translates, roughly, as "Tears of Heaven."

Those Inca were onto something because, true enough, when the equatorial sun flashes off the high glaciers, fat tears of ice water plop onto the black rocks of the mountaintop. Trickles of water thread down the slopes, tumbling and combining into creeks. Eventually, these same bubbling streams, a thousand kilometres to the west, swell into the mighty Amazon River.

We passed over one of these creeks at around four thousand metres. A rickety bridge bent out over the water, and I stopped for a moment, breathing heavily in the thin air. It was our second day on the Inca trail — a four-day march over the High Andes to the lost city of Machu Picchu.

Behind me I heard the porters coming — the slap of their sandals on the rocky trail. These guys were a pretty rough crowd. Their faces were weathered and toothless, but they scurried up the pathways with huge striped grain sacks tied to their backs by rope. In the sacks were our tents and the camp stove, and all the food for the journey.

Besides the porters, there were eleven of us: two Israelis, six Poles, a British girl, and myself. Oh, and a guide named René Huaman Callañaúpa. The last two names are Quechua, the language of the Inca. I asked him about the "René" bit, but he smiled and told me simply that his mother had liked the sound of it. It might have come from a French archaeological team a long time ago. He wasn't saying anything definitive, though.

René was forty or maybe fifty; it was hard to tell. He wore a baseball cap pulled tight over his eyes. When he turned into the wind, looking down over the mountain passes, I could see his Inca ancestry. He had the hooked nose and high cheekbones of the Inca, just like the porters, though René had had the good fortune to be born in a valley town rather than in the high mountains. So, unlike the porters, he'd had a chance to go to school, to become educated and worldly.

Our guide spoke Spanish as well as Quechua. His English, too, was quite good, and after leading treks through the Andes for a couple of decades, he could let fly with smatterings of Italian and Japanese, even a few phrases in Polish, which never failed to send our Polish contingent into fits of astonished laughter.

There wasn't a whole lot of time to talk on the trail, however. We were pushing up to Dead Woman's Pass, and at forty-two hundred metres we were sucking for air. My own pack felt heavy, though I knew it was lighter than what the porters had to deal with. I had a couple of litres of water, a sleeping bag, and a tangle of warm clothes, but it all seemed to be dragging me down. The straps were cutting into the soft flesh between my shoulder blades and neck, and it didn't seem as if my walking stick, clacking on the stones, was any help at all.

I stepped aside at the bridge, and three of our porters bounded past, running at a light jog, their cheeks puffed up with coca leaves. To chew coca is to be a *Runa* — one of the people of the Andes. It's both an anesthetic and a medicine, and of course it's the same plant from which cocaine is derived. René, only the night before in the dinner tent, had told us about the pits in the jungle, about the incredible quantity of coca leaves it takes to create a teaspoon of cocaine. As we'd sat long into the evening listening to him, he'd spun tales of government corruption, presidential planes loaded with the stuff, murders, the CIA, and international espionage.

For our simple porters, though, the coca leaves were an age-old tradition. They provide minerals and nutrients not found in the corn and bean crops of the high mountains. The leaves contain large amounts of calcium. They also have various catalysts that help break down hydrocarbons such as the ones found in corn and beans. Besides the nutritional benefits, coca leaves have quasi-medical properties. They dull hunger and alleviate fatigue, so our porters chewed the leaves relentlessly.

195

The porters boiled warm cups of the stuff in the morning. They made it into a sort of tea, and just after dawn, at about six, there would be a tap on our tent poles and rough brown hands would push in the cups of coca tea. We drank it gratefully. It didn't taste all that great, but it sure got us going.

꼭

A Swedish group was moving along behind us on the trail. We'd already bumped into them once or twice. One of the men wore huge black loafers on his feet. "Comfortable," he said, frowning with disdain at my thick hiking boots. "I got them two sizes too big." He grinned like a kid. "They're big, so they won't give me ... ah ..."

"Blisters?"

"Yeah, blisters."

His face, I noticed, alternated at different times of the day between a blushing red and a sickly white. By the second day, we knew why. He was drinking incessantly. I wasn't sure where he got the alcohol. It was possible he'd secreted it in his pack, but by mid-afternoon he was plainly drunk and was racing along the trails, trying to keep up with the porters, his big black shoes flapping and slapping around his feet. Then, when the altitude and the prevailing hangover caught up with him again, he'd slow to a groaning shuffle. The other Swedes tsk-tsked him, but he became a sort of landmark on the trail. You could almost tell time by his states of inebriation.

We'd already gone a couple of days without showers and two nights with bone-chilling temperature drops. René explained that the trail we were following was probably a route of pilgrimage, a sort of sacred journey from Cuzco, one hundred kilometres to the west. We still had another twenty-five kilometres to hike to Machu Picchu, but just beneath the second high pass we came to the first set of Inca ruins. It was a guard post, René said, and a *tumba* — a resting point for pilgrims.

This network of flagstone roads that we were on was dotted with such rest points. The road itself was one of the hallmarks of the Inca Empire. These roads — twenty-five thousand kilometres of them — wound through the High Andes like strings of thread. They ran from what is now Colombia down through Ecuador, Peru, Chile, and even a little way into Argentina, connecting the farthest outposts of the Inca Empire.

I should say here that *Inca* isn't really the right word. The word *Inca* actually refers only to the ruler, a godlike figure not unlike an Egyptian pharaoh. He was always a direct descendant of the first leader of these people, the Inca Manco Capac.

Names are tenuous things. Of all the bits and pieces of language, they're the words that are most completely social constructions. They're words that we've agreed upon, symbols that refer to specific persons or places.

The people here — what we call Inca — are properly named *Runa*, and their language *Runasimi* — the people's mouth — is what we usually label Quechua. René himself called the language Quechua. He'd been born in the village of Chinchero, not far from Cuzco. As we talked about Quechua, he had some fun trying to get me to pronounce their famous glottal stops. These are a sort of hiccup or gulp that turn up in the middle of some Quechua words. Words like *q'inko*, which means "to zigzag" (the apostrophe marks the glottal stop). I'd asked René about that when I noticed that the porters didn't usually run straight up the stone steps on the trail. Instead, they performed a series of miniature switchbacks, zigzagging up the steepest of the long steps.

197

Some words in Quechua even have a double glottal stop, and René tossed off a few of these, sounding as if he were downing a pint of beer all in one go. He taught me one hell of a word — *huacunaillaihuanhuagracacunacayarcanchu* — which means "Bulls get hungry without grass."

Quechua, like many of the indigenous languages of the Americas, is an agglutinating language. It tacks on word ending after word ending until a single word becomes a whole sentence. Sentences about bulls eating grass, for example. Not that there were any bulls on the Inca trail. There were llamas here, but no bulls. Nor was there much grass, just a sort of dull shrubbery found above the tree line in the high mountain passes.

The Inca, however, were masters of this landscape. Their empire, or what's properly called Tahuantinsuyu, centred itself in these mountain ranges bounded on the west by the Pacific Ocean and to the east by the vast Amazon jungle. Tahuantinsuyu derives from the word *tawa*, which is the number *four*. It means that there were four provinces radiating from Cuzco, the capital city, like a cross. The suffix *ntin* means "together," and it's followed by another suffix, *suyu*, meaning "region" or "province." So Tahuantinsuyu means something like "Four United Provinces."

At any rate, this empire — Tahuantinsuyu — lasted less than a century. By about 1450, the ninth Inca, Pachacuti the Earth Shaker, finally united the separate tribes of the Andes into a cohesive republic. In 1532, though, the Spanish arrived, just in time to witness a civil war between two of the great-grandsons of Pachacuti. There was a terrific power struggle between Huáscar (meaning "Gentle Hummingbird") and Atahualpa (meaning "Heroic Turkey"). Predictably, the heroic turkey trumped the gentle hummingbird, but the whole royal mess left the empire in confusion. And that was the state of things when the Spanish entered the scene.

The conquistadors, of course, saw their advantage, so with a kidnapping here and a murder there, the whole Inca Empire collapsed within a single generation. The Inca call this time the Yawar Cocha — the "Ocean of Blood." And for them the world was never the same.

Ω

The Swedish guy was walking slowly in the morning. He was wearing his white face, and we passed him up beyond the ruins. He gave us a weak grin, and I said, "See you at Machu Picchu." This was to become, literally, a running joke. When he passed us again later — revved up once more on the sauce — he called out the same thing: "See you at Machu Picchu." Inevitably, a few hours later we passed him yet again and threw the same taunt back at him.

At the top of the high pass René gathered us together. We were able now to gaze upon a small set of ruins — a *tumba* —

below us. "What do you see there?" René asked. We had already become familiar with this game.

At the first pass — Dead Woman's — René had stopped us to point out the rock formation that supposedly made up the Dead Woman. It had looked like any other clump of rocks. The only clearly recognizable feature was a mound of rock with a tiny spur on top — what René had claimed was the poor woman's breast. "Look up from there," he'd said. "Do you see her shoulder? Look, there's her chin and her face above it."

We couldn't see anything. Tomir, the Israeli, delighted in at least spying the Dead Woman's breast. Later, because this pausing to see shapes in the rocks happened a lot, Tomir started spotting breasts in everything. Now, when René asked us what we saw in the ruins below us, Tomir offered timidly that it could again be a breast.

"No, it's not a breast." René was a bit indignant. "Use your imagination."

"The walls are in kind of a mushroom shape," I said. The outer walls did indeed form a semicircle, with a hallway coming out from the bottom.

"No." René turned slowly from Tomir to me. "But you're closer. He swept his arm toward the ruins. "These ruins are in the shape of a ceremonial knife. The blade is the half-circle. The handle comes out of it."

"I still see a breast," Tomir whispered, but his girlfriend shushed him.

"In Quechua a ceremonial knife is a *tumi*, so the whole thing down there might be a sort of, what do you call it … a pun. It's a *tumba* and a *tumi*." René chuckled. "The Inca, you see, often made their buildings into certain shapes. Back in Cuzco did you see that?"

I nodded. The entire city had been planned in the shape of a puma, the mountain lion of the Andes. You could see it in aerial photos. Postcards even depicted the shape, outlined in black to

199

make it clear for gringos. At Ollantaytambo, another town in the Sacred Valley, the street plan approximated the shape of a llama. And Machu Picchu, still two days away, had at its centre a rock-and-wall formation in the shape of a condor. These were giant symbols the size of whole cities.

Symbols are funny things. Sometimes we physically construct them — like building an entire city to represent an animal. That's a pretty big metaphor. Words are much smaller, but we build them, too. They're socially constructed, by which I mean that the society as a whole has generally agreed that such and such a symbol represents such and such a meaning. That's largely how it works. So it's not surprising that we take our symbols from the world around us. A condor, for example, happens to be a magnificent bird, a huge raptor, and it's native to the Andes. It was only natural that the Inca took something like that and affixed it with a meaning. We can only work with the materials at hand, the world immediately around us. For the Inca that was largely a mountain world, a rarefied realm of snowbound peaks and high alpine meadows.

Φ

At the height of the Inca Empire, just before the Spanish arrived, the cities and towns held about fifteen million people. Today there are almost eight million people who are fully bilingual in both Spanish and Quechua. The latter isn't generally taught in schools, though it's quite often the language of the home and the street in places like Cuzco. In the high mountains there are still two million people who speak nothing but Quechua.

It's often pointed out that the Inca never developed a writing system, but that's sort of missing the point. They paid almost constant attention to symbols and messages. Their world was a complex one, and symbols were necessary to capture some of that intricacy.

The most famous symbol system of the Inca was the *quipos*, a series of knots tied onto thick wool strings. They're little understood, even by modern Inca, but it's clear they were some kind of system to keep records. There are only a few examples left, and anthropologists and historians fight over them with relish. One recent journal paper claims they might have stood in for syllables — something like hieroglyphics — but that's probably a bit of a stretch. More likely they were an accounting system, though one that could hold a great deal of information. When I asked René about *quipos*, he told me that the colour of the yarn had something to do with their meaning. The knots in yellow yarn signified gold, and these *quipos* were employed to keep track of wealth. Red yarn, meanwhile, was utilized to count soldiers — and possibly workers — to figure out where they were situated across the vast kingdom.

We also know that *quipos* followed a base-ten counting system, much like our own, but beyond that, not much is known about them. What's clear is that they formed a system of representation not unlike a written language. They held information quite effectively, and certainly in an empire of this size, there would have been a lot of information to hold. This was no backwater empire, and if not for the strange quirk of history that had the Spanish conquistadors slam into their midst before the civilization really solidified, well, it's hard to say what they might have accomplished and what they might have become.

Ψ

"Let me tell you now about the Inca world view," René said. We huddled around him a little more closely. A wind had come down off the mountaintop, and our sweaters fluttered under the straps of our backpacks. We were near the top of the second high pass, and the full sweep of the Andes lay in front of us.

201

"Do you know why Machu Picchu is represented by the condor?" René looked around at us. No one would meet his eyes. No one had a clue.

"Because the condor, for us, represents the upper world." René stopped for a moment, obviously considering how to explain all this to us. "There were three worlds. Did you see the steps in the last set of ruins — three steps going up? This is for the three worlds."

"Look," he said, waving his hands out over the valleys below us. "The lower world was called Uju Pacha. It's represented by the snake. When we get to Machu Picchu, you'll see the river far below it. The Urubamba River winds like a snake so that the snake is both the symbol for the underworld and the symbol for water."

The wind whistled across the rocks. René glanced up. "This all around us, this is the middle world, Kay Pacha. It's represented by the puma, symbol of the earth and also of war. Cuzco was the middle place of all things, and that's why it was built in the shape of a puma."

René waved us closer. "But most important is the condor. Have you seen them?" A few members of the group nodded. In Colca Canyon to the south you can sometimes see them riding the thermals. Huge birds of prey, they're in the same family as eagles or hawks, though they're considerably larger and until recently nearly extinct.

"The condors are the keepers of the upper world, Hanaq Pacha. The condor represents the air, the sky ... also peace." René paused dramatically. "We believe that if you've lived a good life, then you'll have a pure spirit. This we call a *chuya alma*, or sometimes an *ura almo*, which means 'white spirit.' And when you die, if you have this pure spirit, then a condor will come and take it up to Hanaq Pacha."

"Like heaven," one of the Poles offered.

"A little bit, yes, but not quite the same." René gazed at the rain-darkened sky. "It's a little complicated to explain."

Just then the Swede appeared from below to break the spell. He'd found his second wind or his second bottle and breezed past us, hopping from rock to rock. "See you at Machu Picchu." He laughed, and then he was gone.

ξ

Our campsite that night was cold. We were still above four thousand metres, and the stars glittered like living things. The crescent moon hung oddly horizontal like a thin smile, and René tried to point out a few of the old Inca constellations. Up in the Pleiades was Colcas, the puma's head, a seven-star grouping.

"Do you see it?" René asked.

Tomir was about to say something, but his girlfriend's hand hooked into his arm and he only squealed softly. Another constellation formed the shape of a llama. These animal symbols were everywhere.

René turned to the south. "Okay, what about up there?"

I squinted, and something familiar formed in my imagination. We were thirteen degrees south of the equator, and there it was again. "That's the Southern Cross," I said, quite proud of myself.

"Yes. In Quechua it's Chacanu. It's like a road map for us." René gestured at the sky. "Cuzco is at the centre, always, and the four arms of the cross point to the different regions, the four provinces of the empire."

What amazes me is how these patterns of stars were given meanings by people around the world. That's to be expected, I guess. The stars are pretty clear to everyone on Earth, and for the Spanish conquistadors the Southern Cross had one meaning, while to the Inca it signified something quite different.

ㄱ

The great cathedral in Cuzco is built directly over the palace of Wiracocha, the eighth Inca ruler. There are a lot of reasons for this. The first is that it was practical. The stout and expertly crafted Inca foundation walls held up well during earthquakes. The Inca walls are famous for their craftsmanship. They didn't use mortar, but the stones were so perfectly fitted together that it's impossible to slip a knife blade between any of the joints. In the early years of the conquest the Spanish experienced a number of minor earthquakes and watched as their own buildings collapsed, while the old Inca walls stood unscathed. It didn't take them long to realize they could incorporate the Inca walls as foundations.

Building the cathedral directly over the Inca ruler's palace, however, was more than a structural decision. The Spanish, of course, were making a statement: "We are more powerful than you," or more precisely, "Our God is mightier than yours."

There were actually many layers of subtle logic at play. The Inca rulers were thought to have descended from the Sun God. When they ascended to the throne, these rulers each took a new name (much as the Roman Catholic pope does today). The eighth Inca ruler — the most powerful ever — chose Wiracocha, which happens to be the name of one of the most ancient Inca gods, a deity that's sometimes called the "Invisible One."

This god was a supreme divinity of pre-Inca origin. Because it's a pre-Inca borrowing, the stories ascribed to this god aren't completely clear. Some stories talk of him as a sort of combination Storm God and Sun God, while others claim he was responsible for creating the sun and the moon. A number of different myths are associated with Wiracocha, but most have him roaming the Earth disguised as a beggar to check on his creations. Most tales say he weeps copiously, and some stories relate that he used these oceans of tears to flood the creations he didn't like. Sound familiar? A flood wiping out creation?

The god Wiracocha eventually disappeared one day over the Pacific Ocean where he was seen walking on the water. One can imagine that some Spanish priests had a real "Aha!" moment when they heard that tale.

These were just the sort of levers the Spanish were able to put to use in their conversion of the Inca to Catholicism. The most important point of all, though, was the one René had told us about: the *chuya alma* — the white soul — and the idea that when a person died his *chuya alma* was carried to another world above.

Ω

On the fourth and last day of the hike we woke up at 4:00 a.m. when there was a rustling outside our tent. René appeared, urging us to hurry. The idea was that we had to get to the Sun Gate to see the sun rise over Machu Picchu. The Sun Gate was still two kilometres away from our campsite, but already the sky was growing lighter in the east as we pulled on our hiking boots, bleary-eyed and heavy with sleep.

205

Below our campsite our group, as well as the Swedes, were joined by a troop of overenthusiastic Australians and Americans. Everyone jostled together, and the final push to the Sun Gate suddenly turned very competitive. We jogged along in single file, our heavy backpacks jumping up and down on our backs. If anyone slowed down even for a second, five or six others would push by him or her. It was crowded, and no one displayed much in the way of manners.

After being pushed along for a while at this rate, I glanced down and realized that one of my bootlaces had come undone. I had no intention of stopping, though. Sweat was now trickling down my neck, and adrenaline was coursing through my system. I managed to get my water bottle out even as I charged along the path. I took a gulp, then realized that my other bootlace was loose. The laces were now flapping spastically, shamefully, and my boots were pulling away from my socks.

The path was carved along a cliff face. We were going up and down long sets of uneven rock steps. The cliff plunged to my right, and gradually, through the morning fog, it occurred to me that I could easily trip over these flapping laces. I could fall headlong off the cliff, so at last cold, hard reason percolated to the surface and I halted to tie up my boots. I grunted menacingly at those who scrambled by me. The Swedish guy sprinted past. "See you at Machu Picchu," he chirped.

"Like hell you will," I spat back. As I stood, though, I realized that the clouds were pretty much socked in, anyway. Half an hour later, when I stumbled into a set of rock ruins, it took me a moment to realize I was at the fabled Sun Gate. Only a few people had stopped there to take token photographs. There was really nothing to see. An immense cloud had settled around us. Somewhere below was Machu Picchu, but we could have been on London Bridge for all we knew.

The pace slowed a lot, though as we descended further, wisps here and there opened in the clouds, and the knife-like peak behind the city — Huayna Picchu — began to appear. Then, to our left, a stone wall materialized out of the fog. Down the hills, the stepped terraces came into view, and at last the whole magical city appeared as if someone had suddenly wiped the condensation off a window in front of us.

So how do you describe something as iconic as Machu Picchu? Who hasn't, at one time or another, had a postcard of it magnetically affixed to the fridge? Who hasn't pencilled in the name on their list of the must-see sights of the world? It's like the Eiffel Tower or the Pyramids of Egypt, and as the sun glinted down on it — the real thing — I couldn't believe I was really there.

Ω

We were significantly lower now. Machu Picchu sits at twenty-eight hundred metres above sea level, and finally we were getting a break from the punishing altitude. What balanced that was that by about 7:00 a.m. the sun was already slamming down on us with an intensity I hadn't felt since I first arrived in South America. Basically, we were only a few hundred kilometres south of the equator, and the screaming sun wasn't about to let us forget that.

René tucked his baseball cap even farther down his forehead and led us through the green eastern terraces. Some three thousand people had once lived here, but clearly the agricultural output of the place was for a population much greater than that.

"Every guide will tell you something different," René told us. "There are a lot of theories about this place, but the truth is that we really don't know much about Machu Picchu. Up until recently it was thought that this might have been a secret refuge for the Inca rulers. The Spanish never knew about Machu Picchu, so everyone imagined that the noble classes of Cuzco came here and lived for many more generations, untouched by the conquest. But that's simply not true. Scientists now say this place was already abandoned by the time the Spanish showed up. We don't know why. Our best guess is that things tightened up during the civil wars, and everyone who lived here fled back to Cuzco. What we do know is that this place was a religious centre. Come, I'll show you why that's so."

207

He led us down a set of precipitous steps. The city now climbed above us, a tumble of terraces and rock walls. We came to a ledge with a cave opening. It looked, though, as if it had been artificially widened and enlarged over the years. In the middle was a series of three steps. They didn't lead anywhere — just up into the air.

René stopped in front of them. "What do you think these are?"

It was clear by now: the three steps, the three levels.

"Here," René said, "you can see the three worlds of the Inca — the Uju Pacha, the Kay Pacha, and the Hanaq Pacha. Now come, I want to show you something more."

He took us up another stairway, and we entered an amphitheatre in the rock. Most of it was left in its natural state, but two great swirls of rock, the result of some cataclysmic geological event, spread out like frozen drapery.

"Do you see?" René asked. "These are its wings."

"Wings?" I said.

In the middle of the swirling rock a small carving was set into the floor. It was hard to make out. "This is its head," René said. "Do you see?"

I squinted, then stepped back for a fuller picture. It took some imagination, but there it was.

"This is the condor." René spoke with pride now. "This whole place is a temple to Hanaq Pacha, the upper world. The Inca trail we've just walked was most likely a spiritual pilgrimage, a holy journey for the people of Cuzco. Maybe a way of purifying their spirits, a way of strengthening their *chuya alma* so that when they died the condor would come for them and raise them into the sky."

René took us to the upper terraces of Machu Picchu after that, to the Temple of the Sun where the rays at the summer solstice angle in through one of its windows. He led us to two small stone circles. What at first were thought to be places for grinding grain are actually tiny reflecting pools. They were filled with water, though the liquid was not for drinking, nor was it strictly decorative. The theory is now that in these pools of water Inca priests observed the stars. They used them as unmoving mirrors to track the movements of the constellations and planets.

"We can't know for sure what these stone circles were for," René told us. "Most of this knowledge is lost. Machu Picchu was rediscovered only in 1911 by an American named Hiram Bingham. The Quechua who lived around here always knew of the ruins on the mountain. The city had long been covered in vegetation, but the farmers who worked the land along the river knew there were ruins here. It didn't take much for them to point Bingham and his expedition up the trails across the ridge."

René glanced at his watch. Our trip was coming to an end. "I want to tell you before we part that I'm Quechua. The truth, today, is that this is a very mixed-up thing. We say sometimes we're Quechañol — a mixture of Quechua and *Español*, or Spanish. But I'm proud of our Inca past. Every time I see this city I'm proud of what my ancestors did. I'll leave you with the three obligations of the Inca way. These are the things you must do if you're to have a pure soul. You must work hard, and this we call *yankay*. You must love, and this we call *munay*. Lastly, you must always keep learning. The word for this is *yachay*." René studied us intently. "You must always keep learning."

Φ

Cuzco is now a bustling tourist hub. Its central square, Plaza des Armes, holds the great Spanish cathedral. A colonnade wraps around the rest of the square, and many of the buildings feature restaurants and cafés with balconies that look onto the small central park.

It struck me that the whole thing was like a layer cake of archaeology. Beneath the cobblestones, at the foundation, were the Inca walls. Above that were the Spanish colonial buildings, many almost five hundred years old. On their rooftops, on their balconies, was the new reality, the third wave, the invasion of tourists.

We sat at a place with the improbable name of Baghdad Café. A series of pisco sours had been set in front of us. These tasted vaguely like tequila, though they were mixed with a froth of steamed milk. They're quite good, dangerously so, and more than a couple of them will soon have a drinker howling down the cobblestone streets with the roving packs of stray dogs.

As we drank, we watched the crowds below us. It was a surprising mix of people. Out on the square a Quechua woman shuffled past with a baby wrapped in a blanket and slung across her back. Her skirts were woven from llama wool and dyed bright orange and red. A woollen cap sat atop her head, and her face was ravaged by the weather and altitude. Behind her was a group of backpackers, draped with day packs and water bottles, each with a Lonely Planet guide opened to the map of Cuzco.

Are we tourists the new conquistadors — sweeping in with our strange clothes and demanding habits, changing the social landscape with our very presence? Were we taking over the place now? Certainly, we were driving the economy. American dollars are accepted everywhere in Peru, and the dubious local currency, the sol, is less and less in demand.

Yet Peru had once been a land of great wealth. Before the Spanish arrived, this whole area was rolling in precious metals. Gold to the Inca was known as "the sweat of the sun" (thus the name of Peruvian money — the *sol* — the sun). Silver for the Inca was called "the tears of the moon."

I went down to see the ruins that were left here, to a fantastic place called Qoricancha. It was just off a busy street in the centre of Cusco. It had come to light again only when an earthquake caused a section of the Convent of Santo Domingo to collapse.

Qoricancha was the Temple of the Sun. It was the most important temple in the Inca world. In its heyday it was covered with more than seven hundred plates of solid gold, each the size of a car door. Qoricancha means "Golden Courtyard," and in addition to the hundreds of gold panels lining its walls, there were life-size gold figures, solid-gold altars, and a huge golden sun disc. The sun disc reflected the sun into the temple and bathed its dark interior with light. Smaller rooms off to the sides existed for the worship of the lesser gods: the moon, Venus, thunder, lightning, and one little cell for the rainbow god.

I can only imagine how the conquistadors' eyes must have bulged when they saw this vast temple of gold. After they kidnapped the Inca ruler, they asked for all the gold plates as a ransom. Then, after the Inca had dutifully taken down the gold and carted it off to the conquistadors, the invaders reneged on their deal and killed Atahualpa, anyway. Then they melted down the gold and shipped it back to Spain. There the coffers of the king and queen overflowed with the riches of the New World and made Spain, for a time, the richest and most powerful nation on the planet.

The gold is now long gone, and the countries of South America are, for the most part, mired in poverty. The tourists come, as tourists do, to gawk at the old ruins, not only Inca ones but Spanish ones, as well. And so it goes.

Ψ

I travelled from Cuzco south to Lake Titicaca, an old name that has been the source of countless jokes in North America. No one really knows where the name originated, but it might be a combination of two words, one from Quechua and another from Aymara, the local language spoken around the shores of the lake.

I took a boat out to a group of islands known as the Uros. They're heavily touristed these days, which is unfortunate because these islands hold one of the most unique cultures on Earth. The Uros have literally constructed the islands they live on from reeds. No one knows how long they've lived on the lake, floating on their artificial islands, but it's at least as far back as the time of the Inca some five hundred years ago.

There are actually only a few hundred people still living on these islands, and from what I saw, that's largely to take advantage of the tourist boats that come out to snap pictures of their unusual lifestyle. It was very strange stepping off the boat and onto the soft mush of the islands. You feel your feet sink a bit into the reeds, and you get the sensation you're still floating. Old peasants, bundled in traditional clothing, huddle over blankets spread with homemade jewellery. Reed huts, emerging almost organically from the reed platforms, show where they live, though at least one, I saw, had a satellite dish for a television.

Apparently, the reed islands rot from the bottom so that the Uros are constantly adding new reeds to the top. They even make their local boats from long sweeps of these *totora* reeds.

No one speaks the Uros language anymore. They traded with the Aymara people along the shoreline of the vast lake, and in time they lost their language and adopted Aymara. Across southern Peru and Bolivia there are still about two million Aymara speakers — not an inconsiderable group. They had been subjugated by the Inca, though there's evidence that the grand Inca architecture might have been based on earlier Aymara civilizations and that the Inca rulers themselves might have been descended from Aymara people.

At the south end of the lake, on the Bolivian side, a bright little village runs up from the beach. It's called Copacabana — not to be confused with its better known namesake in Rio de Janeiro. In fact, there's also a Copacabana in Colombia to the north, another one in Australia, and most confusing of all, a Copacabana in Croatia, just outside Dubrovnik. Go figure.

Anyway, this little village of Copacabana in Bolivia is full-on Aymara. At the local market you can see old women with bowler hats a couple of sizes too small and neatly pinned to the tops of their shiny black hair. Across their shoulders are shawls of llama wool, brightly died in patterns older even than Inca symbols. And up by the cathedral in the central square I witnessed one of the oddest sights I've seen. Tuesday mornings are reserved for the "Blessing of the Automobiles."

If you've ever bought a new car, or more precisely if you've acquired some old piece of junk that is, in fact, new to you, bring it to the cathedral for a blessing before you drive it around. On this morning we saw from the beginning that a long line of cars had been parked in front of the cathedral. Many were decked out with flowers, much like we might decorate a car for a wedding party. They were immaculately scrubbed and polished so that the rust and peeling paint glistened. Their owners stood by proudly and expectantly. Then, at about ten o'clock, a priest came out of the cathedral with a bucket of holy water. One by one, he went down the line of cars. The owners opened the hoods, and the priest paused before the cars' engines, uttering Latin blessings, dipping a small brush into the pail of holy water, and spashing it across the engines and around the entire car while the owners smiled broadly and snapped photos of their young cars' Confirmation.

Copacabana is actually a lovely little town, and I stayed there for several days, relaxing in a place slightly off the tourist trail, a little out of sync with the world, a place where time seemed to slow down and almost come to a complete halt. In fact, the Aymara language itself does the most wonderful thing with time. In English we speak of the past as being behind us and the future, quite logically, in front of us. All this is based on the metaphor we have for time: that life is a journey, a road we travel down.

213

In the Aymara language, things are completely reversed. The past, in Aymara, is spoken of as being in front, while the future is thought to be behind. The very word they use to describe the past is *nayra*, referring to the front. The expression *nayra mara* — meaning "last year" — is literally translated as "front year."

That confused me for a while until it was explained and then it made perfect sense. We already know the past, we have lived it, and therefore we see it in front of us. It's in full view.

The future, though, is unknown. It can't be seen and therefore is behind us, unseen and unknown. The older Aymara people even gesture with their hands, pointing their thumbs behind them when speaking of the future and sweeping their hands forward when talking about the past. The younger Aymara don't do this. This is believed to be because they're now bilingual in Spanish where, of course, the metaphor is the same as English. And so the old ways are being eroded.

To the best of our knowledge, Aymara is the only language on Earth that presents time in this manner. Others — and these include tongues as diverse as Polynesian, Mandarin, and even African Bantu — have been shown in intensive studies to point the arrow of time from back to front. But that doesn't mean it has to be that way.

Humans are incredibly flexible creatures. We construct whole cities out of ideas. We erect meanings out of colours, yarn, and rocks. We build new ideas directly on top of old ones, like cathedrals over ruins, and by the sheer fluidity of our minds, we can twist the river of time and turn its very flow.

10

The Headwaters of the Amazon

Quito lies a bare twenty kilometres south of the equator. It, too, was once part of the Inca Empire. Now it's the capital of Ecuador and is a sprawl of two million people. I'd come by bus through the Avenue of the Volcanoes, some of them still spewing ash and steam. From here, though, I would be venturing east into the headwaters of the Amazon where there are still people who are all but untouched by the outside world.

From Quito I tagged along on a series of increasingly smaller propeller planes. By the time I got to Shell, an outpost on the edge of the jungle, I was shuttled onto one final aircraft, an aging Twin Otter held together with piano wire and duct tape. It reeked of leaking diesel fuel, and the propellers whirred unevenly, spinning us crookedly into the air.

When the plane was aloft, engines whining, windows rattling, we flew over a thick jungle canopy. It stretched to the horizon on all sides like a giant broccoli pizza. There were no roads, no power lines, no signs of anything vaguely smacking of civilization, just the endless green of the Amazon in the borderlands between Ecuador, Peru, and Brazil.

I was going to see a people called the Achuar, who weren't "discovered" until the 1970s. Today, not much more than a single generation after first contact, they still live out of reach of the modern world in thatch huts, hunting monkeys with blow darts, cultivating tiny gardens in clearings on the riverbank.

Their language exists only within a relatively small area of the Amazon River Basin. And that was what I'd been searching for. What sort of language would they construct deep in the rain forest where there were no metal objects, no stones — nothing but roots, fibres, and leaves? What sort of symbolic systems would they create, surrounded as they were by almost endless jungle?

As I've said, languages are socially constructed things. We all agree that a certain symbol, a word, say, has a particular meaning. In Achuar the pronunciation of *ensa* means "river," but that doesn't explain what it signifies for the Achuar — that it's their central means of transport, that it's easier to paddle upriver in a dugout than to try to cut through the jungle with a machete. It doesn't reveal that they orient themselves to the world in terms of upriver and downriver. It doesn't indicate that they count the seasons by the way the stars move over the river.

ξ

The sky was falling into darkness by the time the plane skidded onto a mud strip cut between the trees. Waiting for me was Philippe, who would be my translator. Born in Quito, he had studied anthropology and had gone through a series of rigorous courses certifying him as a jungle guide. He had been living with the Achuar people for just over a year, long enough to get to know their ways and be reasonably accepted in their community.

I followed him away from the airstrip down a muddy path through the jungle. A full moon shone above the dark branches. We still had to hike a short way to the river and then paddle up it in a dugout canoe. When we reached the river, it was silver with moonlight, a long strip of light through the dark forest.

The Kapawi is one of a thousand tributaries that eventually flow into the Amazon. It's a twelve-day hike from the nearest road. As we slid down its muddy banks toward the dugout floating there, we came face to face with Shakai. His face was painted with thin black lines, and he didn't look at us or smile. He was short but powerfully built, coming from a stock of often brutal and ruthless warriors.

Shakai was Achuar and would be our guide for the next five days. He was somewhere around thirty, I guessed, and he would have grown up in a world of green leaves and parrots, of slithering anacondas and unrelenting heat. We climbed awkwardly into the dugout. Shakai got in at the front and remained standing, easily balanced, gazing only at the river without the slightest acknowledgement of our presence.

I'd already learned that this was part of Achuar culture. Eye contact is seen as aggressive. Through many centuries of almost ritualized warfare with the surrounding peoples of the rain forest, the Achuar had taken on a cautious, wary air. Everything was potentially dangerous. Death hid in the water, in the forest, and even, as I was soon to find out, in their dreams.

Philippe sat in front of me, hands gripping the edge of the dugout. He spoke some Achuar, and Shakai now uttered a bit of Spanish so that between them they had worked out a sort of understanding that Philippe would then try to translate back to me in English.

The electric buzz of insects had come up with the setting of the sun. The draping trees on either side of the river swelled with life. We moved through the water slowly, and after a time Shakai began to let out a strange whistle — five descending tones that trailed off sadly, almost eerily. To our right, deep in the forest, a call came back to us: the same five-tone descending scale.

"What's that?" I whispered at Philippe.

"Shakai is calling to one of the birds — the common potoo. This bird only sings during the full moon."

Shakai whistled again, mimicking the bird call exactly.

"It's one of their myth birds," Philippe continued. "They call her Aujujai."

"And Shakai knows its call?"

"He can imitate the call of many animals. This bird, though —" Philippe turned to look at me "— is an important one. The Achuar believe Aujujai is in love with the moon. Maybe you'll hear the story later ... when they get up for the telling of their dreams."

"Dreams?"

"Later." Philippe turned back toward the front of the boat. "In the early morning — that's when they tell their dreams."

Under the full moon the river was now a ribbon of pale, shimmering light. The forest on either side was lost in blackness, and even Shakai had become a silhouette against the starry sky.

An hour later we approached a grouping of huts set along a swampy lagoon. A few more Achuar men came down to greet us. The Achuar are one of four tribes in this part of the Amazon. Collectively, they're known as the Jivaro, and they all speak slightly different dialects of the Jivaro language. To the west, slightly closer to civilization (and therefore slightly more habituated to the Western world), are the Shuar, who are famously known as headhunters. They were the ones who shrunk the heads of their enemies in a practice known as *tsantsa*. The Achuar, even deeper in the forest, don't believe in such rituals. They think of them as cannibalistic and barbaric. Instead, they simply bash in the heads of their enemies and leave it at that.

Achuar men are meant to possess *kajen*, a predisposition toward anger and violence. It's expected. Until relatively recently an almost endless series of personal and family vendettas ravaged the forest. Today, even, meetings between groups of people, anyone outside one's own family and friends, are carefully ritualized. Eye contact, as I said, signals aggression. Eye contact between males and females is even more problematic. It signals desire. Desire begets jealousy, and so in a heartbeat, we're right back to violence again.

These old ways, though, are already showing the first signs of change. Only a generation ago the Achuar lived in family groupings deep in the forest. Now they've started to congregate in larger communities, villages almost. Our plane had bumped down into one of these "new" places. The Achuar there had cleared the landing strip, and an array of huts and tin shacks had sprung up.

This wasn't the Achuar way. Already their social constructions were changing. With the arrival of airplanes, and more specifically, cooking pots, machetes, and medicine on these planes, not to mention white adventurers like myself, their world, the very organization of their way of life, was already evolving into something new.

219

We had journeyed past that "new" village to a place much farther upriver where the people lived in much the same way as their ancestors had for centuries. Everything they needed came from the forest. They hunted and fished and constructed their huts according to a set of belief structures that were unlike any I'd come across before.

꠹

The next morning Shakai and Philippe took me on a jungle hike. Shakai went first, hacking through the vines with his machete.

Philippe trudged behind him, and I trailed in the rear. The canopy was filled with wildlife, and Shakai stopped occasionally to point into the trees and name the animals and birds. To describe the forest only in visual terms, though, is to miss much of it. Whole symphonies of sound swelled and thrummed around us. It was muggy. My clothes, from the first hour there, were never quite dry again. They clung dankly and began to smell — a musty odour not of sweat so much as a sort of earthy scent, like that of wet grass or mushrooms.

We tramped along slowly. I felt as if I'd spent too long in a hot tub — thoroughly weighted down with the heat of the place. Everything was various shades of green. Even the sky was obscured by the forest canopy. A sort of mulch was underfoot, and if I peered closely enough at the rotting leaves and branches, I quickly discovered they were alive with wriggling things: ants and spiders and creatures I had no name for. Occasionally, butterflies as big as two hands flitted through the trees. They were a shimmering, iridescent blue, and the hue was startling in the midst of all that green.

Philippe plodded behind Shakai, translating his few words. In the long silences my attention drifted to a square box Philippe had strapped to his back. It was about the size and shape of a hardcover book, and I could see an electrical wire sticking out of the zipper.

"What's in the box, Philippe?" I asked.

"Oh." He stopped and proudly flipped it opened for me. Two little paddles were in there, and a battery or something.

"What is it?"

"A portable defibrillator. Look at this — twenty thousand volts!"

"Jesus, are you expecting someone to have a heart attack?" I glanced around. There was no one there except me and my companions. The air was as thick as water, and I'd been marching along lethargically, my heart thumping in my ears.

"No, we don't use it for that. It's for snakebites."

"What?"

"Snakebites. It's pretty new. They've just discovered that the jolt of electricity somehow dissolves the venom."

"Are you kidding me?"

"Yeah, twenty thousand volts. I haven't had a chance to use it yet."

"I hope you don't."

Philippe's English was perfect. To my surprise he'd lived in America and even worked for a time not far from my own home in the Canadian Rockies. He had gone through an intensive training program to become a guide and interpreter with the Achuar, though he fully admitted that his knowledge of the jungle wasn't even a hundredth, not even a thousandth, of what the Achuar knew.

A German research team had been down here the year before, Philippe told me. The team's members had isolated a single tree and fumigated it. When the insects dropped off, hundreds of them, the Germans found that 80 percent couldn't be identified — and that was just from a single tree!

Shakai stopped suddenly in front of a strange tree. He glanced at Philippe, then started to explain something. Philippe translated. "He wants you to know this tree is called the walking palm. It's the only tree that walks."

I wrinkled my brow. "Walks?"

"Yes, if you look at the roots ..." Philippe began. Shakai was gesturing at the base of the tree. It was held up on a thicket of branches, a cage of root fibres. "Everything in the forest competes for sunlight," Philippe explained. "The roots don't have to go far to find water. It's everywhere. But the canopy can become so thick that all life here must find ways to get to the sunlight. In this case, if a larger tree grows over the walking palm, the roots on one side will die off and it will grow new roots on the other side. Since you can see that the tree is held up by the roots, it literally walks back over into a patch of sunlight. The tree can move about sixty centimetres in a year, about five centimetres a month."

Shakai said something again. Philippe leaned toward him. "He wants you to know that the jungle is always changing. It's evolving all the time." Shakai reached for a leaf from the next tree over. To me it looked like all the others. Philippe translated. "This kind of leaf is toxic. In fact, almost everything is poisonous here in the forest. In this case, the ants — see here, there are little holes where they've eaten a part of the leaf in the middle — know this leaf is toxic in certain doses and they know exactly how much they can eat before it kills them.

Shakai spoke again. The language sounded clipped and staccato, vaguely like Japanese. "He's saying now that a few months ago they started to notice that the leaves of this plant were growing in a different way. The leaves started to grow with the little holes already in the middle of them. The leaves were mimicking the holes made by the ants, and now the ants will come to one of these new leaves and think that leaf has already been eaten. So the ants move on to the next plant. Do you see?"

He held up the leaf. A scattering of tiny round holes were clearly visible. "The eco-system is incredibly dynamic here. It's like a race between the predators and the prey, one always trying to stay a step ahead of the other. The Achuar understand this. They're a part of the place."

Ω

Throughout the day Shakai showed us the medicines, or *tsuak*, that are harvested from the forest. One leaf, dried and crumpled up, smelled exactly like garlic. The Achuar use it to boost their immune systems. In another case, a parasite that causes a form of flesh-eating disease is treated with the roots of a particular cactus plant. At another little clearing Shakai dug his machete into the white bark of a large tree, and it bled. A bead of thick red liquid dribbled from the wound, exactly like blood.

Shakai dipped his finger into the fluid and invited me to do the same. I tasted it. It was vaguely sweet. "In Achuar," Philippe explained, "this is called *arushnumi numi*. *Numi* is the word for 'tree.' In Spanish we call this *sangria de dragon* — "dragon's blood." Now there's a medical company interested in this 'blood.' It's a natural antibiotic. The Achuar use it to clean wounds. It's good for mosquito bites, too. It makes the swelling go down." Philippe paused. "In my trips into the jungle I've counted more than fifty-two different plants that the Achuar use as medicines."

"What about malaria?" I asked.

Even Shakai turned at the sound of that word. *"Chukuch,"* he muttered.

"That's the word for malaria," Philippe told me. "For this they take *wayusa*. They make it into a tea, and every morning they drink it. That's also when they tell their dreams and myth stories."

"Yes," I said, "you were going to tell me the story about the bird that was in love with the moon."

"Ah ..." Philippe began, but just then Shakai turned quickly and grunted something at him. "Rain is coming," Philippe translated.

We both looked up, and it was true: something was different in the air. Shakai began to pick up his pace, and we hadn't gone more than a few paces before we heard a distant clap of thunder.

"When we get back to the huts, remind me to tell you about the *wayusa*, but now I'm sorry ... we have to move quickly." He darted after Shakai, and I sighed and clumped after them.

Before we reached the dugout the sky opened up. Rain splashed down unmercifully. Even the birds grew silent. Huge cracks of thunder rolled across the sky. They rumbled on and on before finally tapering into the soft slap of the rain on the river.

Φ

The first extended contact with the Achuar came in 1976 when a young Frenchman named Philippe Descola came to study them. Descola was a student of the great anthropologist Claude Lévi-Strauss, who taught him to look for the underlying meaning of things, to search for the fundamental structures on which Achuar society was built.

Descola stayed for two years, and from his field notes he cobbled together a remarkable book called *The Spears of Twilight*. I had an English translation of it, though it was already musty with jungle air. I read it with my flashlight when I couldn't get to sleep.

The Achuar, Descola contended, don't have the same sense of space we have. They have no place names to speak of except the names for their rivers — the Kapawi and the Pastaza. They wouldn't be able to tell you where they were born, not because of forgetfulness or ignorance but because the place had ceased to exist. There are no large rocks in the jungle here. Everything is organic material, so there are no landmarks of permanence. Even the lifespan of a broad, tall tree isn't long in comparison with trees in temperate forests. Things grow incredibly fast so that any given patch of jungle will look completely different, in fact, will be completely different, in only a few months. Remember, this is the place where some trees can literally walk.

The jungle is ever-changing. Even the various twists and bends in the river transform as large trees fall into the river, pulling away the earth underneath them, eroding the bank, and altering the course of the river. A typical Achuar settlement has garden patches of manioc, yams, and sweet potatoes, but these last only five years or so. House beams resist the elements for perhaps ten years, and when their homes eventually collapse, the Achuar simply move on and leave the remains to the encroaching jungle. Nothing in the environment can be counted on as an unmoving point of reference. Everything constantly grows and changes.

The Achuar don't even have directional terms for north, south, east, and west. Instead, their only words of direction are the relative terms for upriver and downriver.

By the time I arrived, all that was beginning to change. Forty years ago there were no metal tools here. Now everyone seems to own a machete. Shakai was especially adept with his, swiping away overhanging roots and vines, or with a simple tap of its sharp tip, cutting off a piece of fishing line.

I asked Shakai about his machete through Philippe, and for a moment the Achuar seemed perplexed. He didn't know where the machetes had come from. In his youth they had used stone axes. These new tools were much better. The Achuar dubbed them "polished stone axes," or simply adopted the Spanish word *machete*.

Certainly, a long metal blade is a handy piece of technology in the forest — so much so that it's now almost indispensable to the Achuar. What's more, this piece of technology — and to us an extremely primitive one — has radically changed the Achuar way of life and their whole sense of space. It's now possible for them to move through the forest quite easily. The singular importance of travelling solely by water no longer holds the precedence it did only a couple of decades ago. The Achuar can clear out landing strips for airplanes, and invariably villages of a type that never existed before spring up along these same airstrips. Permanent villages. I'd already seen the one where we'd landed. There was a clapboard school there, even a soccer pitch. All of this was completely new.

225

It's almost scary to think how much a new implement like a machete can change a way of life. And think of the barrage of technology facing the Achuar in the very near future. All of them are now aware of the airplanes coming in from some unknown outer world, great metal birds that carried both the strange and powerful white people, as well as their goods — cooking pots, machetes, and weapons far superior to anything the Achuar had ever previously used.

So, though languages and cultures are both socially and environmentally constructed, one might also say there's an element of something we might call technological construction. There's a lot of overlap between these different sources of cultural construction, of course. That a hut is built along parallel lines with the river is environmental. The family groupings that occupy them are societal constructions. But the tin roof I saw near the airstrip is a technological innovation. And clearly this sort of thing, this introduction of metals, is going to have a profound and irreversible effect on the Achuar way of life.

$$\Psi$$

No one really knows where the Achuar people originally came from. The Amazon River Basin is perhaps the least-studied linguistic area on Earth. As many as three hundred languages are spoken here, belonging to some twenty different language families. In addition there are a dozen or so isolate tongues.

Some things seem quite simple in Achuar. This language, for example, classifies all animals into two general groups: *yojasmau yatia*, which means "animals that smell good," and *yojasmau yuchatai*, which means "animals that smell bad." Essentially, it's their coding for animals that can be eaten and animals that can't. Monkeys, for example, are widely consumed, taken from high branches with lethal blow darts. Strangely enough, though, the word *hunting* doesn't really exist. A vast range of euphemisms and circumlocutions are used instead, the point being that any word directly referring to the chasing down and killing of an animal might anger the spirits of the forest. So, for instance, an Achuar hunter might come to a place underneath a tree and say, "The parrots have pissed here." This is a code, almost slang, and anyone familiar with this particular group of Achuar would know instantly that it means there's a monkey in the branches above them. They don't want to alert the monkey's spirit, the animal's *wakan,* to the dangers of human beings. Something about an animal's *wakan* still understands human speech, so it's best not to say anything out loud. It's prudent not to refer to them directly.

All living things in the forest are invested with *wakan.* A loose translation might be "soul," but such words are loaded with cultural baggage and translation of this term into English is particularly difficult. For one thing, when an Achuar dies, his or her *wakan* will be lodged in a particular spot in the body. It seems to move around, this *wakan,* and according to Achuar belief, if the *wakan* at death resides in a human's liver, then it will next become an owl. If it's stuck in the human's heart, it will become a grosbeak, a small yellow bird. And if the *wakan* is in the flesh or even in the shadow of the dead person, it will then become a small red deer. Sometimes a person's *wakan* can even end up in the ears or eyes, and when that happens, it reincarnates into one of the huge neon-blue butterflies I'd seen. The Achuar are vaguely afraid of those butterflies. They know these huge insects carry the souls of the dead so that when I pointed one out to Shakai, asking what it was, he shied away from the question and said it wasn't important.

227

ξ

That afternoon we went still farther upriver to visit another Achuar community, specifically the house of a man named Naanch. Achuar names are really quite beautiful. They're meaningless on the written page, so I urge you to try them out loud. They need to be heard to be fully appreciated. Men's names crackle with consonants, names like Kawarunch, Washikta, Tsukanka, Wajari, Jimpikit, and Yurank. Women's names, as in many cultures, seem softer and lighter: Atinia, Entza, Chawir, and Senur.

The jungle around the Kapawi is constantly alive with sounds, and the Achuar language mirrors it. Achuar dialogues are peppered with onomatopoeia, words that sound like the thing they're describing. *Pak* is the sound of something cracking, like a twig when it's stepped on, and *puj* is the noise of falling water. Of course, the written letters here are based on Spanish pronunciations so that the final *j* in *puj* is an aspirated *h* (just as in the Spanish name Juan). The sound then of *puj* is more like *poohhhhh*, letting the *h* rasp a bit at the back of the throat so that it does sound vaguely like flowing water. With the same aspirated *h*, the Achuar say *juum, juum, juum* to mimic the growl of a jaguar. They're a very aural people and live in a world without books, without written texts, so their words and phrases are often borrowed from the noises around them.

Achuar is also a highly ritualized tongue, and we were about to see one of those rituals. A visit to another man's house is an elaborate affair, studded with regulations and protocols. Philippe told me, as we were getting out of the dugout, that there were very strict rules for our visit to the hut of Naanch. There was to be no photography, for one thing. Once, said Philippe, a tourist took a photo of a pet monkey, and a few days later the monkey died. Some Achuar believed the camera was to blame for the animal's death.

"Also," Philippe continued, "when we go into the hut, you must follow Shakai carefully and do everything he does. At the doorway you must say '*Winiajai*.'"

I'd already learned this word. "Isn't that the greeting — like hello?"

"Well, yes, sort of, but it's really used only when a visitor has come, and only the visitor will say it. It means, literally, 'I come.' And then Naanch will answer you with '*Winitia*.' That means 'Come' — like 'Come in.' This is part of the ritual."

Inside the thatch hut the mood was vaguely tense, slightly uncomfortable. In the middle of the dirt floor perched on a small carved stool like a throne sat Naanch. As we paraded in, each of us stopped at the door and pronounced the ritual greeting.

Shakai had gone in first. This wasn't Shakai's village, but he was apparently known and accepted here. A long, low bench was wrapped around the outside of the hut, at least on the side where the door was. Shakai sat and then I did likewise beside him. Philippe parked himself on the other side.

We were sitting in the front part of the house, known as the *tankamash*, the men's area. All Achuar huts are divided carefully along an imaginary line down the middle, a demarcation that usually runs parallel to the direction of the nearest river. Behind the imaginary line lies the women's area, the *ekent*. This division of the hut is still apparent in all Achuar homes. It's the kind of social construction that anthropologists delight in, though, truthfully, they aren't strictly women's and men's areas.

The idea of the *tankamash*, the so-called men's area, is that it's the part of the house where visitors are received. The *ekent*, meanwhile, is the sleeping and cooking area. Naanch, the husband, plainly lived in the women's area, though no other adult males, besides himself, were allowed in that area.

229

Naanch was on a stool directly on the line between the women's and men's areas, and behind him in the *ekent*, his pregnant wife scurried about getting the *nijiamanch* ready. *Nijiamanch* is a sort of beer made from manioc roots. It's fermented by human saliva, and as Naanch's wife crossed into the men's area to hand out our wooden bowls of the stuff, I got my first close-up of it. Long, cloudy threads swam in the soupy mixture. I couldn't bear to look at it, much less raise it to my lips. Philippe took a few tentative sips and tried not to grimace too noticeably. Shakai gulped it down with relish, and the pregnant woman hurried over to him with a second bowl. She also had a baby hanging from her hip, and two other children, both girls, played behind Naanch in the *ekent*. The oldest daughter, a girl of about five, was fiddling with a sharp machete. It was as long as her arm, but no one snatched it from her. Neither of the parents even looked at her. It was perfectly natural for a child to twirl this dangerous slice of metal. Its cutting edge glinted in the shadows, and I had to fight the impulse to get up and take it away from her.

When we were all served our bowls of manioc beer, the ritual dialogue began. This ritual dialogue is called *aujmatin*, and it goes on for quite some time. Shakai spoke without gazing at Naanch. Naanch, in turn, answered, keeping his eyes firmly off to the side.

The *aujmatin* carries little real meaning in itself. It's a repetition of stock phrases designed to point out some aspects of the Achuar value system: things like the importance of a visit, rules of hospitality, the duty of relatives to help one another, and most important, the obligation of men to display bravery.

Translated, the start of the *aujmatin* sounds something like this.

"Brother of my brother-in-law, I have come."

"Haa. You have come to visit. It is right. I have been waiting."

"Aih."

"To do what I should be doing, I am here, waiting."

"Brother of my brother-in-law, you are here for me."

"Haa. Without knowing the news you bring, I am here. I am at home."

"Aih."

"I am waiting here for you to tell me the news that you bring. That's why you have come."

"Aih."

And the ritual continues like that for quite a while.

As Shakai spoke, Naanch punctuated the speech with frequent grunts of "Aih" and "Haa," which basically meant "It is true." When Naanch talked, Shakai performed similar sets of punctuation. Neither one really got to any sort of point, but that was the point. The language was highly ritualized, a sort of disarming of any possible tensions before the real purpose of the visit commenced.

I peered into the wooden bowl on my lap. Naanch's wife kept her eyes on our bowls, waiting to refill them should they become empty. A chicken lurched into the house through a hole in the fencing that served for walls. Naanch's wife shooed it out and ordered the second child to take the baby from her.

Shakai sipped at the sloshing white gunk in his bowl. I considered mine, and a lump built in my throat. Occasionally, Naanch, as the host, turned in his conversation and spat. Even this was part of the ritual. It underlined, accentuated, what they were saying.

At last the ritual talk began to slow, and for the first time Naanch's eyes drifted toward us. His eyes glanced off us and darted away. His voice, finally, started to loosen up a little, the mood to lighten. Shakai began to turn toward us more often. Naanch acknowledged our presence now and even asked me a question. Did I have children? he wanted to know. When I answered no — translated through Philippe into Spanish and then through Shakai into Achuar — Naanch seemed momentarily confused. How was that possible? I must surely not be much of a man.

231

We drifted back downriver in our canoe. Shakai was listening to us, though I didn't think he was picking up many English words yet. Clearly, though, he was learning.

Philippe was explaining some of the misunderstandings that crop up from time to time. "There's a medical team that comes in here every few months to check on things. The last time they were here they told the Achuar to boil their water before drinking it."

"That sounds reasonable."

"Yes, but I noticed that after the team was gone, the Achuar weren't doing what they said. They certainly weren't boiling their water. It took me quite awhile to finally figure it out."

"Figure what out?"

"Well, what was really going on was that the Achuar thought the white doctors were telling them to drink boiling water."

"You're kidding."

"No, that's how they understood it. And, of course, they thought that was pretty crazy to do, so they ignored the advice and went on drinking their manioc beer."

That's how it goes with misunderstandings.

"Another time," Philippe continued, "someone brought in a little TV and a VCR. They must have rigged it up to a car battery or something. The Achuar were entranced with the movies. Whoever it was had also brought a bunch of Jackie Chan movies." Philippe laughed. "So here were these Achuar men huddled around a little TV screen. Jackie Chan was dubbed into Spanish, and only a few of them even understood that. They liked the fighting, though. They thought it was pretty fierce. I think they watched the first movie about a dozen times, but when they got to the second Jackie Chan movie ..." He laughed again.

"What?" I prompted.

"Well, this one guy came up to me. He asked about one of the minor characters, some actor in the movie. Well, I guess what happened was that this character — a bad guy, I suppose — got killed off in the first movie. And then in the second movie, a whole different one, different plot, different story, well, there was that same actor again. The Achuar didn't get that. They thought he was killed in the first movie."

"Wow!"

Philippe chuckled some more.

"Philippe?"

"Yeah?"

"Will you tell me the story now?"

"What story?"

"The story about the bird that fell in love with the moon."

He nodded. "Okay, tomorrow. Bright and early in the morning."

Ω

That night we saw the yellow eyes of caymans, a kind of crocodile, popping up from the surface in the lagoon beyond the huts. The evening sizzled with crickets and the curious plops and croaks of nocturnal frogs. It washed over the whole forest and lulled me into sleep.

In the very early hours, long before dawn, I got up with the Achuar. In a little shelter up from where I'd been sleeping, they had already stirred the coals of a fire. They had gathered for one of their most important practices.

This was the time for drinking *wayusa* tea. Each day starts like this, and the rituals around it serve many purposes. The first is medical. The Achuar served up the *wayusa* tea in steaming wooden bowls that they held in both hands near their faces. The air was surprisingly chilly, and we huddled around the fire. They talked as they drank.

233

Shakai showed me some *wayusa* leaves. They smelled a little like tobacco — the kind found in good cigars. Philippe was there, too, and said something to the effect that *wayusa* contained traces of quinine, an age-old remedy for malaria. I might have heard that wrong, because quinine is supposed to come only from the bark of the chinchona tree. At any rate, the Achuar drink this tea in large quantities until the sun comes up, then go outside the hut and vomit it all up.

That's not because it makes them sick. Shakai told me, through Philippe, that their bellies get so full of the stuff that after a while they have to throw it up. And that's the point. It's a cleansing of the system. Shakai told me, by way of Philippe, that they actually think of it in the same way we might brush our teeth. It's a daily ritual, a cleansing, and it's one of their many methods to ward off the countless parasites and bacteria that infest the rain forest.

However, that's only one element of the *wayusa* ceremonies. What's even more important is the talk that goes on in the pre-dawn darkness. This is the time for the telling of dreams.

The dreamtime they have just awakened from is, for the Achuar, something to pay careful attention to. A dream, a *kara*, can be an omen for hunting. Through an elaborate and highly creative deconstruction of dreams, the Achuar determine which species is best to hunt on a given day. They also predict from their dreams where these animals might be found and in what numbers. This, of course, is called a "hunting dream."

There's another sort of dream, as well, and it's the most important kind. These dreams are called *karamprar* or "true dreams." In a *karamprar* dream the Achuar believe they've been visited by a spirit, a *wakan*. It could be the *wakan* of an animal, especially a representative from the animals they often hunt, or it could be the soul of a human who has died.

I was told by Philippe the story of a young man who, in youthful exuberance, shot an *iwianch japa*, the kind of small red deer that inherits a person's *wakan* if it resided in the person's muscles upon death. The young man in this story only wounded the deer, in itself a sort of disgrace, and later had to chase it down with dogs. He was too young to realize that this animal shouldn't be hunted because it could hold the *wakan* of a dead person. That night the boy was visited in his dreams by a dead man he'd known. The dead man's head was bloody, and he complained loudly that a great injustice had been done to him. The boy, I presumed, never shot at another deer.

The verb *kajamat*, "to dream," also applies to the vision quest that all males undergo. The women of the Achuar can also go on these vision quests, though it isn't mandatory for them. For the *kajamat* the Achuar ingest a variety of hallucinogenic plants. One in particular, called *juunt maikiua*, induces several days of intense hallucinations and is used primarily to contact a being known as an *arutam*. This, apparently, is a sort of ancestral spirit, an ancient "warrior soul."

It's a complicated rite, but it seems that if one of the Achuar has killed another (which was, until a decade or two ago, a fairly regular occurrence), then that warrior's *wakan* must be rebuilt or at least strengthened again, and this can only be done through contact with the mysterious *arutam*. It can only be accomplished through a vision quest.

This *kajamat*, or vision quest, is often described by the Achuar as "setting off on the path," and I can't help but notice similar practices among many of the indigenous peoples of the Americas. The vision quest, wherein a young warrior sets off on his own, starving himself, taking hallucinogens, until finally being "visited" by a spirit being is a rite found thousands of kilometres away in peoples with wildly different languages and beliefs. Why this should be isn't clear. Was it a practice that developed spontaneously in different places, or was it a useful idea that was traded across the lands and peoples — like a new piece of technology?

Anthropologists such as Claude Lévi-Strauss, who famously worked throughout the Brazilian Amazon, tend toward the idea that such practices and ideas develop spontaneously, that they arise almost naturally from some deep structural hardware in our brains. There are all sorts of cultural rituals that seem strangely similar across cultures, vision quests and creation stories being two. In fact, much has been made of the presence of flood myths around the world. But whether they developed spontaneously in different cultures (being somehow hardwired into our genes), or whether they migrated across continents and centuries, is a question that's very difficult to answer. The point is they're everywhere ... and that makes one ponder the phenomenon.

235

Φ

As the first tendrils of light started to inch across the river, and even as the first bird calls tentatively peeped out of the shadows, the Achuar turned slowly from the examination of their dreams to the myth stories of their people. Another round of *wayusa* bowls was raised, and everyone settled in to listen.

These stories are called *yaunchu aujmatsa mu*, and all of them begin with the single word *yaunchu*, sort of an all-purpose "Once upon a time ..." On this morning the Achuar had arranged a telling just for me — the story at last of the bird that fell in love with the moon. A younger man named Wahai spoke it. He sat well back from the fire. His face was in darkness, but every once in a while the crackling fire flared up and I saw him clearly, eyes glistening with the telling.

In the myth time the animals of the forest were all humans, and a man named Nantu was married to a woman called Aujujai. Nantu went out hunting every day, while Aujujai cultivated the crops on a little patch outside their thatch hut. She grew squash there, which was Nantu's favourite food.

Unfortunately, it was her favourite, too, and after she finished cooking it, inevitably, she would eat it all herself. Terrified of her gluttony being discovered, she sewed her mouth partially closed so that her husband would see she couldn't possibly have eaten it all. To further hide her transgression, she picked some unripened squash — green squash — and cooked it up as well as she could before Nantu returned from hunting.

When Nantu arrived, she fed him the green squash, but he knew immediately that it wasn't ripe. "Where is the good squash?" he asked.

"There isn't any," his wife lied.

After that happened a number of times, Nantu knew something was up. So one morning, rather than go out to hunt, he hid in the forest near the hut and watched Aujujai as she cooked the good squash. She undid the stitches on her mouth and stuffed in the squash. Then she sewed her mouth shut again and set about harvesting the bad green squash for her husband.

Nantu had trapped Aujujai in her lies and selfishness, and he decided to leave her. She pleaded with him, crying pitifully, but he wouldn't relent. He gathered up his things and departed their house forever. Aujujai followed him, begging him not to leave, but Nantu's mind was made up.

He walked to the Monkey Ladder, the Auju Watairi, a giant vine attaching the earth to the sky, and began to climb it. Halfway up, he spotted his friend, the squirrel, and said that if Aujujai tried to follow him up the Monkey Ladder, the squirrel should bite through it.

Aujujai, of course, did try to climb up behind her husband. The squirrel nibbled through the vine with his sharp teeth, and the earth and sky were forever sundered. After this Nantu became the shining moon and Aujujai, in despair, became a bird. To this day, at the full moon, one can still hear Aujujai's plaintive call — the five-note descending scale — that she sings throughout the night to the distant moon.

The bird (*nyctibius griscus* in its scientific delineation) does have a beak that looks as if it's been stitched shut. In Achuar the bird's name — *ahjou jou jou* — mirrors the sound of the bird singing. That was the same cry I'd heard Shakai imitate in the boat on my first night in the forest.

Many Achuar myth stories are morality tales, not unlike Aesop's fables. In fact, from this particular myth, from the name of the bird, the Achuar people take the word *ujajai*, which means "I warn you" or "I advise you." The stories are meant then to instruct as much as entertain. This one tells us that deceit and gluttony can't be allowed in the forest, nor can selfishness. The community and the family, in particular, require that everything be openly shared. It's critical for the Achuar's very survival.

Ψ

The rains came on the day I was to leave. The skies grew thick and exploded in a torrential downpour. Philippe came meekly into my hut to tell me that it was impossible for the plane to land. He had radioed ahead and was told that the landing strip was a slop of mud and that even if the sun came out it would take another full day for everything to dry.

There wasn't much to do, so Shakai took us fishing after the rain stopped. The Kapawi River actually takes its name from the hand-sized silver fish that are abundant here. The Achuar indicate directions from the Kapawi, and through this river they also mark time. It so happens that the star cluster known as the Pleiades moves across the sky throughout the year in a direction that follows the river from upstream to downstream.

To the Achuar the Pleiades are the Musach, and that's another one of their myth stories. The Musach were seven children, orphans, who fled from an angry stepfather downriver on a raft. It's a tale, I suppose, that's vaguely Cinderella-esque … at least in its portayal of an evil step-parent. The raft in the story is represented by the constellation Orion, and the father by the star Aldebaran — ever chasing them across the sky.

The word *musach* is also the Achuar name for counting a year. But it's nothing like our own sense of time. In the Achuar language there are five forms of past tense. One of them is called *yáanchuik wémiaje*. This is the remote past, a time that can't be remembered. Quite often it's the same thing as the myth time.

Few Achuar know the names of their great-grandparents. Anyone who was alive before they were born isn't remembered, so family lineages aren't critical. In fact, when a person dies, there are a number of ceremonies performed to erase that person's memory from the group. That's not cruel. It's actually related to the Achuar's conceptions of the freeing of a dead person's *wakan*. It's a process in which the *wakan* is let loose to inhabit the form of another creature. So anything that took place more than two or three generations ago, or even as recently as thirty years, is already relegated to the remote past, to the time of the myths.

I'd found in the Achuar a people as untouched as I was likely to find on this spinning green planet of ours. But the world was surely sneaking in on them slowly and inexorably, but not completely yet. Our own fine technology — the great silver bird to get me in and out of here — was still no match for the rain forest's torrents. We were, for the moment, stranded in the jungle. I was a twelve-day hike from the nearest road, and there was nothing to do but sit back and enjoy myself.

"Time," Philippe Descola wrote in one memorable passage, "is not cumulative." By that he meant the Achuar aren't caught up in the idea of progress. They orient themselves in a time and space that aren't fixed. There's nothing here beyond the stars and the flow of the river to mark the gradual turn of their days.

PART FOUR

To the North

11

The Lost World of the Maya

I'd flown into Belize City, a ramshackle shantytown on the edge of the ocean, and from there I'd taken a ferry to Ambergris Caye, one of the many islands sparkling across Belize's barrier reef. Belize has the second biggest barrier reef in the world, after the Great Barrier Reef off Australia. This one extends from the Yucatán to the northern edges of South America.

Thousands of young British soldiers did their jungle training in Belize when the place was still a British colony, and some of them came back, remembering it, I suppose, as a place of ample space and beauty. One of them was Dave, whose dive shop, painted bright blue, sat between the beach and the main street.

Dave was a dive master, meaning he could certify people for scuba diving. He was also an ex–Royal Marine, tough as nails and sure to let everyone know it. Dave was the kind of guy who could kill with his left thumb blindfolded. He was short but was jacked up with muscles, most of which bore navy tattoos.

I recalled the tattoos of the Polynesian islanders, but Dave's tattoos were different. They had no sacred connotations, though they marked a certain something. They indicated a brotherhood of the sea that said very distinctly, "Don't fuck with me and don't fuck with my mates."

Scuba diving, too, isn't to be taken lightly. If you mess up and get the bends, you're in serious trouble. You'll die a horrible, excruciatingly painful death. So I was okay with Dave barking dive tables at me. Tucking my head down, I frequently said, "Yes, sir" or "No, sir." In the end, I learned what I needed to know.

I passed all my tests, and on our first real dive he took me down to a submerged wreck. For our second dive Dave extended his tattooed arms widely and told me we were headed for Shark-Ray Alley. That sounded ominous, and Dave explained, as we chugged through the water toward our destination, that it was a break in the reef where sharks came to feed.

"Say what?" I blurted. "Sharks?"

"Yeah, but they're just big reef sharks. They won't hurt ya." He could have followed that with "You poncy big baby," but he didn't.

When we got to the dive site, there wasn't much to see on the surface. A couple of other boats bobbed in the surf. Dave eyed me and said I was going in first. *Fine,* I thought, trying to appear brave. I sat on the edge of the boat and tipped off backward, just as he'd shown me. My tanks crashed into the water, and I was sucked in behind them.

As I splashed into the tropical waters, way out of my element, it took a moment for the bubbles to clear around me. Then, Holy Mother of God, I took a deep gulp of oxygen from my regulator and my heart missed a beat or two. Just below my feet were five or six really big sharks — most of them at least two metres long from teeth to tail. They circled slowly, not moving like fish at all. Fish flit and jerk through the water. Sharks look more like cruise missiles, slicing neatly through the water in deadly, unstoppable straight lines.

Underneath the sharks, a manta ray glided along the bottom. Its giant wings swept the water. It moved more like a bird than a fish, only centimetres off the sandy ocean floor. Manta rays aren't as dangerous as sharks, of course, unless you have the misfortune to step on them. Then their whiplike tails can plunge razor-sharp barbs into you, leaving you paralyzed.

A snorkelling boat bobbed above me. The water wasn't that deep, and a local guide from that vessel was already in the water. He had a handful of meat and was chumming the water to entice the sharks through the break in the coral. *Now,* I thought, *is this really a wise idea? I mean, you've got to be kidding, right?* Here was a man swimming not two metres from me with a bag of meat floating from a rope tied around his waist. I watched as the manta ray circled around him and, amazingly, took the chum from his hand as playfully as a dog would.

The sharks were different, though. They circled in as well, but when one veered toward the man, he let go of the soggy meat and jerked his hand away just in time so that the meat was left floating, slowly descending to the bottom. The shark arrowed in on it, and it was gone in one great unhinging of its jaw.

I swam a little way off while the other divers splashed into the water around the boats. Underneath me great fans of coral waved in the currents, and the brain coral, lumpy bits of underwater oatmeal, shimmered with tiny neon fish. My own silver bubbles percolated toward the surface, and the deep intake and exhalations of my regulator formed a Darth Vader soundtrack.

It was then that I noticed a shark coming at me. I tried to hold on to the thought that it was just a reef shark and not dangerous, but this one definitely had its eye on me. It was big

245

and was bearing down on me. As the shark's mouth, still closed thankfully, came within an arm's reach of my face, a very curious thing happened. I placed my hand on top of the shark's head and pushed down. I had no idea why I did this. I only remember that the feel of its skin was a lot like sandpaper. It wasn't smooth or slimy like a fish's skin. It was rough and hard.

I pushed, and the shark went down. I continued to press, applying a slight pressure downward, and the shark disappeared beneath me. It kept on going forward, shooting between my legs, and then off behind me into the murky depths.

I'm pretty sure now that it thought I was the one chumming the water with meat. Obviously, it didn't realize I was mostly made of meat. In retrospect I think the shark might have been old … or sick. Perhaps it was slightly wonky with age. Whatever the case, the shark swam off and I kept all my limbs as well as the odd kinesthetic memory of the creature's leathery skin on my hand.

246

ξ

Belize is a fascinating mix of people and customs. It's the only country in Central America where English is spoken as the official language. Historically, though, Belize was the land of the Maya, as interesting a people as one is ever likely to come across. There are a few left, mostly in the south. There's also a large population of mestizos who are of mixed Spanish and Mayan descent. Then there's the Garifuna, descendants of escaped slaves from Africa, and finally there's the ever-growing contingent of expatriates from the British Isles.

The patter between the different groups is a lilting Creole. In linguistics this means much more than broken English. It's true that when the first British arrived the local islanders picked up a few words of the new language in order to trade their goods. This is called a "pidgin" language and would have been merely a simplified, stilted version of English. The word *pidgin* is thought to be a Chinese bastardization of the English word *business*. And that's exactly what it was used for: "You buy? Me be selling dis."

Creole, however, is something else. We have to go back to Noam Chomsky to understand it. Language, he said, is hardwired into the brain, and Creole languages are as neat a proof of that as one is likely to find. In Belize an amazing thing occurred. When the first trading encounters took place, while the would-be merchants were struggling with their broken pidgin, the children at their feet picked up something more.

Languages emerge from children's brains like butterflies from cocoons, and for the offspring of "pidgin" speakers something completely new developed quite naturally. It had all the grammatical finesse, all the embedded phrasing and past perfect tenses, all the conditionals and modal verbs, everything that exists in any proper language on the planet. Somehow their infant minds wired and spliced together a new language from stunted pidgin, and Creole was born. Today it's no longer merely a broken approximation of English with a few Mayan or English words stuck into it; it's a fully functioning language in its own right.

247

⅃

I took a creaky bus up to Orange Walk in the north of Belize and from there, one early morning, went down the crocodile-infested New River with a Mayan guide unaccountably named Mario. He was short, barely coming up to my shoulders, but he was stocky and laughed so deeply that his whole body shook. Mario took me in a dugout canoe up the lazy brown river, stopping every few hundred metres to point out something in the water, turning off the thumping little outboard engine he'd rigged to the rear of the boat, and gliding for a moment in perfect silence. He pointed out the Jesus Christ birds hopping between lily pads and appearing, I suppose, as if they were actually prancing on water.

Mario showed me spider monkeys and cormorants, and orchids and trees with roots that dripped off branches like melted wax.

At one point in the rain forest canopy a great bird took off into the blue, and Mario whistled. "Jabiru," he said.

"What?"

"A Jabiru stork. She's the largest bird in the western hemisphere." The stork had the wingspan of a small plane, and with a great *whoompf* it pulled itself above the treetops and was gone.

The trip upriver took much of the day, but in the late afternoon the dugout canoe pulled into a widening in the river. A wooden dock stuck out from the bank of trees ahead. This was Lamanai, the ruins of a Mayan settlement deep in the jungle. The name itself is an ancient word that means "Submerged Crocodile." The muddy water swirled around the boat as we pulled into the dock, and I did indeed spot a small crocodile sunning itself on the opposite bank.

Lamanai is still a full-fledged archaeological site. In fact, I would be staying at the Lamanai Outpost Lodge with the very archaeologists working on the Mayan ruins here.

The golden age of the Maya was from about 300 A.D. to maybe 900 A.D., though there are Preclassic cities much older, and in the Yucatán there are later ruins, remnants of a final phase that petered out completely with the arrival of the Spanish. By all accounts, in their Classic phase, the Maya were the most advanced civilization in the western hemisphere. They developed the only clearly defined writing system in the New World and created a fairly complex set of mathematical charts. The charts were used to predict eclipses of the sun and the moon accurately. The Maya also calculated the exact orbit of Venus with an error of only fourteen seconds per year and knew the planet was alternatively the morning and evening "star."

It's believed that the Maya were the first society on the planet to employ the notion of zero in their mathematics, represented in their writing by the glyph of a seashell. That's pretty good for a people who were basically still living in the Stone Age. The Maya never mined or used metals. Nor is there any indication they used the wheel for the transport of goods. Much of their writing and mathematical calculations were carved into solid rock. They were also unbelievably bloodthirsty, performing unspeakably cruel acts on prisoners they had captured from rival city states. So, I thought, here was an interesting culture. What kind of butterfly had emerged out of this cocoon? The Maya had absolutely no contact with the European world (or the Asian one, for that matter), yet they developed a highly sophisticated society with a writing system and a profound knowledge of mathematics. How did that happen? What exactly was their story?

Ω

Out of the shade, the sun was blistering. The air was thick and musty, filled with the scent of ever-growing vines and tendrils. Mario took me through the jungle, pointing out spice leaves and a particular berry burned by the Maya for incense. He crushed another leaf in his hand and held it up to me. It smelled exactly like root beer. Butterflies as big as my hand fluttered past us. Down one trail, Mario showed me a tall ceiba tree with smooth white bark. For the Maya the ceiba was sacred.

"This tree," Mario said, "we call Yaxche, or the World Tree. It stands at the centre of all things. For us, you see, there are five directions."

I paused for a moment because I could only think of four — north, south, east, and west. Mario was waiting for my question and chuckled even as I turned toward him in puzzlement. "And the fifth direction?" I asked.

Mario pointed at the tree above us. "The fifth direction is vertical. Up and down. You see, the roots reach deep into the earth, down into the underworld, and then the ceiba's trunk rises through our world into the sky. Did you know that the blossoms on this tree come out only in the evening? Small white flowers like stars."

"Really?"

"Yes, and the branches of the tree ... well, do you know the Milky Way?"

"The Milky Way? The stars, you mean?"

"Yes, the branches of the World Tree form the Milky Way. The underworld is the realm of death, but the sky is the place of creation. And that's the most important thing. We Maya think a lot about creation and destruction."

I nodded. "I heard that the ancient Maya believed the world was created and destroyed four times."

"The ancient Maya?" Mario slapped his paunch merrily. "We're not gone, my friend. Look at this fat belly. We haven't gone anywhere. I'm still here. We're all still here."

250

Φ

Trudging through the jungle trails, we eventually came into a clearing. In it sat a great stepped pyramid — typical of Mayan temple architecture. It was fronted with a steep stone staircase. To one side, over a stone carving, a thatch shelter had been set up by the archaeological team. The archaeologists weren't working there at the moment, so we went in to look at the carving. Mario told me that it was a giant stone mask depicting Lord Smoking Shell, one of the ancient leaders of Lamanai. The Maya had great names like that, names the archaeologists have managed to transliterate from name glyphs. I glanced up at the huge stone face, noting the hooked nose, the arrogant sneer, but I couldn't see any resemblance between it and Mario's calm smile.

Back out into the hissing sun, we clambered up the stairs of the temple. The stones were pocked with holes and the steps were littered with loose pebbles. The steps were ferociously steep, so we stayed on all fours, moving almost crablike to the top platform where the priests would have enacted their rituals.

I gazed out over the jungle below. To the yellow south I spied the lagoon sparkling in the sun. It was too hot to stay up there long, so after breathing in the view for a while we climbed down to the shade of the jungle.

Alongside another temple, farther in, was a strange valley of stone ledges. Mario sat on one of these and patted the space beside him, indicating I should join him. "Do you know what this place is?" he asked.

I looked up at the slanting walls and narrow thoroughfare between them, then shook my head. It looked familiar, but I wasn't quite sure.

"This," he said, spreading his arms expansively, "is the ball court."

"Oh, yeah?"

"This one is largely symbolic. It's too small for an actual game. Under the centre stone the archaeologists found a large amount of mercury, like silver water. It told them this was an important place."

"Is it true that the loser of a ball game was decapitated?"

"Yes, sometimes. That was a great honour. How can I explain it? The ball court is more than just a ball court."

"It's a metaphor?"

"Sort of. It's the entrance to the underworld, you see. It's like a glass-bottomed boat over Xibalba — that's the name for the underworld. Listen, I'll tell you a story ... Once upon a time, just after the third destruction, two boys were playing ball on a court much like this one. With all their yelling and running around, they disturbed the gods of Xibalba. The gods there, you must understand, are the gods of death. They're the scary ones. Anyway, these gods were angry at being disturbed and dragged the boys down into Xibalba."

"Like Hell."

"Yes, a little bit like that. There were nine levels in Xibalba, and the boys were taken to the very bottom. It's a long story, but these two boys had many adventures getting back to the top again. They played riddles with the gods, outsmarted them, and gradually returned to the surface, taking with them all the warriors who had been previously killed. In the end, these two boys — the Hero Twins, we call them — were raised into the sky. One became the sun and the other became the moon, and the many warriors they resurrected became the stars."

"But ..." I paused, confused. "I thought the Maya understood astronomy. I mean —"

"That's your science, not ours. It's true we were able to understand the movements of the skies to a great degree, but it wasn't science as you understand it. We were trying to work out the cycles of creation and destruction. That's all. We were trying to work out the great clock of the universe."

$$\Psi$$

Mario and I plodded through more ruins. A dog followed us for a long time. It was friendly, though I wondered how it could bear the heat. On a stela, a standing stone marker, Mario showed me the number system. It was actually quite easy to read — a series of bars and dots.

"Mayan mathematics," Mario explained, "is almost completely taken up with the measurement of time. You could say we were quite obsessed with it. Have you seen the Mayan calendars?"

I had. There were replicas in the shops in Belize City — fantastically complex charts, rows and rows of strange block glyphs.

"It takes fifty-two years to run through a complete cycle," Mario said. "The day you were born on, according to these calendars, is very important. It determines your life. Say you were born on seven Ahau."

"Seven Ahau?"

"Yes, that's the name for one of the days, one day in the fifty-two-year cycle. So, say you were born on that day. It determines everything about you — the name you receive, the day you're married, everything. And these fifty-two-year cycles keep rotating over and over. This we call the Long Count."

"I've heard of that."

"You can read our calendars and, still to this day, you can work it out. The start of the Long Count, in your calendar system, would be August 11, 3114 B.C."

"That's pretty exact."

"We're an exact people."

"Do you know the end of the Long Count?" I asked.

"I do, yes."

"And?"

"The Long Count will end in the year 2012."

"But that's only a few years away." I must have looked worried.

"Yes, I know." Mario became thoughtful. "It was all worked out more than a thousand years ago by the priests here. The priests were the mathematicians, the astronomers if you like. In your year 2012 there will be a planetary alignment and then ... that's it. That's the end of the Long Count."

"So that's the end of the world?"

"That I don't know," Mario said, beginning to rise. "That I don't know."

ξ

I flew out of Belize in a four-seater Cessna, a propeller plane that mosquitoed into the light blue sky and headed west into Guatemala. A world of unbroken greenery rolled beneath us. The Petén is a vast area, almost completely undeveloped, at the centre of the peninsula that squiggles between North and South America. This endless canopy of leaves and vines once held the very heart of the Mayan world. Deep in the jungle was the great city of Tikal.

We landed on the shores of Lake Petén, and I was mobbed by taxi drivers. I ended up paying one of them an exorbitant $20 to take me to Tikal. The trip took about an hour on a thin road that sliced into the jungle deeper and deeper until we finally arrived at the lodge where I was staying. I dropped my bags in one of the lodge's rooms, a cavernous concrete cube with mosquito netting over a cot and a solitary flickering light bulb hanging from the ceiling, then set off to explore.

A dirt path led from the lodge into the jungle. A little wooden shack stood beside the path. In it was a guard who was supposed to check that I had a pass for the archaeological site at Tikal. The guard was fast asleep, his chair leaning against the side of the shack. For all the many times I passed by, this guy was always sitting there, head lolling on his chest, gently snoozing.

Just past his shack the jungle took over, and pathways led into the green tunnels of intense vegetation. I scrambled down one trail, wondering where it would take me. Through the deep foliage, here and there, I could just make out a collapsed wall, a line of stone in the tangle of vines and leaves. At a little clearing there was a structure not much bigger than a modern house. A tree had wrapped itself around the crumbling walls, its thick branches caressing and holding the stones. The doorway was a triangular archway, a corbelled vault, and I knew I was on the edge of Tikal.

Tikal, more than a thousand years ago, was one of the most important Mayan city states, a sort of New World Rome or Paris. At least five major temple pyramids stand in the city centre. Spreading out from them are hundreds, if not thousands, of other buildings. Only something like 5 percent of Tikal has been excavated, and in the dense jungle, radiating for hundreds of kilometres in every direction, are mounds and crumbles still waiting to yield their stories.

Sixty thousand people once lived here, which was hard to imagine now in the silence on the sun-dappled paths. The name Tikal comes from the Mayan word *ti ak'al*, or "at the water hole," and it's true that these people constructed great water reservoirs between the palaces and temples. No river flows through Tikal, so all the water in the reservoirs had to be supplied by rain. But that wouldn't have lasted long. In no time the water would have burned off under the treacherous sun or bled into the porous limestone. The bedrock here is riddled with caves and wormholes. It's the land of spirits, of Xibalba, the dark underworld.

A gecko skittered over the stones, and in the underbrush butterflies floated through the thick air. I trudged down another trail, and more ruins appeared. When the jungle opened up, the sun overhead scorched me. Ahead I spotted the back of the first high temple. Circling it, I came into the central plaza of Tikal.

I must have stood there for a while in jaw-dropping amazement. Two massive temples, about fourteen storeys high, faced each other across a grassy area the size of a football pitch. It was like Red Square in Moscow or the Temple Mount in Jerusalem — a grand plaza in the heart of the city, liberated once more from the vines and roots, a vast tumble of stairs and limestone palaces.

To the east of the plaza was the Temple of the Giant Jaguar, a nine-stepped pyramid with a central staircase rising steeply up its front face. On the top platform a dark doorway led into the temple proper. Only the high priest and the king would have entered here, and deep in its shadows they would have performed the bloodlettings — horrendous self-mutilations.

Blood was thought by the ancient Maya to be the source of life, the font of energy, which of course it is. But for them it was something even more. It possessed magical properties. It was liquid soul.

The Temple of the Giant Jaguar was built around the year 700 A.D. at the very height of the golden age of the Maya. It looked over a plaza that was once paved with mortared white lime. Across from it is the Temple of the Masks, slightly blunter and not quite as high. The two temples, facing each other, their staircases swinging madly into the sky, presented a unique metaphor for the Maya. Bookending the broad plaza, they became the walls of a massive ritual ball court, while the vast open space between them served as the playing floor.

At the height of its power Tikal often found itself at war with other Mayan city states. Captives from the hated cities to the east were brought up these high steps and ritually bound in hemp ropes. They were tied up tightly and rolled down the steep steps of the temples, crashing to their deaths. In this way the metaphor was pushed even further. The captives became human game balls, bouncing off the gigantic slanting walls of the ball court.

Real or metaphoric, the ball court always represents the story of the Hero Twins and their victory over the gods of the underworld. It is, as Mario told me, one of the central themes of Mayan cosmology — understanding the cycles of creation and destruction in order to escape from them, to find a way to stave off the inevitable.

I sat halfway up the temple steps and thought about everything. Gazing across the plaza, the door to the underworld, I wondered about the Mayan myths. Some of the elements seemed vaguely familiar — heroes resurrecting themselves from death, a deep and terrifying underworld, home of the gods of death. Is there an underlying grammar in myths? As in Noam Chomsky's view of language, are there deep structures, fundamental configurations, in myth stories around the world?

Luckily, the Maya wrote their stories down. The Mayan texts were there to decode in their original form. In bits and pieces they lay all around me.

Tremendous strides have been made in the past couple of decades to decipher and understand the strange block glyphs of the Mayan writing system. The bulbous, twirling shapes are quite unlike any other writing method on the planet. However, the breaking of the code was made infinitely more difficult by a disastrous series of events in 1549. Bishop Diego de Landa, a conquistador/missionary, publicly burned hundreds, if not thousands, of Mayan books in the central plazas of the Yucatán. It's said that the population watched and wept as the books, many of them bound in jaguar skins, curled in the flames.

Only four of these books, or codices, survive. They're made from fig bark pages covered in a thin layer of lime. The so-called Dresden Codex is in the best shape. It still has a full seventy-eight pages that can be read. Two of the other codices are more fragmentary. They're kept in museums in Paris and Madrid. A fourth is housed in Mexico City, though its authenticity is doubted by some authorities.

The Dresden Codex features an almanac of good and bad luck days, tables charting the orbits of Venus, predictions of solar eclipses, and even warnings about diseases. Ironically, much of what we do know was written down by the book burner Bishop de Landa. His own journals contain a complete account of Mayan ways at the beginning of the colonial period, a description of the workings of the calendar accompanied by recognizable pictures of the glyphs for *kin*, or "day," and the names used for various days and months. These are the only clues, a sort of Rosetta stone, by which the strange glyphs could be decoded.

De Landa, not surprisingly, got a lot wrong, haughtily supposing that the glyphs were based on an alphabetic system. In fact, the glyphs are more like Egyptian hieroglyphics or even Chinese characters. They're based on logographic symbols, the oldest of which are actually pictographs of the things being referenced.

This is only the beginning, though, because in Mayan glyphs, as in other logographic writing systems, the main feature usually has various affixes. In the Mayan block glyphs there are prefixes to the left or above the main character, and suffixes to the right or below. These generally alter the meaning in predictable ways not unlike how we negate a "thing" by adding the prefix *no*, as in *nothing*.

To complicate matters further, the central glyphs in Mayan writing are often based on homonyms, similar-sounding syllables, almost like puns, so that a central glyph of a fish in Maya, while representing the large fish *xoc*, might under other circumstances stand for the homonym root *xoc*, which is used in the words for to *count* or to *read*. Similarly, *ah kin*, a bearded circle, represents the sun, though it can also refer to a day.

At any rate, despite the burning of the books by Bishop de Landa, there are still thousands of glyphs carved into stone throughout the many Mayan sites. There are glyphs on walls and on staircases, and most important, on stelae, or standing stone markers, found all over the city and just waiting to be read and understood.

258

Ω

Besides the famous four codices, another book exists — a copy made by an unknown Mayan priest, who transliterated the most important stories from the ancient glyphs into the new Latin script. This book was discovered in 1702 by the Spanish priest Francisco Ximénez, and rather than burning it, this cleric, unlike Bishop de Landa, treasured it and even had it translated into Spanish.

This rare and fabulous fifth book contains the magnificent Popol Vuh epic — the creation and destruction myths of the Maya. Here we get our first full elaboration of the Mayan view of the world. It begins in a fantastic string of alliteration: *"Are utzijoxik wae, k'ak atz'ininoq, k'akachamamoq, katz'inonik, k'akasilanik, k'akalolinik, katolona, puch upa kaj."* This translates roughly as: "This is the account of how all was suspended, all was calm, all in silence, all motionless under an empty sky. The surface of the Earth had not appeared; there were only the ripples and murmurs of the unending sea."

Beautiful! This is the story of how things started, and like many beginnings, it kicks off with the creation of the world. Before that there was nothing. The Mayan glyph for zero is a stylized seashell, and that makes sense here. Emptiness is the lack of land; there is only the emptiness of a vast and dark ocean.

Much of the Popol Vuh text then goes on to deal with the creation of the first people. The gods initially attempted to construct creatures out of mud and earth, but they kept falling apart. They just wouldn't stick together. So the gods tried again. According to the Popol Vuh, they wanted to create a being that would speak to them with respect, something that would worship them. They made their second creatures out of wood, but these stupid beasts ate and fought and shat and had no idea of the gods' existence. So the gods destroyed these disrespectful creatures in a great flood. Sound familiar? It's the flood myth again. The story goes on, however, to explain that the wood creatures who survived went into the trees and became monkeys.

259

Lastly, the gods tried making men out of yellow and white corn, and this time they were successful. These beings were intelligent. In fact, they were too intelligent. They saw as the gods themselves saw, they understood as the gods themselves understood, so they didn't respect the gods and believed they were their equals.

Here I can't help but think once more of the Tower of Babel. "Behold," said the God of the Bible, "they are one people and they have one language and this is only the beginning of what they will do. Nothing that they propose to do will now be impossible for them."

Like God in the Old Testament, these Mayan deities also grew wrathful. Humans were much too clever and something had to be done. In the Popol Vuh there's no talk of scattering their languages, for in the Mayan world there was only one common language. Instead the gods "took them apart just a little." They blinded their intelligence as the reflection in a mirror is "blinded by a breath on the face of it."

That's an astounding metaphor: clouding the mirror with the hot breath of the gods.

$$\Phi$$

Do you remember all that stuff I was saying about Creole languages? The real point is that the human brain is hardwired to produce language. Our brains churn out grammars, formulaic structures, and our words — whatever they might be — simply get slotted into their proper places. This was Noam Chomsky's suggestion, and it puts him firmly in the camp of the structuralists.

Structuralism is a field of sociological theory that looks for common elements in cultures and, ultimately, the universal structures of the human mind. Structuralists say that no matter how strange the customs of a place, no matter how bizarre the food, manners, and behaviours, there are always underlying structures, deep structures, that are components of basic human experience. We all eat, sleep, and need shelter. So when we look at the kinds of symbols found in creation myths, marriage rituals, or funerals, we see that some of the elements are the same. Or at least that's the theory.

The Popol Vuh as a creation myth is a pretty good example. It's no coincidence there's a flood myth in the Popol Vuh. The structuralists contend that these stories, these archetypes, are hardwired into us — well, not exactly the concept of a flood perhaps, but the idea of the gods being angry at us, the notion of being cleansed. I tend to be skeptical about structuralism, but still the evidence is there. We would be hard-pressed to find a civilization more untouched by Western ideas than that of the

Maya, yet we still find an astonishing similarity in their myths and stories, if we're willing to dig for them.

It's a fascinating idea. From Claude Lévi-Strauss to Margaret Mead, from Carl Jung to Noam Chomsky, these sorts of theories are found. Joseph Campbell, in his book *The Power of Myth*, says that all people seem to have wonderfully similar foundation stories. The differences are only in the surface appearances, and even these can be accounted for in predictable ways. For instance, Campbell noted that cultures that thrive in deserts, in the dry, barren places of the world, often develop religions with a single god. The religions of the jungle, meanwhile, where richness and fertility is a fact of everyday life, usually have a pantheon of gods — hundreds and sometimes thousands of spirits — that reside in all the abundance around them.

Such structuralist theories rest on the idea that we're all — underneath the cultural and linguistic baggage — essentially the same, that we, as humans, construct our understanding of the world in specific ways. And it's true. We all have tales of destruction and resurrection. We all have stories of love and death, of heroes and gods and poor players on the mighty stage of life. And though they seem on the surface to be wildly divergent, their underpinnings really all fit into the same solid formulas. They're all different expressions of the same essential human traits.

Like, for example, fear.

Ψ

It was already getting late in the day and the sun was slanting at a precarious angle through the branches. I remembered something Mario had told me. He'd said that you could climb up something called the Cat Temple. You could scale to the top and from there watch the sun set, a great gob of fire dipping into the jungle canopy. "It's amazing," he'd told me.

I didn't really have any idea where the Cat Temple was, but I strode down a path that led away from the central acropolis into the jungle to the west and to the far-flung ruins that lay there. The air was heavy and silent in the heat of the dying afternoon. Only a narrow red dirt trail slithered through the thick foliage, and I knew that a couple of steps off the path would leave me completely lost in the foliage. Roots and vines dripped from the branches, forming organic stalagmites. Leaves the size of small cars blotted out the sky.

Mario had made me a little hand-drawn map, but I couldn't quite make it out. I passed by one set of ruins and then strayed into another maze of trails that seemed to go the right way. Except for my own breathing and the thump of my feet on the trail, it was as silent as it ever got in the jungle.

Soon I *was* completely lost. The sun had sunk below the canopy, and the shadows were growing thickly. I stopped and heaved off my backpack. I didn't have much — some water, a camera, and a guidebook to the region. I hoped the guidebook might have a better map, so I fished it out of the pack. The pages fell open in my hands to a section that spoke about jaguars.

Now the Petén is a huge region that's pretty much untouched rain forest. At dawn and at dusk the forest begins to swell with bird calls and the patter of tiny animals. I'd already seen a peccary waddle by near the first set of ruins, a sort of large rodent-like creature with a snout like a horse. There were armadillos and grey foxes, spider monkeys and anteaters. And apparently there were jaguars.

Jaguars are spotted and are almost the same size as the tigers of Asia. The difference is that, in adapting to the jungle where running at full speed is unnecessary, indeed impossible, they lope along a little lower to the ground. They've developed massive forearms that look something like the biceps of a heavyweight boxer, and they can jump. Boy, can they jump.

So I was down on one knee reading the excerpt on jaguars and it said that, though jaguars are reasonably plentiful in the jungle, there's no need to panic. Jaguars only come out at night. They're fully nocturnal.

I glanced up. The sky was definitely growing dark.

Furthermore, the guide said, in the extremely unlikely event of coming across a jaguar, you shouldn't move. You should stay calm and not make any sudden movements.

At that precise moment, overhead, a low growl rumbled through the foliage. It began as almost a purring, but soon erupted into a throaty roar.

I turned and ran for all I was worth, careening down the jungle trail, sweat almost obliterating my field of vision, while all around me the jungle shadows got deeper and deeper.

I must have run a kilometre or two, and somehow, through sheer luck, I came out at the little booth where the guard was still snoozing. His head bobbed once as I raced by, but I only stopped when I got to the safety of my concrete cubicle in the jungle lodge. I stood there and shook for a while, then the generator shut down and the single buzzing light bulb snapped off. I crawled in under the mosquito netting over the bed and gradually fell into a dreamless sleep.

263

ξ

I was awakened at dawn, as I was every morning, by a terrific symphony of bird calls. Hurriedly, I pulled on my clothes and walked down the path and into the forest. Up above in the trees, literally hundreds of parrots squawked and shrilled. The air was electric with sound. A tapir ambled in front of me, looking much like a pig except that it had a snout almost like a stunted elephant trunk. It passed across the trail in front of me, unconcerned, and disappeared into the forest. Wild turkeys scurried in and out of the underbrush, their tail feathers shot through with luminescent and neon hues. The place was thick with life.

Up in another tree I heard the same low rumbling of the previous night. It wasn't a jaguar at all, of course. It was a howler monkey. These creatures, much bigger than spider monkeys, have adopted the strategy of mimicking large predators, and failing that, they sneer at you and piss, carefully aimed I might add, so that many explorers have had unwelcome showers.

I found the Cat Temple later that day. Stupid me. It wasn't *cat* at all but *cuatro*. Spanish for *four*. I guess I was still thinking of jaguars. At any rate, Temple Four stands ninety metres above the forest floor and is probably the tallest Pre-Columbian structure in the western hemisphere.

Temple Four is a wild crumble of stone now, draped in its lower quarters by vines and branches that enable you to climb it as you might scale a tree. Here and there steps lead up a little way and then break off into ruins again, forcing a climber to find another way up. In places some kind souls have left ropes or bits of ladders. Halfway up I came level with a family of howler monkeys skittering and barking in the trees. I barked right back at them, and they were silent for a moment. Through the branches once I caught sight of a toucan with its multicoloured beak. That was the cartoon bird I recalled from my youth — the bird on a Froot Loops cereal box.

Then, finally, at the top I came out onto the temple terrace. I was above the trees now, and the jungle canopy was a green felt carpet stretching on all sides to the farthest horizon. To the east I could see the roof combs of the Temple of the Giant Jaguar poking above the greenery. Here was a shot employed by George Lucas in *Star Wars*. He used this place as his rebel base, and though it was certainly otherworldly, that no longer seemed right.

Watching the sun set over the deep jungle, I heard the monkeys below me and felt the trees swell and ripple with life in the purple twilight. I stayed until the first star appeared in the skies over the canopy and then knew I had to go.

꒕

The last stone marker, or stela, was erected in Tikal in 909 A.D. Then there was a great collapse. No one quite knows what happened. And it wasn't just Tikal. The entire Mayan world throughout Central America completely disintegrated.

It's bizarre, really. It seems the Maya, whose every particle of being was consumed with the measurement of time, whose astronomical calculations were single-mindedly focused on predicting the cycles of birth and destruction, had — in one of the many great ironies of history — completely miscalculated their own collapse.

Mayan mythology speaks of four cycles before them, of four destructions. They were fanatical about trying to predict the fifth, and sure enough the fifth did come upon them. After 900, in the space of a generation or two, the great cities imploded. The people left and disappeared without a trace, and the jungle took over once more.

There are many theories, of course. Most centre on the idea of ecological collapse. The thin forest soil could no longer sustain the agriculture it took to feed the cities. The plots of corn became barren, and in addition, all those vast temples and plazas had been coated with thick layers of lime plaster. It took young trees, green wood, to burn a fire hot enough to melt the limestone into plaster, and for this literally millions of trees were cut down and burned.

Added to the ecological collapse was the fact that the city states were seemingly in an almost constant state of war with one another. Furthermore, the kings and astronomer priests grew rich while the peasants, overwhelmed by a harshening environment, grew poorer and more desperate. The final events are unknown. Did the underclasses rise and slaughter their masters? Did hunger, disease, or war sweep across the continent like a forest fire? Perhaps we'll never know for sure.

265

Ω

Scattered along the beaches of the Yucatán in southern Mexico, there are Post-Classic Mayan ruins, and it seems that at least a dribble of the civilization was still around when the Spanish landed in 1511. There's a famous story that says when the first Europeans finally arrived and saw the stone temples shining in the sun already falling into ruins, they asked the Maya what the place was.

The people answered by saying, *"Malatinaʼat katʼan."* As nearly as I can figure it out, the prefix *maʼ* is the negation *not*, and the root *naʼat* means "to understand." *Tʼan* in the second word means "language" so that what the Maya were actually saying was something like: "Sorry, but we can't understand a damn thing you're trying to say to us." The Spanish thought they we're hearing the name of the place and jotted it down quickly, writing it as Yucatán, and the name has stuck.

At a place named Xcaret, on what is now called the Mayan Riviera, there's a sort of Mayan theme park built directly over the ruins of a few beachside temples. I don't know what to think of that. The place is like a giant wax museum, like a ride at Disneyland — Maya World. It's all a bit unsettling. On the other hand, I snorkelled through an underground river there, through caverns and passages that reminded me of the stories of Xibalba, the underworld, and that at least wiped away some of the place's tourist facade.

In the centre of the theme park a reconstructed Mayan village dredges in sightseers. A young Maya sat in front of a thatch house, carving masks out of wood, and I struck up a conversation with him. I asked him to teach me a few words in Maya. There is, surprisingly, really no single word that directly translates as *hello*. Instead the Maya greet one another with *baʼax ka waʼalik*, literally meaning "What do you say?" Nor is there a word for *yes*. In Maya you merely rephrase what's been said positively: "Are you from Canada?" "I am from Canada."

I asked the Maya if he could go back to the Classic age of his people, would he be able to talk to them. "I would be able to talk to them," he said, reforming the positive. "Of course, there would be some differences. If we want to say *yes* now, we all use the Spanish *sí*. It is common. But I think I would understand most of the old words they spoke. A turtle is still *'áak*, and a snake is still *'kung*. Even your English word *jaguar* comes from our old language. We call the jaguar, *chac war*. You see? You have borrowed this word from us."

He held up the small face he was carving and told me to look at the moon later that night. It would be full, he said, and he told me that just as we say there's a man in the moon, the Maya say there's a *tu'ul* up there — a rabbit.

That night, when I gazed at the full moon, I clearly saw in the shadows and craters the two long ears and wiggling snout of a rabbit. I don't know why no one in our culture has noticed it before. It's really quite obvious.

267

Φ

One thing is certain. The various peoples of the world construct their symbols and languages according to specific internal logics. There are always reasons for their semiotic choices. And whether or not they actually form the bedrock of some sort of universal human consciousness, they're the fundamental building blocks of our cultures, the foundation of our many world views.

When I consider the Maya, I think mostly of their calendars and endless rounds of ritual — like that of the ball court. I wonder what those stepped temples with stone buttresses rising against time really tell us about the culture of the people — not the kings and high priests — but the stonemasons and the corn farmers.

A thousand years from now, after our own Long Count, what will visitors make of the shells of our modern skyscrapers? Surely, the suburbs will be gone, all the carefully manicured lawns, the strip malls, and gas stations. But what will the towering steel scaffolds of office buildings and shopping malls really tell future archaeologists about our time on Earth?

I suppose shrewd observers will know they're monuments to finance, to the wild market economy we live under, and if they do, they'll have nailed down something true about us. Certainly, it's plausible to suggest that we're obsessed with money, with the acquisition of wealth and material things.

In the same way, Mayan temples, markers of their obsession with time, really do illuminate something essential about the Mayan view of the world. The Mayan calendar, all fifty-two spinning years of it, was marked by an almost continual round of ceremonies, each day having its own special meaning. That makes me think, in my very best Joseph Campbell imagination, that maybe we aren't really so different from them at all.

Haida: The Surface People

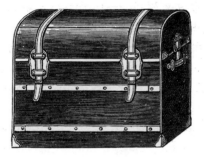

A dark shadow appeared in the water. From high above, the ocean seemed green and still, but the shadow cruised below the surface, moving at a good clip. The pilot dipped the plane toward it. "Humpback whale," he said, turning to me. As he spoke, the whale broke the surface. A spout of water shot up like a geyser. The creature must have been twenty metres long, as big as two buses parked end to end.

We circled toward the underwater beast, and four or five more whales materialized, breaching the waves behind the first one. The pilot glanced at me and grinned. My mouth had formed a silent "Oh." I'd never seen whales this size before.

We were flying in a floatplane, a Cessna, one hundred kilometres off the Alaska Panhandle, heading across the open ocean to a chain of islands known as the Queen Charlottes or, more properly, Haida Gwaii — the land of the Haida.

The Haida are celebrated for their totem poles. They were great artists, these Haida, and they lived in one of the most remote places on the planet — on the very knife edge of North America.

The pilot took the plane down farther, and we sailed over a rocky outcropping, the first sign of land. On it several hundred sea lions wallowed in the rare sunshine. They stampeded off the rock and into the water at the sound of the airplane. Ahead of us the mountains of Haida Gwaii swelled into view, and a few minutes later we landed, skimming across the water to stop at a place called Rose Harbour at the extreme southern end of the island chain.

An inflatable Zodiac bounced out through the waves to meet us. Rose Harbour used to be an old whaling station, but the only person who lives there now runs tourists from here out to the Haida ruins. We clambered out of the plane, standing for a moment on the float before stepping into the boat. In the relative safety of the harbour I was handed a survival suit to put on. It looked like a large orange snowsuit. I struggled to get it over my clothes and finally sat down, feeling ridiculous, encased in something like a full-body life jacket.

Still, this was the only way to get there, and should we be hit by a sudden squall, or should I tumble into the ocean, I'd have a few minutes at least before the dark waters of the North Pacific sucked my life away.

The Zodiac launched out of the harbour and into the swells. We had twelve kilometres of ocean to cross before we reached our destination.

Ψ

An eagle glided from the black line of spruces, soaring across the beach and over the water toward us. We were approaching the island, skipping across the surf. Overhead, the eagle circled and flew in front of our boat, as if guiding us into shore. When the Zodiac finally beached on the rocks, I lumbered awkwardly and gratefully off the front and onto solid ground again.

This island is called SGaang Gwaii in the ancient Haida tongue — the Wailing Island. On stormy days waves the size of four-storey buildings surge through a hollow in the reef. In the winter the rushing waves give off an eerie, wailing sound, a mournful, haunting noise like the breaths of past spirits.

I managed to get my survivor suit off, not an easy task and not a graceful event to watch, and left it sitting, almost human, on the beach. A small trail wound into the forest, and we set off on it, almost immediately finding ourselves lost in a grove of old-growth cedars, among the tallest trees in the world. Their trunks were carpeted in moss, and a reverential silence accompanied our footsteps. This was untouched northern rain forest, and it reminded me of a giant green cathedral.

Before long the trail led into a clearing. A small wooden cabin sat there. This was the watchman's home. All the abandoned Haida villages have watchmen, guards who watch over the old totem poles. They're keepers of the spirits, these watchmen, and they know these islands better than anybody.

A young man stepped out of the cabin. James was the watchman here and wasn't at all what I had expected. He was about twenty-five and wore a hockey jersey and big basketball shoes. James clomped onto the porch of the cabin and waved us up. There were various forms to fill out, since this is a protected place, a United Nations World Heritage Site, in fact. James didn't say much to begin with, though the forms made it clear he would guide us to the village site and that we couldn't deviate off the trail. We weren't to touch anything and we were certainly not to take any souvenirs. The poles we were about to see were fragile.

Many of them were almost two hundred years old. They were wind-worn and cracked, and in a few more years they would be completely gone.

James finally spoke up. "How many of you have seen the poles in Vancouver?" he asked.

I put up my hand like a dutiful student. I'd been to the Museum of Anthropology in Vancouver only a few days earlier. The poles there were well preserved. They even had some of their original colour still on them.

"Those poles were taken from this village," James said, not pleased.

I put my hand down quickly.

"The totem poles," he went on, "are meant to be here. They're not meant to be kept in museums. They're supposed to decay. When a totem pole falls over in one of our villages, we don't put it back up. It comes from a tree, and it's meant to return to the earth." He took a deep breath and shook his head, easing up a little. "It's hard now. We want to preserve our history, of course, but we must respect the old beliefs. So please, you're welcome to take photographs, but you must only walk where I tell you to. You have to do what I tell you."

James wasn't particularly tall, but he was barrel-chested, a strong guy who could kick the crap out of most anyone if he ever felt the need to. He got up and signalled us to follow him. Down the steps we went, back into the forest. SGaang Gwaii is a small island, and I realized that we had come in on the far side of it. We were going to walk across the island from one beach to another on the other side. It didn't take long. Through the trees ahead we soon saw the ocean again, and as we came out of the forest, the old village appeared.

All along a grassy pitch, just up from the beach, were the totem poles, many slanting over with the weight of years. Twenty-six poles still stand at SGaang Gwaii llaana, and they're all that remain of the great village that once stood here.

This was the village of the Gan<u>x</u>iid Haida, the Red Cod People. (The underlined letters are voiced uvular stops, sometimes written as *gh* or *xh*, and they're sounded way back in the throat.) The Red Cod People were terrifying warriors, pirates really, who launched their war canoes from here, raiding up and down the coasts of British Columbia and Alaska, even going as far south as California.

They weren't to be messed with. When the first European ships arrived offshore, the Gan<u>x</u>iid battled them ferociously. In the space of five years the Gan<u>x</u>iid destroyed two of these ships and got into vicious scraps with two more.

James led us to the remains of one of the houses. It was only a tumble of fallen cedar timbers now. In front were four or five slanting totem poles. James halted in front of one of them. A column of mythical spirits gaped at us, and even though the pole tipped precipitously, even though its cedar grain was weathered and cracking, exposed to two centuries of fierce sea winds, the mastery of the carving was evident.

"This is the pole of Chief Xoyah's clan," James said. "Do you see? It's a sort of family crest, though we don't really know much about this chief, really. *Xoyah*, in Haida, means Raven." He looked at us seriously. "That's probably not the chief's real name. It's his group."

"His clan name?" I asked.

"No, his group." James paused for a moment. "There's not really an English word for this. Look, all Haida are born either Raven — *Xoyah* — or they're Eagle. An eagle in Haida is <u>Gud</u>."

"So that's like a person's tribe?"

"No, no. Look, in this town, S<u>G</u>aang Gwaii llaana, half the people would be Raven and half would be Eagle. Even in one house, even in one family, you're going to have some people who are Raven and some who are Eagle."

I must have looked pretty confused. James was doing his best, though. "If a young woman is a Raven," he continued, "then she can only get married to an Eagle. All her children will be

Raven, though. They don't take this from their father. It comes through the mother's line."

I still didn't completely get it.

We moved over to another group of totem poles. "This one," James said, "is a mortuary pole. Do you see at the top there?"

I glanced up. There was no figure at the top. Instead it had a sort of hollow carved out of it.

"Up there," James said, "they would have stored the bones of an important person, one of the elders, maybe a house leader. And these carvings would have been his or her personal crest. Some people say you read totem poles like books — you know, from top to bottom or whatever — but that's a load of bullshit. They're more like a coat of arms — either the symbols of a family or the personal crest of a single powerful person."

I studied the figures carved into the pole carefully. The only one I could identify with any certainty was the small human being near the bottom. The rest were animal spirits. I really wanted a good crack at figuring out these symbols. I wanted to do a sort of Joseph Campbell analysis of them, but I didn't even know where to start.

"Can you tell us what all these animals are?" I asked hesitantly.

"Well, some of them are real creatures. Some even come from the mainland. This one —" James pointed at a figure halfway up the pole "— is a grizzly bear. But we have no grizzlies on Haida Gwaii."

"And this one?" I indicated a large figure below the grizzly. It seemed to be holding the human in its arms.

"First you have to know that some of the animals are mythical spirit beings. Many of these spirits lived under the water. This one is a sea wolf. The old Haida believed it was a creature that lived at the bottom of the sea, and when people drowned —"

"So you mean … like this guy?" I pointed at the little human figure. Maybe it was meant to be inside the belly of the sea wolf or perhaps lying on its chest.

"Yeah, like that guy," James said. "The people who drowned would be caught in the fur of the sea wolf, and they couldn't get themselves untangled. On this totem pole you can see that the grizzly bear has come down to shake the sea wolf and free the drowned person from his fur. Maybe it means that this mortuary pole is for someone who drowned. I don't know for sure."

I nodded sagely.

"On the other hand," James continued, "like I said, don't go thinking the totems tell stories. This one is about as close as you're going to get to any kind of story. Probably the grizzly bear was the person's personal animal, and that's why it's depicted as coming down to free the soul from the sea wolf. It's usually not like that, though."

I scanned the beach. There had been seventeen houses here, each holding an extended family of maybe twenty or thirty people. The houses were important things, too. They each had their own names, wonderful ones like "House That Is Always Shaking," or even more poetically, "Clouds Sound Against It (as They Pass Over)." The house at the far end of the beach had the impossibly fine name of "People Think of This House Even When They Sleep Because the Master Feeds Everyone Who Calls."

Names are important here — marking a particular identity within a clan or the moiety groupings of Raven or Eagle. This obsession with identity is a key to understanding the Haida and their totem poles. The totem poles aren't stories. They're signatures, ubiquitous markers that say, very clearly, "We were here."

275

ξ

The Haida did have stories, of course. At the turn of the nineteenth century an anthropologist named John Reed Swanton showed up with pen and paper and set about taking down Haida myths. He transcribed them in Haida phoneme by phoneme, sounding out the unfamiliar words, making sure he got each one exactly right.

The translations show them to be works of great virtuosity. One of the elders Swanton interviewed, a man by the name of Ghandl, had lost his sight to smallpox. This brings to mind Homer and his great epics, and the comparison is apt. Haida tales can go on at length, even being told over several nights of sitting. There are stories of heroes and monsters, and a creation myth in which the beings of the world emerged from a cave — a consistent theme among many First Nation creation stories.

So are these structural archetypes? Are they fundamental components of human myth-making? That's the conclusion the structuralist camp offers, but it's a view that's largely fallen out of favour with academics. Now there's post-structuralism, deconstructionism, and postmodernism, and what they're all saying is that the differences between cultures and languages far outweigh any perceived similarities.

And it's true. The Haida myth stories are, for the most part, unlike anything I've ever read before. They're called *qqaygaang* or *qqayaagaang* — both of which come from the root *qqay*, "to be old or full or ripe." The infix *aa* changes the mode of the verb so that it emphasizes a state or a condition over a process or an action. *Qqayaagaang*, it seems, are things that continuously ripen with the telling.

A storyteller is a *nang qqaygaanga llaghaaygaa*, and Ghandl was one of the best. His stories float on a bed of the surreal. The Haida are a people who live on the edge of three worlds. In fact, in the old Haida pronunciation, the name of the land Haida Gwaii is called Xhaaydla Gwaayaay — land on the boundary between worlds. Out in front of the villages is the great Pacific Ocean. Killer whales — *sghaana* — are the primary visible forms of the spirits of this place, and when a Haida paddles on the ocean, he's literally a tiny island floating over the roof of heaven. The dark temperate forests behind the villages form another edge of the spirit world for the Haida. The deep inlands of the islands were once places where the Haida never went. They were the place of the spirit bears and the deer and all manner of mythical creatures. And above the villages was the third world — the sky — the spirit place of the Eagles and Ravens.

Humans in the old Haida language are called *xhaaydla xhaaydaghay* — surface people. It means that they live on the edge, on the shiny bubble surface between three different spirit worlds. The human territory is at the boundary where the earth meets the ocean and where the sky meets the land. A few strokes on the paddle, a few steps into the woods, or if it were possible, a few flaps of the wing into the sky, and one would be in the spirit world.

In reading the Haida myths I often have the sensation of dreaming. A canoe cuts through the ocean waves in one passage, then a line later it floats through a great cedar house. Creatures morph from shape to shape, sometimes in mid-sentence. A bird becomes a girl, a spear metamorphoses into a rope, a tree transforms into a ladder leading to another world.

This *is* different. The Haida are a people living on a thin sliver of reality, the knife edge of inhabitable land between the vast open ocean and the cloud-capped mountains. And they're truly original.

277

There are fifty-three aboriginal languages spoken in Canada, and almost half are found along the coast of British Columbia. The Haida were once a singular people, remote and isolated on a chain of islands far off the coast. They traded with (and raided upon) the peoples of the mainland, but they were distinct. They were something unique.

We tend to lump the aboriginal nations together in a kind of television image of the "Indian," but they actually differ considerably more than we think. They're a lot more different, say, than the French are from the English. To compare the different First Nations is more like contrasting the English with the Turkish.

They have distinctly different languages, different customs and religions, whole different ways of being in the world.

Part of the problem is that the English language has borrowed words from various nations and used them to apply to all indigenous peoples. *Teepee*, for example, is a Sioux word, but we use it to apply to any sort of animal hide structure. *Moccasin, tomahawk, powwow*, and *toboggan* all come from the Algonquian family of languages, which includes Cree, Mi'kmaq, Blackfoot, and many others. *Kayak* comes from the word *qajaq* and is Inuktitut, the tongue of the Inuit.

They're all different, but in our rush to understand and to label we seem to have all aboriginal peoples living in teepees, wearing feathered headdresses, going to powwows, smoking peace pipes — all the stereotypes. The first order of business is to throw away that mental baggage. Each First Nation has its own story, its own House of Being, its own Palace of Words.

Words, we have to remember, don't label things. They label meanings. A canoe in Haida is *t'luu*, and it's really quite a different thing than the canoes used to paddle in the Great Lakes and on the rivers in central Canada. *Totem* comes from the Ojibwa word *ninto:te:m*, and though James used the word *totem*, the old Haida would never have employed such a word. For them the poles were called *gyaaghang* or *zhaat*, depending on their use, depending on whether they were clan poles or mortuary poles.

The poles, of course, are complex symbolic systems in their own right. They don't tell stories exactly, as James told us, but they do identify the people and the clans quite precisely. Their figures, their symbols, are derived from the stories of the Haida's own particular spirit world.

Ω

Like many First Nations, the Haida experienced great tragedy with the arrival of the Europeans, and I'm not talking about the battles between the Red Cod People and the European ships. No, many of the other Haida villages had far more amicable first encounters. However, with the white men came disease. Typhoid, measles, and syphilis all took their toll, but by far the most deadly disease was smallpox.

The variola virus that causes smallpox has now been eliminated on Earth, except for a few vials hopefully carefully protected in a few select laboratories around the world. Smallpox, of course, is highly contagious, and for a people who had never had contact with the disease, it was catastrophic.

The first sign is a fever. A person's temperature rises quickly after the initial infection, and in a few hours he's immobilized by a temperature that soars to well over a hundred degrees Fahrenheit. Then come the "spots." Raised bumps appear on the skin, growing until they cover large parts of the body. The lumps are hard, as if small pebbles are lodged under the skin, and this is when the disease is at its most contagious. Survivors, and there were very few among the Haida, would have borne the scars of these bumps for the rest of their lives.

279

When the first Europeans sailed through the straits, there were about twelve thousand Haida living in hundreds of villages up and down these coasts. Within a couple of decades the population dropped to about six hundred desperate souls. In fact, their numbers dipped so precipitously that it looked as if the Haida and all their meanings might be wiped off the face of the planet.

On SGaang Gwaii the population plummeted from three hundred or four hundred to about fifty and finally to five ragged survivors, all in the space of a few years. All along the island chain of Haida Gwaii, the few survivors fled their villages, and by the end of the nineteenth century, congregated in two safe places: Skidegate, in the great fjord that runs between the two main islands, and Masset at the tip of the northern island.

To this day Skidegate and Masset are the only villages where the Haida still live in any great numbers. Some say there are now only two Haida dialects, one in the north and one in Skidegate, but that's actually not quite right. It's a bit more complicated than that. At Skidegate the descendants of villagers all up and down the southern islands, including SGaang Gwaii, banded together. They held on to their ancestries so that today the elders actually speak a tumble of different dialects. In Skidegate there are at least six ancestral chiefs among the population, that is, the chiefs from six different villages. They're all in one place now, the survivors. This is what remains.

Φ

We sat on a log on the beach in front of the abandoned village. A mist had come in off the ocean. I looked at James. As I said, he was a big guy. Except for the hockey jersey, I could well imagine him in a war canoe, thumping at the gunnels as it rushed toward the beach of an enemy village.

"So," I asked, "what are you?"

"What?"

"Are you a Raven or a —"

"I'm an Eagle," he said without hesitation.

"And do you speak Haida?"

"Well, they teach it in the schools now. The elders come in and teach the kids right from kindergarten. But that was after me. I only had it in grade eight, so I only know a few words. Not much."

In truth the Haida language is on the edge of extinction. There are only a few hundred people still fully fluent. But a concentrated effort is underway not only to teach the children but to assemble a sort of language bank before it's too late. The elders meet and argue over the ancient words, as there are many dialects and accents. The spelling, too, is problematic, and there are at least four different writing systems in place.

The very last speaker of the dialect of the Red Cod People died in 1970, so the tongue of the Wailing Island is already gone. I had assumed that James was from this place. "No," he told me. "I have a one-month shift here ... living in the watchman's cabin." He glanced up at the sky. It was hard to tell if it was going to rain or not. "I've only been here for three days, so I've got, what, more than three weeks left." He heaved a sigh. "There's not much to do."

Funny. I had the impression there was nothing James would like more than to shoot some hoops with his friends, maybe play some video games. This was a job for him, a responsibility, and he didn't seem to be taking a great deal of pleasure in it. That wasn't to say he didn't have the greatest amount of respect for the place. It was just that, back in Skidegate where he lived, there was a here and now.

Seeing James sitting there on a clump of driftwood, his back to the ancient totem poles, distractedly tossing rocks into the water, all this reminded me that cultures, and languages for that matter, are pretty abstract entities. The world, in reality, is made up of individuals, and the way that individuals actually fit into these cultures and languages is sometimes problematic. James was a good example.

281

Post-structural theory talks about the individual as a "subject" caught in the "object" that is culture. One of the big problems with the old theories about culture say the post-structuralists, are that they're very much bogged down in Western preconceptions. A Western preconception that really stands out is that we tend to think in dualities: this and that, us and them. We think in terms of individuals as separate from cultures. But the fact is, they're not divisible.

What's needed here is a collapsing of René Descartes. The French philosopher, of course, was the one who uttered the immortal "I think, therefore I am." He was contrasting himself, his own consciousness, with the great outside world, the ghost in the machine, if you will.

But the post-structuralist line of thinking says that he got it all wrong. Consciousness doesn't come first. Consciousness, after all, has to be conscious of something. It's a sort of chicken-and-egg thing. We're immersed from the very beginning in our culture's sets of symbols — its beliefs, its ways of seeing and encoding the world. It's the water we swim in. We can't escape it because it precedes us, envelops us. It's the world we're born into no matter what sort of mental gymnastics we attempt to avoid it.

The world has already been defined for us through our language and through all the other semiotic systems of our culture. Such symbols might change over time, certainly, but we're quite inseparable from them.

So what happens to the person who's caught between two cultures, or three, or four? That's where things really get interesting. I suppose the post-stucturalists would say we're making arbitrary divisions again. A person exists within a world, not a world made up of two cultures but of a single blended culture — one with televisions *and* totem poles, one where you fish for salmon *and* surf the Internet. This is life in the twenty-first century, the world that James lives in.

Ψ

A long fjord separates the two main islands of the Queen Charlottes. It's called Skidegate Inlet, and I'd come here to go sea kayaking, skimming over the spirit world in a Haida canoe.

So I found myself up at dawn one morning, standing at the dock with fog hanging over the inlet. Out in the water I could hear a small skiff puttering into shore to pick me up. A tall man, his feet in gumboots, jumped out to greet me. This was Patrick. His long black hair was tied in ponytail, and he spoke with a French-Canadian accent. He wasn't Haida. Patrick turned out to be, of all things, Mohawk.

He was taking me to a small island owned by another man, his friend and mentor, Louie Two Elks. Louie, who was going to be my kayaking guide, wasn't Haida, either. He was Métis, part Cree and part I wasn't sure what, but I thought it might be Italian.

So here I was in Haida Gwaii, land of the Haida, about to go on a kayaking trip with two Native guides. One was Cree and the other was Mohawk. Now that seemed weird. But things don't always fit into the neat conceptual boxes we build for ourselves. What exactly does it mean to be Haida? The answers aren't always so straightforward.

"How many days you staying at Louie's place?" Patrick asked as we set out across the inlet.

"Three days."

Patrick nodded. A man of few words, he turned back to the tiny outboard motor and puttered out to a chain of three tiny islands. Louie Two Elks lived on the middle one. The island was perhaps four hundred metres from edge to edge. You could walk around it in a couple of minutes. Patrick steered the boat around the edge of the island and there, on the little beach, was Louie. He was about a third of a metre shorter than Patrick, but he also had his long hair tied back in a ponytail.

Louie waved to me from the beach and then helped to pull the boat in. I couldn't help but see that Louie was wearing a Che Guevara T-shirt, and when I commented on it, his face lit up in a big grin. "Did you see *The Motorcycle Diaries*?" he asked. "I'm a big fan of Che." And that made sense. Louie was a bit of a rebel himself.

He took me up to his cabin, actually quite a nice little house. Louie had been living here with his family and Patrick for twenty years. "We're completely off the grid," he told me. They didn't get their power or their water from anywhere except nature. On the roof was a set of solar panels. Out back was a big rainwater tank, and for the winter, Louie had rigged up a system for heat — all of it very neat and tidy.

"When I first came out here," Louie said, "I got a job on a tramp steamer going up the Inside Passage of Alaska. Well, I'd never been on the ocean before and I got real sick. You know, some people, they get sick …" Patrick nodded at the story. I was sure he'd heard it a thousand times. "Some people get seasick for a day or two and then they get their sea legs. But a certain percentage of people ... they just stay sick. There's nothing you can do. They never get over it. And that's what happened to me. Finally, they just dropped me off at the Queen Charlottes, and I've been here ever since." He looked at me and chuckled. "Me, I'm a freshwater Indian."

Louie, as near as I could tell, was from northern Saskatchewan. His grandmother was full-blooded Cree, and though he was born Louie Waters, he was given his Native name in a ceremony a few years back.

"Two Elks," he told me, "is perfect because, to me, it means I walk in two worlds, the white one and the Native one." In fact, Louie had eventually married a lovely woman named Joy. She was non-Native, but a few years later they adopted two full-blooded Cree kids. Then along came Patrick, who had wandered out from Quebec, and they sort of adopted him, too. He was something between an uncle and a brother to the kids.

Louie, besides occasionally guiding kayaking trips, lived largely off the land, hunting and fishing. Sitting on the deck of the cabin on the first evening, we watched the salmon jump out of the water. They passed by here for most of the year, each according to its season. The spring salmon arrived first and then the coho. After that the chum salmon made their run until finally September brought the sockeye. That was one of the secrets of Haida civilization. For thousands of years they had lived here, hunting and fishing, and the food was so plentiful that it allowed them lots of time to develop their consummate arts and storytelling.

Lounging on the deck, Louie and I got to know each other. He told me about the guy on the next island over. This man had a commercial greenhouse operation, a large, almost industrial complex with a barking dog and lots of NO TRESPASSING signs. He was the polar opposite of Louie's eco-friendly little slice of paradise. A few years back this guy searched some legal papers and discovered he actually owned the rights to Louie's little island. Within days Louie received an eviction notice.

Well, Louie was already into his second decade there and wasn't about to move. Across at Skidegate the Haida heard about Louie's impending eviction and came over to rescue him. One of the elders, Chief Skedans, a full ninety-two years old, was the first to help.

Chief Skedans arrived and looked around at Louie's little island. "I think," he said, "there was an old Haida village here once." In fact, that's pretty much a sure bet. Just about all the islands, at one time or another, had villages. At any rate, Chief Skedans claimed the island as Haida, and after that the guy next door couldn't face the prospect of a legal battle to prove otherwise. Even the Canadian government doesn't try to tackle land claims like that.

Louie told me that the Haida were in a different position than most of the other First Nations in Canada. Land treaties were never signed here. There was never an agreement with the provincial or the federal governments. The islands were too remote. So with a declaration by Chief Skedans, Louie's island became Haida territory — as simple as that.

285

But there was more. Chief Skedans offered to adopt Louie's family. This was a great honour, and Louie still gets quite moved when he talks about it. An ancient potlatch ceremony was held, and Chief Skedans, who is a Raven, formally adopted Louie Two Elks' family. They would now be Haida, or at least Joy Waters and the children would be.

Now think about that for a second. If Louie's wife and kids became Raven, that meant Louie himself would have to be an Eagle, because a Raven can only be married to an Eagle and vice versa. Therefore he was the sole one in the family who couldn't be adopted because Chief Skedans was Raven and couldn't speak for the Eagle moiety.

"So," Louie said, laughing, "I've been here for more than twenty years. My wife is Haida. My children, who are Cree, are also Haida. And me, I'm still not a bloody Haida." Louie's eyes twinkled at the telling. "I actually went out and bought me a little pipe carved with the figure of an eagle. I guess I thought I could become an Eagle on my own. And on the first day I had it, I dropped it and it shattered. That told me it wasn't up to me. You can't just say, okay, they're Raven so that means I'm an Eagle.

"But I do go out in the winter and feed the young eagles," he continued. "Kind of trying to pile up the karma, I guess. That doesn't make me Haida, but, you know, I'm happy just to be the Haida's honoured guest here. That's enough for me. It's all about respect, you see. It's all about respect."

ξ

Professional linguists are having a hell of a time placing the Haida language. Some want to claim that it's part of the Na-Dene family of languages, but that might only be because the Haida have borrowed a lot of words from their mainland neighbours (the Tlingit, for example, whose language is definitely Na-Dene). Another group of linguists say that the Haida tongue is a language isolate, one of those very rare languages that don't seem to be related to any others on Earth.

The Haida themselves think they're unique. They believe they've always inhabited these islands. Through the long years they've certainly traded with many of the mainland cultures. As artists, they imported beaver teeth for chisels and porcupine hair for paintbrushes. As cooks, they traded for sheep and mountain goat horns to manufacture bowls, ladles, and spoons. Raw copper came from Alaska and abalone shell from Oregon and California. On their totem poles and in their storytelling, many of the spirit animals were actually mainland creatures like the grizzly bear, the beaver, the mountain goat, and the wolf.

So the Haida were never completely isolated. In fact, their most important cultural ceremony is one found up and down the coast — the famous potlatch.

When Louie's family was adopted by Chief Skedans, a potlatch ceremony was held. Louie sat me down one night and showed me the videotape of it. There were songs and dances, and Chief Skedans, old and wise, appeared in his finest headdress. It was a fantastic ceremony, and along tables in the back of the hall were piles and piles of everything from towels to toys for the kids.

These were the material goods to be given away in the potlatch, and that's the whole point. Whoever puts on a potlatch gives away huge amounts of wealth. That's something completely counter to our own sense of economics. Why would you hold a party in which you give away everything you own? It doesn't seem to make sense.

Ah, but it does. It works precisely according to logic far outside our own, but logic all the same. Very basically, wealth and power for the Haida aren't determined by how much is acquired in a lifetime. It's the opposite. Wealth is displayed in how much one is willing to give away. Rather than our system of "conspicuous consumption," the Haida display their wealth, power, and respect in the community by a system we might call "conspicuous disposal."

Even that's a bit of simplification. All across Haida Gwaii there are potlatches for various sorts of events. There are potlatches for the election of a new chief and there are potlatches for naming ceremonies, sometimes the naming of a person, sometimes even for the construction and naming of a new house. At all of these occasions the person putting on the potlatch gives away vast amounts of wealth. They usually give it away to the members of the opposite group so that Chief Skedans, being a Raven, would give it away to members of the Eagle group.

It's a sort of legal payment given for the act of "witnessing" the ceremony. Like a signature on a legal document, the other group is called upon to verify the ceremony. And this is what they're being "paid" for. It all seems to balance out, it all seems to even up over the years, so that it's a tightly knit, perfectly functioning economy.

That's the case now and it was the situation before the arrival of the white man. However, potlatches were actually made illegal by the Canadian government from 1885 to 1951. Obviously, white authorities couldn't understand what the Haida and other West Coast people who held potlatches were up to and therefore figured they were up to no good. It's a perfect example of cultural misunderstanding, and it's only now that some of the more ceremonial objects from the potlatches are being returned to First Nations people, sometimes from museum collections as far away as New York and Sweden.

It occurs to me now that when Louie was talking about respect he was really speaking about understanding. To respect something is to give an honest attempt at understanding it. It's as simple as that.

The word *potlatch* actually comes from a Nootka word. The Nootka were a people who lived on the west coast of Vancouver Island. The root is *ppaatlppiichi'atl*, which means "to transfer property in the context of a public feast, to buy status."

288

The Haida use a different word for it, in fact, a number of words depending on the exact ceremony performed. A *waahlghal* is employed when a house is built, though it's also used for adoptions, like that of Louie's family. Unfortunately, it's one of the many words that have almost been lost. Even the Haida today will probably just call it a potlatch so that *waahlghal* is all but a dead word.

But I didn't want to let that word go. It's quite something to hold a word like *waahlghal* on your tongue, a word with such meaning. In the rugged mountains and fjords of Haida Gwaii, there are, as I've said, only a hundred or so elders who still speak this language with any fluency. That means these words, each and every one, are as rare as diamonds. They're jewels we need to hold on to, if only to present them to the light and let them sparkle once more.

Like the weathered totem poles, they deserve respect.

꒝

Louie, like James the Haida watchman, lives in a strange world, one that didn't exist before. To press a point, I might call it a postmodern world. Two hundred years ago it would have been quite easy to say what was Haida and what wasn't. The people in villages spread across Haida Gwaii, though they spoke different dialects, were all definitely Haida. Everyone else wasn't.

Now it's not quite so simple. Today the Haida live in a blended world. Most of them speak English and no more than a handful of Haida words. They live in modern, centrally heated houses. The dense forest has been logged and scarred, and the totem poles are mostly gone.

The Haida, at least in terms of defining the boundaries of their ancestral lands, are better off than most First Nations peoples of North America. Living on remote islands has left them with a clear sense of what is Haida land and what isn't. But what is the Haida world? It's not the old world. That's gone. Bits and pieces remain, especially in their great art, but for the individual ... what is it to be a Haida in the twenty-first century?

After Louie's family went through the potlatch ceremony, after it was formally welcomed into the Raven moiety, Chief Skedans took it upon himself to commission a totem pole. That's a rare event and not something that's carved for tourists or on some pretense of showing off their culture. This totem pole was to mark the new family clan that had been created. It was carved by an artist with the Haida name of Skil Q'uas, and it now stands proudly on a promontory at the edge of Louie's little island, looking out to sea.

Louie took me out to it. From the bottom up there's a killer whale, a grizzly bear, and a mountain goat. These are the totems or symbols of Chief Skedans's clan. At the top is the figure of a moon, Chief Skedans's personal symbol, and tucked under the paw of the grizzly, almost around at the back of the totem, a little

289

carved frog seems to clamber up the cedar trunk.

Louie chuckled. "We always say the little frog is for Patrick. French Canadian, you know."

There are other figures and abstract lines on the totem pole, and I found out later that in the crest of Chief Skedans's clan there are two types of clouds and a rainbow. At the top of the whole thing is a stylized raven, and as if that isn't enough, a real raven appears to sit atop the pole, gazing at the ocean, conspiring to trick the universe with another one of his stories.

᠊᠊

The canoe slipped easily through the water. Louie sat in the back, steering with his knife-edged paddle. I worked the front. The canoe was painted black and had a stylized raven near the bow in white. In Haida this is a *t'luu*, exactly the same as the ones that have been used here for thousands of years.

We paddled up Skidegate Inlet. Along the shoreline Louie pointed out how the tops of hemlocks bowed over while Sitka spruce stood straight. Cedar, he showed me, had needles that were soft like lace. Where there were alders and sometimes even crabapple trees the soil had been disturbed. That meant there had been a village once.

Louie told me many things about the land. He revealed how spruce pitch, a sort of gooey tar from the Sitka, would have been used to heal battle wounds. "It sticks the skin together like stitches," he said, "and it's sterile."

He held up his paddle. It was sharpened at the end to a point. "Do you see this?" He waved it at me menacingly. Water droplets arced around it. "The Haida used these as both paddles and weapons. I'd use it still if a bear showed up on the beach. Did you know," he continued, suddenly fixing upon this idea, "that the bears here are a sub-species that are different than any other ones in the world? They're a kind of black bear."

"Yeah?"

"But much bigger than the mainland black bears, especially their jaws. They've developed huge jaws to bite into the clams and mussel shells they find along the beaches."

Louie certainly knew a lot about this place. I began to see that not only had Louie (or his family and his island, anyway) been adopted by the Haida but that Louie himself had adopted the Haida ways — their land, their ideas, their understandings.

We dipped through the placid water for several hours, switching sides when it got too tiring. The old Haida could go on for days like this. The little canoe we were in would have been the kind they used every day, the sort they puttered in to their neighbour's place to borrow a cup of spruce pitch. But there were bigger canoes.

"A five-hundred-year-old cedar," Louie said, "could be carved into a canoe that would hold thirty or forty guys. These were the war canoes, the ones they paddled in on their raids along the coast."

"Does it ever get rough in the straits?" I asked.

"In the winter, yes. The winds come in off the Pacific and churn up the straits pretty good. Between here and the mainland of British Columbia ... whooo boy!"

"Hecate Strait?"

"Yeah, it's supposed to be one of the most dangerous stretches of water in the world. Some people say it's like rounding Cape Horn in South America. Different currents and weather patterns all colliding —"

"But the Haida used to go across it in canoes?"

"In their war canoes, yeah."

"But still, crossing the ocean in an open canoe?"

"The Haida were tough guys — that's for sure. Here, steer into the beach for a second. I want to show you something."

We entered shallower water and hopped onto a rocky stretch of land, pulling the canoe a little way out of the water. "Look at this," Louie said. He showed me how the front of the canoe was cut away. It didn't have the rounded hull of a normal canoe but was concave at the front. "That's for ploughing through the surf. It handles really well in the ocean swells but then —" he pointed at the back of the canoe "— if you're going up still water, you just turn the canoe and the rounded end becomes the front."

Ingenious, I thought. That was what happened when you lived in the same environment for a few thousand years. You got to know it well.

ㄱ)

At the east end of the inlet, where the bay meets Hecate Strait, the actual town of Skidegate rises from the beach. It's where most Haida still live. It's not a reserve. It's a town like any other.

I walked up the highway to Skidegate on my last day in Haidi Gwaii. It began to rain, but I had one more thing I wanted to see. The rain grew harder. I hadn't planned on that, but I plodded wetly up the road. In the trees, ravens cawed, and large, dark clouds had come down to touch the sea.

Near the edge of Skidegate there's a large carving shed. In it is one of the treasures of the modern Haida — a massive war canoe named *Loo taas*, "Wave-Eater," another jewel.

It was pouring now. With every step my sodden boots sloshed and my coat was soaked through. Up ahead I could see that the doors of the canoe shed were thankfully open. I dashed toward it and found myself in a long room, well lit, constructed entirely of cedar. In the rain it smelled wonderful, and there, like a centerpiece in the hall, was *Loo taas*.

The canoe, just as in the old days, had been carved from a single tree. It was eighteen metres long, as big as a whale. In the middle it was two metres wide, so it could comfortably hold as many as twenty burly paddlers. Along the hull it was painted masterfully, and I knew this was the work of Bill Reid, the greatest modern artist of the Haida.

Reid's work is now so well-known that one huge piece sits in the Canadian embassy in Washington, D.C. Another is the centrepiece of Vancouver International Airport, and many smaller pieces are found in museums and galleries around the world. Almost single-handedly, Reid has taken the great Haida traditional forms and patterns out to the world, and his work is indisputably magnificent.

I was alone in the carving shed for a few minutes before a young Haida woman came in. "Go ahead," she said. "You can touch it if you want to." Evidently, the look on my face was of reverence, and she found that a little comical. She slapped heartily at the side of the canoe. "They paddled this one all the way up from Vancouver, you know. That's seven hundred kilometres of open ocean. I think it can handle you poking at it."

She chuckled again and introduced herself as Kim. She was in her mid-twenties, about the same age as James. She took me around the huge canoe slowly, showing me how a carved channel just under the gunwale served to keep waves from splashing into the boat. She explained how a carved notch in the front was used for ropes, as well as for steering the canoe, like a sighting on the barrel of a rifle.

293

"One time," she said, "we took it out in the bay and loaded it with the heaviest guys in Skidegate. They tried to tip it over but, you know, they couldn't. It's pretty sturdy."

The rain continued to pelt down, so I stayed in the warmth and continued talking with Kim. She was born in Skidegate, and I asked her what it was like growing up here.

"It's weird," she said, "we're just like anyone else. We go off to the big cities to university. We email one another. We do all the things everyone else does. But that Haida thing ... it's always there." She glanced at the floor. "Some people don't like it. You know, it's always hanging over us. People expect us to be such and such a way." She studied me for a moment. "But I like it. I go up into the woods sometimes and I walk the path of the ancients."

Those were her exact words: "I walk the path of the ancients." That was beautiful. I asked her about Haida names, and she laughed. "Yeah, it gets complicated. I was born with both a Haida name and an English name. You know, to make it easier for you white guys." She waved her hand at me, and I smiled. "Then you get another Haida name when you grow up. Sometimes, if something important happens, you even get another name after that. I got another name when I got arrested."

"Arrested?" I must have looked alarmed, but she only chuckled again.

"Naw, it's not what you think. I was at a blockade on the south island. We were blocking the loggers from going in. Right after that they made the whole area a national park, and now the logging companies can't touch it."

"You did that?"

"Yeah, I was real young, but I got a new name for that. I'm very proud of it."

The rain had let up a little. Kim phoned a friend of hers who ran a company called Eagle Taxi, and a guy turned up in a battered van to take me back to the ferry landing.

I flew out of Haida Gwaii later that day. Beneath me a mist lapped around the islands, and the old propeller plane whirled out over the ocean. I didn't see any more whales, but I left the islands with something more than I had come with, something like understanding.

May You Walk the Trail of Beauty

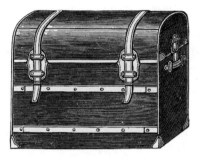

We set off down the trail on our skis. It had snowed heavily the night before and a wonderland of fresh powder lay before us. We'd planned this trip carefully. Two days of food, sleeping gear, loads of warm clothes, all stuffed into our backpacks. It was about fourteen kilometres to the hut — a rustic wooden cabin deep in the Canadian Rocky Mountains. We'd spend the night there, build a fire in the cast-iron stove, have a few drinks and laughs, and then ski out again the next morning.

I was with a friend of mine, a lanky musician named Mark. The trouble is, neither of us had done a whole lot of cross-country skiing. We had only the most rudimentary knowledge and no map.

But Mark said he'd been here before, and it wasn't a particularly difficult route. We started off well. Someone had skied ahead of us so that we simply followed their tracks into the dark forest. It was very still. The snow muffled sound. Our skis whispered and shushed underneath us, and our breath came in clouds.

The world was incredibly simplified here. The tree branches were black against the sparkle of snow. The shadows were watercolour purple, and a slate-grey sky hung above the treetops. Both Mark and I collapsed into our own thoughts. In single file we set up our rhythms, gliding down the quiet trail and into the heart of the mountains.

We stopped for lunch four or five kilometres in. The light had flattened out, and it had begun to snow. At first it was beautiful. Great fat flakes drifted down. We grinned at each other and ate our sandwiches under the boughs of a giant spruce. Everything was fine. We set off again with the whole afternoon ahead of us. The temperature had dipped — hovering around minus ten degrees Celsius — but there was no wind and we had all the gear we needed. We were well dressed for the cold and kept up a good pace, feeling the blood surge through our legs and arms.

The snow was falling more thickly, but it was as pretty as a Christmas card. The only problem was that the tracks we were following were slowly being filled in. After a while, they were just shallow depressions, hard to see in the low winter light. And at last they vanished altogether.

Four hours in we came to a wide valley swinging off to the north.

"Is it this way?" I asked Mark.

"Um … um …" he hummed. I could tell he was looking for a sign, something he recognized. "Yeah, I think we go this way."

"I thought you were here before?"

"I was … but it was summertime. I don't quite …" He glanced back at the way we'd come, then down the valley again. "It must be this way."

The snow was around mid-shin by now, which meant the person going first had to break through it, pushing one ski boot through the deep snow and then the other at no more than a walking pace. The skis were no longer gliding. There was just too much snow. It was hard work, and after ploughing this way for another hour, Mark suddenly stopped. "Um ..." he began again, and this time I knew we were in trouble. "I don't think this is it, after all. I think we need to be in the next valley over."

Both of us gazed at the sky. Snowflakes the size of potato chips drifted all around us. Even our own tracks, just behind us, disappeared as soon as we left them.

"What should we do?" I asked.

"Well, we can't stop here. We have to go back."

So we tucked our heads down and turned around. Back at the entrance to the valley, we toyed with the idea of returning to the car. It was now late in the afternoon, but we could make it there not too long after nightfall if we really hurried. On the other hand, the hut — by our best calculations — couldn't be more than another couple of kilometres into the next valley.

It seemed reasonable to keep going toward the hut. We were warm enough. In fact, we were dripping with sweat, and the first tiny sparks of fear were beginning to appear. It was hard going. The skis were now almost useless. They sank into the knee-deep snow, but we pushed on, taking turns breaking the trail. It was almost impossible to advance more than two hundred metres before the other guy had to take over. It was like playing soccer with a bowling ball. My thighs ached, and we had to stop often, grasping for our water bottles, trying to keep ourselves focused.

If the hut was two kilometres away, I reasoned, we could still make it. It was just a matter of hard work. I began to count off my steps, figuring that two full steps equalled about a metre. I counted off ten metres and then twenty ... all the way up to a hundred. Only ten of these would make up a kilometre. Counting off the numbers gave me something to think about.

An early-winter twilight was descending, and though we had flashlights, we knew we had to make the hut by nightfall. The hut was at the top of a cliff. Mark had joked about that from the beginning. "It's the last hundred metres that are the hardest," he said. "You have to go straight up to get to the hut."

That final thought almost killed us.

My mind was numbed. I could only think of the numbers, measuring off my steps. We'd been skiing now for almost eight solid hours and the last two had been excruciating. Everything below my neck was sloshing with lactic acid. I would count two hundred steps, then turn the lead back over to Mark. Two hundred more steps and I would return to the front. Slowly, I counted off a full kilometre.

Just as I yelled this proud fact to Mark, who was now in the lead, he collapsed into the snow. The white stuff underneath him had given way. We had crossed over a stream without knowing it. Mark was now sunk to his shoulders in snow, and his feet and skis were in a metre of water below that.

"Jesus!" he yelped.

I clipped out of my skis and got onto my belly. I'd seen this in movies before. It was how you were supposed to rescue people who had gone through ice. Mark's feet were on the bottom, so he wasn't going to sink anymore, but still he wasn't able to move and I thought he might go into shock or something. Mark let loose with a blue streak of swearing, and I told him to calm down while I gripped one of his arms and began to haul him out.

It took a while, but he managed to squirm up and out onto the surface of the snow again. His pant legs were soaked through, though, and already they were crusting with ice.

"Shit," he muttered, looking around. "How far do you think we are from the fucking hut?"

"At least a kilometre ... and then, you know, it's straight uphill for the last bit."

Mark's face was pink with rage and frustration. "Shut the fuck up!"

"Okay, okay … what are our options here? What should we do? We need to think."

The shadows had enveloped us now. There wasn't much light left in the sky. "Should we push on?" I asked. I was worried, actually, that I wouldn't even be able to reason with him anymore. As bad as I felt, I knew he was having a worse time of it. Hypothermia was a real possibility.

"No," he growled. "We have to —" He shook his head.

"We have to what?"

"We have to build a snow cave."

"Are you kidding me?"

"I don't see that we have much choice." He inhaled. "Look, we dig a hole in the snow and cover it up with spruce boughs. Maybe we can light a fire or something. We've got our sleeping bags. We just have to get through the night and then we can get out of here in the morning."

I looked around. The snow hadn't let up at all, and it was now most definitely dark. "Okay," I said.

"Take off your skis," Mark said. "We'll use them as shovels. We'll dig over there — in that big drift." The temperature was falling. "C'mon, dig. Help me dig."

ꓹ

You can't really have a book about language without mentioning the Inuit and their sixty-four words for snow. Or is that one hundred and twenty-eight? I don't know. Each time the story gets told the number gets bigger. I call it the Great Inuit Snow Hoax.

The Inuit constitute a number of different groups, from the Kalaalit in Greenland to the Inupiaq of Canada, the Alutiiq in Alaska, and the Yup'ik in Siberia, whose similarity in language is perhaps the best argument for the land bridge migration hypothesis over the Bering Strait.

For a long time the Inuit were called Eskimos, a term still used in parts of Alaska. The word *Eskimo* comes from a derogatory term thought to be from an Algonquian language to the south. Some say it means "eaters of raw meat," though no one is quite sure because the word has come to us third-hand via an early French trader's approximation of it: *Eskimaux*.

As for the Inuit and their words for snow, they don't really have that many. The original field research comes from Franz Boas, a famous anthropologist and linguist who, in 1911, wrote that "Eskimos" had only four words for snow: *aput*, expressing snow on the ground; *qana* for falling snow; *piqsirpoq* for drifting snow; and *qimuqsuq* for a standing snowdrift.

The whole thing is a misunderstanding. Even Boas's catalogue of four words greatly misses the mark. The language of the Canadian Inuit, Inuktitut, simply doesn't work the same way English does. Boas was looking for nouns. In the bias of an English-speaking world, nouns rule. The subject and the object have always been at the heart of English sentence structure. We tend to divide the world into things rather than actions or properties. Inuktitut, and most of the indigenous languages of the Americas, work quite differently.

In Inuktitut the verb *to snow*, *qanniq*, can be modified by literally hundreds of different suffixes — anything from who's talking about the snow (and who they're talking to) to the time, causality, and speed of what's happening. Even then it's just as likely that a conversation about snow would be based around different verb roots like *to freeze* or *to blow* or *to drift* or even *to clump together*.

These long, extended verbs often form whole sentences and really can't be thought of as single words at all. So to talk about how many words the Inuit have for snow is quite ridiculous. You might as well try to count how many sentences in English contain the word *snow*. It just doesn't make sense.

Try this sentence on for size: *Qanniqlaukaluaqtuq anitunga*. It means: "Although it's snowing very heavily, I'm still going out." That's a whole sentence in English, a sentence of nine different words, a sentence Mark and I had foolishly managed to act out.

Ω

Mark and I dug out a pit in a snowdrift, covered the roof with spruce boughs, lumped more snow on top of that, and then built a small fire by the entrance. In fact, it wasn't that bad. My feet were cold, but only because I'd stubbornly kept my socks on. They were damp, and even down there in the sleeping bag, they just never warmed up.

At the first light of dawn we skied back out to the car. It took four or five hours, and my legs were like blocks of cement. They had become so stiff from the cold, cramped quarters, and gallons of lactic acid gushing through them that when we at last got to the car I could hardly bend myself into a sitting position. We drove after that, as quickly as we could, to a hot springs not far away. When I dipped myself in the steaming water, I actually screamed — a curious mix of both pleasure and pain.

301

Φ

A people's environment does, obviously, have a huge impact on their language. It's not always as simple as counting words, though. A word is like a chess piece. It doesn't really matter how a chess piece is carved — whether it's shaped like a horse or a castle. It doesn't matter what it's called — a rook or a bishop or a knight. What matters is how it's used, how it moves.

Languages function within a certain environment. They're tools for surviving within that environment. But that's not to say they don't migrate. In fact, despite all my talk of territoriality and environmental construction, languages tend to move around a fair bit. They're organic things, and like all living things, they roam endlessly, searching for places where they'll be most successful.

The ancient world was a pretty fluid place. Things moved and changed all the time. Peoples and ideas swept across different landscapes, as they do today, interacting with one another and the new environments, creating new worlds out of old. Languages have always had to change and adapt. They are, as the Inuktitut might say, not so much things as actions.

Φ

Where the tundra meets the great boreal forests, where the Inuit lands end, we find evidence for one of the most astonishing language migrations in the New World. All along the Mackenzie River in the Northwest Territories are the Dene. The word *Dene*, of course, means "People."

On the northern banks of the Mackenzie, at a junction with Great Bear Lake, there's a little Dene settlement called Tulita. Great Bear Lake is the third biggest lake in North America. People forget that, I suppose, because it's frozen over for a good part of the year. In fact, supplies are trucked into Tulita over ice roads, making for a precarious crossing in the spring months.

Tulita used to be called Fort Norman. It was a trading post, but now it's home to about three hundred and fifty people. Most of them are Willow Lake Dene. They have satellite TVs and telephones. Out on the fringes of town, however, there are a couple of dozen people from the Mountain Dene band, and they still tend to live on the edge of things, making their living by hunting and trapping, much as they've done for thousands of years.

Both speak a Dene dialect called Slavey. At the little schoolhouse there they still teach the kids how to hunt caribou, how to sew the skins together, and presumably how to avoid spending the night in an improvised snow cave.

Grizzly bears come down into Tulita a couple of times a year, and when this happens, everyone unties their dogs. Not so the dogs will attack the grizzlies. The dogs wouldn't have a chance, no matter how many of them there were. No, it's to give the dogs a fair chance of getting away. Even at that, four or five dogs never seem to return after the night the grizzlies hit town.

It's a rough life for everyone up there. One woman I know of had already had six children. She was twenty-eight years old. She was having her seventh, already several more than she could handle. But there's an unwritten law in this community. If the next baby is a girl, she'll keep it. If it's a boy, then she'll give it up and someone in the community will always take it. They take care of their own here. Even in the language you can see this. In Slavey there are two different words for brother, depending on the birth order. An older brother is a *sɣnaghe*, while a younger brother is a *sechee*. They're different because of what they do. An older brother carries responsibility. He can take care of the younger children. He can hunt with his father and carry part of the family's workload. A younger brother is, well … not exactly a burden but someone who is, at least for the time being, less useful.

303

So words are less about things and more about what things do, what things mean. The Dene language describes the way of life in the Far North. It's a language at home in the long winter, a tongue spoken at the very edge of the Arctic Circle.

What's surprising then is that this same language — or dialects of it, anyway — can be found in pockets all down the long spine of North America. On the Great Plains where the buffalo once roamed in herds of millions, there are Dene. And farther south, in the sunbaked canyons of Arizona and New Mexico where they grow corn and live in pueblos, there are more Dene.

We can follow this linguistic trail for thousands of kilometres through a series of wildly different landscapes. And what that means for the people and their language is as fascinating a story as you're likely to find in the study of the world's languages.

Ψ

The winter was a long one. The ice was thick on the great lake, and the people moved out across it in a long line. A wind howled across the ice but, wrapped in thick buffalo robes, the people plodded on. Beneath their feet the ice shifted sometimes in thunderous cracks, but still they moved on across the long lake to the safety of the farthest shore.

One small boy rode on his grandmother's back. Only his little pink face peered out from the bundle of robes, but with his clear young eyes he spied something black in the ice, just off to the side of the long trail of people. "*Isu,*" he called through the wind. "Grandmother, there's something in the ice."

The grandmother stopped and squinted into the wind. It was true. Something black was sticking out of the ice.

"It's a bone," the boy cried. "Or a horn. Can I see it?"

The grandmother let the boy skitter off her back and onto his feet. He tottered across the ice toward the odd thing sticking out from the ice, and she could do nothing except follow.

When they arrived, they saw that it was a large horn, though not the horn of a ram or any other animal they could identify. The boy danced around it. "Can I have it? Can I have it?"

So, not wishing to let anything go to waste, the old woman began to chip away at the ice around the horn, hoping to free it. In her mind, as she worked, she wondered what animal it might have come from and how it came to be there.

Even as she pulled on the horn, trying to release it, the ice started to crack. With a momentous shudder the crack ran through the ice sheet and across the whole length of the lake. In a moment it split wide open, leaving half of the long line of people to the south of it and half to the north. Each half scattered, running in opposite directions. Those who were caught in the north remained there. Those on the other side, those to the south, well, they kept on going, moving farther and farther into the lands of the sun.

The above is a story that was told by Helen Meguinis, who was one of the elders of the Tsuu T'ina band. The Tsuu T'ina live in southern Alberta several thousand kilometres south of their Northern Dene cousins. Their treaty lands are on the southwest edge of the oil-rich city of Calgary. T'ina is one spelling of Dina — that is, Dene.

The Tsuu T'ina live in a completely different world. When the ice split on the lake, whether metaphorically or literally, the Tsuu T'ina were the group who headed into the grasslands in the middle of the continent. It's difficult to say when this happened. As an oral history, the story dates back hundreds of years, and over those many centuries, the Tsuu T'ina lost their northern ways. Like the other nations of the Great Plains, especially the Blackfoot and the Stoney who are their nearby neighbours, the Tsuu T'ina adapted to the ways of the buffalo hunt. They lived in teepees and learned to ride horses, all words and concepts that don't even exist in the dialect of their Northern Dene cousins.

305

ξ

Tsuu T'ina, by their own accounts, means simply "Many People," which is ironic considering that only about two thousand people still live on the Tsuu T'ina reserve. And fewer than one hundred are still fluent in the Tsuu T'ina language. Even Helen Meguinis passed away, sadly, in 2007 at the grand old age of eight-three.

Of the three hundred aboriginal languages spoken in North America at the time of European settlement, one hundred and fifty have disappeared completely, and only a handful of the remaining ones are still acquiring new speakers. And that was why I jumped at the chance to go to a powwow on the Tsuu T'ina reserve one dusty summer day. I drove out of Calgary and headed west to a point where the long prairies turn into the forested foothills of the Rocky Mountains.

This was to be a huge powwow. Several thousand people were going to be there. Dene representatives were coming down from the north. There would be Cree and Ojibwa, too. Even the neighbouring Blackfoot would be arriving in their trucks and campers.

Powwow is derived from an Algonquian term *pau-wau* or *pauau*, which referred historically to a spiritual gathering. It was generally a sort of religious ceremony, usually for the purpose of curing and healing. Powwows are practised across North America now, and many, like this one, are referred to as Gatherings of Nations. They feature dance competitions and drum circles. The people of many First Nations come from as far away as Yukon Territory to the north and Arizona to the south. All are welcome, even skinny white guys like me.

Not a drop of alcohol was to be found anywhere on the huge fairgrounds. No one snuck it in, either. They had some pretty strict rules about that. The people here had come to be together, to converse, to meet, and to extend the hand of friendship across many nations.

I drove across a rattling cattle gate, and someone waved me into a field to park my car. There were other cars there and loads of campers and tents. Several thousand people had come for the three-day event, and I could hear drums beating in the distance. It was dusty and hot, and I drove around a little until I saw a piece of grass where I could pull my car up and out of the way.

I'd just turned off the engine when a woman in a buckskin coat hurried over to me. "You can't park there."

Shit! I thought. I'd been there ten minutes and already I'd made some sort of mistake. I'd dishonoured something. I wondered if I'd somehow parked my car on a bit of sacred land. There must have been a reason why no one else parked there. It was a big green space, so maybe it was a teepee ring, a medicine wheel, or something.

"I'm so sorry," I muttered. "I didn't mean to disrespect anything. I ... ah ..."

The woman glared at me as if I were a complete idiot. "You can't park there," she said, "because you're blocking the ice-cream truck." And sure enough, I saw that I'd parked against the opened side window of a panel van. A gaggle of dark-haired little children had surrounded my car. They gazed up at me expectantly. Could I please get out of the way so they could get themselves a snow cone? Was that really too much to ask?

ㄱ

Remember the anthropologist Franz Boas? He's the one who came up with the four Inuit words for snow. Well, he had two students whose names are infamous in linguistic circles. One was Edward Sapir and the other was Benjamin Whorf. I actually spent a lot of time at university looking into their theories — what we now collectively and rather unimaginatively call the Sapir-Whorf hypothesis.

Essentially, it says that a language sets up the categories and organizations by which we understand the world around us. "We dissect nature along lines laid down by our native languages," Whorf wrote. We sort out the wild chaos of data that our sense organs bring in using the structures of the language we speak.

The naming of colours is a good example. Colour actually exists along a continuum — the rainbow or, if you like, white light refracted through a prism — and the dividing line between, say, yellow and green isn't an exact point. It's open to cultural or even individual taste. There are no borders in a rainbow.

So different languages tend to divide up colours in different ways. For example, the Haida have only four colour terms. The word *ghuhlghahl* corresponds well to the Chinese *qing* or the Dene *dootł'izh*, but not to any single word in English. It covers most of the range that English divides more specifically into terms like blue, green, purple, and turquoise. *Ghuhlghahl*, instead, is the colour of the sunlit living world, including the blues and indigoes of the sky, the greens and blues of the sea, the summer colours of the mountains, and the greens of needles, shoots, and leaves — clearly distinct from white and red, though it can sometimes include hues of yellow, brown, and even black.

All of this is distinctly marked in different languages, so the Sapir-Whorf hypothesis says that colour — our way of thinking about it and even our way of seeing it — is organized by the language we have for it.

In my graduate work I came across a quintessential set of experiments on colour. Two researchers, Brent Berlin and Paul Kay, tested speakers from ninety-eight different language groups. There were a few rare tongues with only two words for colour (the Dani language of New Guinea, for example, has only words for black and white, their jungle world being almost entirely composed of darker or lighter shades of green). A few more languages have colour words for three hues: black, white, and red. Languages with a fourth colour name usually include specific words for yellow or green. It goes on until you hit languages like English that generally speak in terms of eleven broad categories for colour: black, white, red, green, yellow, blue, brown, pink, purple, orange, and grey.

But the thing is, even among speakers of languages with only two words, all people are equally able to distinguish between a broad range of hues. The Dani speakers of New Guinea make almost exactly the same mistakes as English speakers on a colour memory test involving more than forty colours, which shows, pretty conclusively, that the Dani speakers are no better and no worse than the English speakers in their perception of real colours.

So what do we make of all this? Sapir and Whorf would have predicted that different language speakers really see colours in different ways. And they would be dead wrong. A strong version of their theory — linguistic determinism — had to be thrown out for a very simple reason. There are lots of things in our thinking that are outside the control of language. Colour is one of them. It doesn't matter if the Dani don't have a word for red. They can distinguish between the red of one flower and the pink of another, especially if they know that the red one is poisonous and the pink one isn't. They figure that out pretty quickly, language or no language.

But that's not to say there's nothing to the Sapir-Whorf hypothesis in general. Language rides pretty high in our consciousness, and to admit that it has at least some effect on our thinking is really a matter of common sense. Just what that effect is, though, is pretty hard to pin down.

Researchers like Lera Boroditsky at Stanford University are still doing some pretty convincing tests (as recently as 2007) on the influence of language on colour in English as opposed to Russian, the ideas of time in English, Greek, Spanish, and Mandarin, and even on the gender of toasters (yes, toasters) and other inanimate objects in Spanish and German. Linguistic determinism is dead, but the view that language somehow still affects us is widespread and, in some cases, even provable. It's a notion called linguistic relativity.

309

In the summer of 1922 Edward Sapir himself appeared on the Tsuu T'ina land. Treaty Seven had already moved them into a particular two-hundred-and-fifty-square-kilometre reserve, and their language was already showing signs that it might disappear.

Sapir worked with a Tsuu T'ina interpreter named John Whitney. Together they spoke with many of the elders of the nation and managed to fill seven notebooks with an incredibly detailed account of the Tsuu T'ina grammar system.

What they failed to record, though, is how the Tsuu T'ina lived. They said nothing about the other semiotic systems under which the Tsuu T'ina make their way in the world — the tastes of their food, the clothing they wear, their haircuts, their dance patterns, the symbols on their teepees. All of these comprise a much larger grammar, something Sapir and Whorf never quite imagined, and all of it makes up their true House of Being.

Ω

The central point of the powwow was a huge circular covered area. I sat cross-legged on the floor. There were no seats left, but I was in time for the Grand Procession. Representatives from all the attending nations would be dancing into the centre. Four or five different drum circles were dotted around the enclosure. Each drum circle had five or six guys, and the drum circles took turns playing. First, near the entrance, one circle went at it, banging out a fantastic rhythm like the swelling of a heartbeat. They chanted, too. I had no idea what they were saying. I didn't even know if they were all Tsuu T'ina or whether some of the other circles were guest drummers from other nations.

In time the first drum circle closed off its performance, and the group next to me started up. It had a few younger guys and one older man, not quite an elder but clearly middle-aged, who called out instructions to the younger ones. "You're cutting it off too soon!" he bellowed, and one of the younger guys, his hair in two long braids that came down over his shoulders, bent into the chant more conscientiously, his face contorted with the effort of getting it exactly right.

Then the dancers came in, dozens of them, hundreds of them, each doing a version of their own nation's dances. There were Cree and Blackfoot, Ojibwa from the East, and even a couple of Navajo from the far reaches of the southern United States. The range of costumes was incredible. They flashed with colour. Feathers and beads bobbed and tinkled. Some had headdresses, others wore furs. Elk skin moccasins pumped to the hypnotic beat of the drums. One young boy danced in, and all along his chest on a sort of leather jersey, he (or his mother more likely) had sewn blank silver computer CDs — a note from the present.

It took almost an hour for everyone to enter. The drummers pounded on. The dancers wove and twirled until finally everybody was present. The drums quieted and the assembled were invited to sit. Then one man stood up at the front. I didn't know who he was. He wore a lightly tanned rawhide jacket, the kind with leather tassels coming down from the hems. This man made the most amazing announcement. "We've now raised the money," he said, "for a Calling Home Ceremony. Eleven groups will go."

Just as I was wondering what a Calling Home Ceremony might be, he began to explain. "Elders and representatives from eleven nations will be going this summer to Normandy."

Normandy? I thought. *Like in France?*

"Many of our brothers fought in the world wars," the man continued. "Many of them lost their lives in Europe. Now it's time to call their spirits home. We will be a strong group — the Inuit and the Métis, the Cree and our gracious hosts the Tsuu T'ina. We're going to bring our brothers' spirits home at last."

There was great applause, of course. The man's words left an indelible image in my mind: the elders of many nations standing on the beaches of Normandy, chanting softly for the spirits of their ancestors, those who sacrificed themselves along with all the other Canadians on the beaches of D-Day. That was a beautiful thought.

311

Toward the end of the welcome speeches, one of the Tsuu T'ina elders got to his feet. His name was Fred Eagle Tail. He's one of the small group of people who are still fluent in the ancient Tsuu T'ina language. Fred gave a prayer in the old language, but then switched into English for his speech. It was his final words that stayed with me. "Children of nature," he said, "be strong. Remember always to hold your heads high."

Φ

I once travelled to a site just to the south of the Tsuu T'ina lands. On a long cliff rising unexpectedly from the prairies there's an archaeological dig with the fantastic name of Head-Smashed-In

Buffalo Jump. For many thousands of years the first peoples here ran small herds of buffalo off the cliffs.

Sixty million buffalo once roamed the Great Plains, and life in the grasslands — for the Blackfoot, the Tsuu T'ina, or the Stoney people, who live just to the west — depended almost entirely on the migrations of these huge herds. The buffalo was their chief source of food, fuel, clothing, and shelter. Everything was used — from the horns to the tail. Nothing was wasted.

Two spearheads found at Head-Smashed-In date to almost nine thousand years ago, making the site far older than even Stonehenge or the Pyramids in Egypt. I stood there on the lip of the cliff. On the western horizon the Rocky Mountains rose. To the east and south the wide grasslands stretched off unimaginably. I closed my eyes and tried to picture the place as it must have been.

Today the Head-Smashed-In site is on Blackfoot land. Blackfoot is the literal translation for the name they call themselves — the *Siksika*. They speak an Algonquian language distantly related to Cree and as different from Tsuu T'ina as English is from Arabic. They're from completely different language families, and yet both were intrinsically dependent on the buffalo.

Neither the Blackfoot nor the Tsuu T'ina were likely the original users of the cliffs at Head-Smashed-In. No one knows who those first spear points really belonged to. It seems that wave after wave of migrations probably passed through these lands over the millennia, and as the people came, their way of life adapted to the prairies. All seemed to find a way to drive the buffalo off the cliffs. It was an economic windfall, a wealth of hides, food, and bone implements that would see them through even the cruellest winters.

Buffalo in the Tsuu T'ina dialect is *xāná*. As the band spread into the grasslands, *xāná* must have come to mark a central concept, a crucial piece of vocabulary in their whole way of being. *Xāná*, though, isn't a word found in the Northern Dene dialects. There were simply no buffalo up around the Arctic Circle. In order to refer to a buffalo the Northern Dene use the same word they employ for a musk ox — *hotélį ejeré*.

So where did the word *xāná* come from? When the Tsuu T'ina were presented with this new source of food and livelihood, who came up with the word to name it? Well, there are really only two ways in which a new word can enter a language. First, a new piece of language can be deliberately constructed — anything from the formal construction of a new word (like the Hebrew construction of the word *airplane*) to the more informal elements of slang (like the computer slang of *surfing, hacking,* or *spam*).

The second way in which a new word comes into existence is just to borrow it from another tongue. A buffalo in the Blackfoot language is an *iiníí*. The middle *n* and the surrounding vowels in both *xāná* and *iiníí* may point to a shared cognate.

Blackfoot, though, is distantly related to Cree — both are Assiniboine languages — and you would think that the Cree word might offer up some clues. However, it's *paskwâwimostos*, which obviously bears no relation at all. It's a mystery then. Both the Tsuu T'ina and the Blackfoot have adapted these words, but from where we're not certain.

In English I've been using the word *buffalo*, but that's technically not correct, either. The animals in North America are more properly called *bison*. Still, this is exactly the point. Pretty much everyone here calls them buffalo. Languages are like free markets. They're democracies wherein a thing gets named by whatever most people choose to call it.

Of course, I'm still stuck on single words here. I don't think the Dene dialects are quite as verb-heavy as Inuktitut, but still I'm probably making more of the individual word stems than they really deserve. The Tsuu T'ina language would be wrapped around a wide variety of phrases and sentences — everything to do with the way they hunted the buffalo and the way they

313

butchered them. The language — all the slang and swearing, all the wordplay and joking, all the various comments and utterances that might have taken place around the fire after a big kill — that's the real stuff. Even the grunts and shrugs between the words would hold communicative content.

To understand it all, we would have to be there. We would have to be brought up in that particular society, in that particular place, at that particular time. It's something lost to us, probably lost even to those few souls who still speak the Tsuu T'ina language today with any fluency. No one now on the Tsuu T'ina lands speaks only Tsuu T'ina. They're all bilingual and speak English more and more in their everyday lives. No one hunts the buffalo anymore, and though they do keep buffalo on the Tsuu T'ina nation — I've seen them between the trees — the times are long gone when they would run them off cliffs, when they would butcher them and live in teepees made from their hides.

Words change with the world around them. It's a central feature of all languages. Nothing stays the same for long. *Buffalo* in the Tsuu T'ina dialect today is *xāná-tíyí*, which means *real* buffalo or *natural* buffalo. This serves to distinguish them from the domestic cattle that now range across the ranchlands.

And so it goes.

314

Ψ

When the powwow was over, I walked around the grounds for a while. The setting sun cast long shadows. Children played with water pistols. A few of the older kids were out behind a shed, sneaking cigarettes. One old battered Winnebago sat on the field not too far from my own car. It had Arizona plates, and when I came around the side, a family had a barbecue going. They were cooking hamburgers — everyday normal beef — and the scent of it drew me closer.

"Hi," I said.

They looked up from their cooking. One guy had a metal spatula in his hand, and except for the braids in his hair, he could have been any father barbecuing up a storm in the suburbs.

"You from Arizona?" I asked.

"Yeah."

"You drove up here all this way?"

"Yeah, sure."

"Are you ... Navajo?"

The father flipped a burger over. "Yup, that's us. Do you want a burger?"

"Um, okay."

"Ketchup ... mayonnaise?"

"Maybe a little mayonnaise, please. Thanks."

He passed me the burger. It was delicious.

"So," I said, "can I ask you ... do you also speak the Dene language?"

"Navajo is a Dene language, yeah."

"So can you understand the Tsuu T'ina?"

"Well, a little, yeah. If they speak really slowly, I can make out a few of the words. They've got a funny pronunciation, though."

Water in the Tsuu T'ina dialect is *tu*. In Navajo it's *tó*. The sun and the moon are *Sa* and *Tɛdhɛzaɛ́* in Tsuu T'ina. In Navajo they're *Shá* and *Tłéhonaaʼéí*. Clearly, they're dialects of the same language. But here's the thing. The Northern Dene, like the Willow Lake people at Talita, live in a land where winter still rules. They hunt caribou and cross frozen lakes for a good part of the year. The Tsuu T'ina live on the Great Plains and hunted, for centuries, the great herds of buffalo. The Navajo, meanwhile, are an agricultural people living in pueblo villages, growing corn and beans, and wearing jewellery of turquoise and copper.

Halfway through my burger, I remembered a phrase I'd studied in Navajo. Very likely my pronunciation of it was horrendous, but I tried, anyway. "What," I said, "does *sǫ́ǫh naaghái bikʼeh hózhóʼ* mean to you?"

315

He looked up quickly. "How did you know that?" I sensed a little edge in his voice now, and I thought for a moment that this was something I shouldn't have asked about. This time I really was parking, so to speak, on sacred land.

"Those are words we use in our ceremonies," he said. He didn't correct my pronunciation and he didn't seem as if he wanted to say more about it. On the other hand, he didn't seem ready to grab my hamburger and tell me to get lost. I changed the subject, and we chatted about things that were a little less personal ... a little less sacred.

Later I watched their Winnebago trundle off across the field, throwing up a cloud of dust behind it. They had a long way to go home — three or four days of straight driving. Now they could follow the blacktop all the way down, but a thousand years ago, more or less, the Navajo really would have moved south from here, right through here. It might have taken a few hundred years to get all the way to Arizona, stopping here and there, adapting to new ways of life. But something kept the Navajo pushing farther and farther down the continent. Something made these Dene speakers finally lose the ways of the ice and snow, lose the ways of the buffalo and come, at last, to the canyon lands of the far south.

I should say here that most Navajo, and I suspect a fair number of Dene and Tsuu T'ina people, won't be happy with all this talk of migration. It doesn't help with legal land claims. Many First Nations peoples have oral histories and creation stories saying they've always been in the same place, and they surely have for many hundreds of years. I'm just saying that the linguistic records — and a few of their own oral histories, such as Helen Meguinis's lovely story — point to a long, slow movement down the continent. Again we're talking slow here, over hundreds and hundreds, probably thousands of years. So the point is kind of moot.

An even longer record, the DNA one, shows that all peoples move, given enough time. People travelled from Africa into

316

Asia. Some looped from there into Europe. Others, out on the far edges of Asia, moved at last into the new continents of North and South America. And so it goes. We're a wandering species. We go where the food is cheap and the weather is bearable. We just don't go very quickly.

ξ

The Navajo are now the largest First Nation in the United States. *Dinétah*, or the land of the Diné people — the Navajo — stretches over the four corners between Arizona, Utah, Colorado, and New Mexico. It's a reservation as big as some states.

Navajo is thought to be a Spanish term, possibly from the archaic Spanish word *nava*, meaning "secluded valley," something like the Old English *dell* or *vale*. A document from 1620 refers to the Navajo as the Apachu de Nabajo. Their lands now encompass about seventeen million acres, covering most of the so-called Colorado Plateau, a high desert of red rock canyons and waterfalls, of rattlesnakes and sandstone arches under a brilliant deep blue sky.

The Navajo language has somewhere between one hundred and twenty thousand and one hundred and fifty thousand speakers, making it one of the most widely spoken indigenous languages in all of North America. It's also one of the most carefully documented. One of its early proponents, in fact, was Benjamin Whorf.

"The world," Whorf wrote, "is presented in a kaleidoscopic flux of impressions which has to be organized by our minds. We cut nature up, organize it into concepts, and ascribe significances as we do, largely because we are parties to an agreement to organize it in this way — an agreement that holds throughout our speech community and is codified in the patterns of our language."

Like the colour studies, many tests were done on Navajo speakers, but pretty much all of them failed to show that a

317

strong version of the Sapir-Whorf hypothesis can exist. After all, Noam Chomsky and his crew have pretty much shown that grammars — all grammars — are simply variations of something fundamental, something that's hardwired into the brain of each and every human being no matter what language they speak.

But there's much more to language than grammar, and there's got to be something in the ideas of Sapir and Whorf. It's just a matter of common sense to believe that when we think in a language — English, say — the peculiarities of that language may serve to shape our thoughts … or if not our thoughts exactly, something about our way of being in the world. The Sapir-Whorf hypothesis says we can't think outside of the box that is our language. A more acceptable theory is simply to admit there is a box, whether or not we think outside of it.

And that's the essence of linguistic relativity.

From the town of Santa Fe in New Mexico you can see a silver line of mountains — the Sangre de Cristo range. These mountains are the southernmost spur of the Rocky Mountains. It's here that the spine of the continent finally peters out.

I'd come down in January, hoping to escape winter. The photos I'd seen of New Mexico showed a red rock desert with stunted spruces and cactus-like shrubbery. It was a pretty, sun-splashed place, so I was a little surprised to step off the airplane and into an icy blast of wind. What I hadn't counted on was the altitude. Sante Fe is more than two thousand metres high. While the afternoons at least approximated warmth, the mornings and evenings were bone-crackingly cold.

I'd come down to meet up with an old friend once again. Lesley, the English doctor, the one I'd travelled through Italy with, was here visiting her father. He was a physicist from Oxford University, and he, too, had his reasons for being here.

Lesley picked me up at the airport, and we drove down into the centre of the old town. We walked into the central plaza. At one end is the Palace of the Governors, an old adobe structure that dates back to 1610. Out front, under a colonnade, a long line of women hunched under blankets, selling copper and turquoise jewellery. Most of them were Pueblo Indian, but a few were Hopi, and a couple of the women at one end were Navajo.

We shuffled along, looking at their wares. I bought a few things, and we chatted merrily with the old women. They all had faces that were darkened and cracked by the sun, but their nimble hands darted over the blankets, offering up this or that piece of jewellery. I asked them about the designs and found out that many of them were hundreds of years old, shapes that were carved into the rock in the surrounding canyons, petroglyphs of strange humpbacked stick figures, of turtles and rabbits and eagles. One set of earrings had a spiral pattern that was the Hopi symbol of migration.

Lesley and I pored over the stuff, buying bits and baubles for the people back home. A man in the square was roasting corn over a brazier, and that got me thinking again. The Navajo root word for corn is *naadą́ą́ʼ*. It's a word that didn't exist for the Northern Dene or the Tsuu T'ina. The entire concept of agriculture simply didn't exist on the northern plains, but it's central to the Navajo (and to the Hopi, of course), so here was another little litmus test for language. Corn is as basic to these people's lifestyles as the buffalo were to the Tsuu T'ina. It's the very building block of their culture.

The Navajo still have a word for buffalo — *ayání* — a term closely related to the old Tsuu T'ina. Evidently, it's a word that followed the southward migration of the Dene people, even though there are no buffalo in the Navajo lands.

Lesley and I went over to where the man was selling roasted corncobs, and Lesley turned to me. "Did you know," she asked, "that the Hopi have over a hundred words for corn?"

"Oh, good God!" I groaned.

"What?" Lesley looked at me, puzzled. "What did I say?"

Ω

We drove north and west of Santa Fe, past a place called Los Alamos. It's right on the edge of the Navajo lands. Even as we wound down the road toward it, something about the name jogged at my memory. Los Alamos. Why did that sound so familiar? Then it came to me.

Los Alamos is where Americans built and exploded the first atomic bomb. During the dying days of the Second World War, Robert Oppenheimer and his team unleashed a new kind of weapon, one that forever changed the world.

Los Alamos today is an unremarkable little town. Two fingers of land — the south mesa and the north mesa — stick out over a series of dusty ravines. At the edge of the south mesa the Los Alamos National Laboratory still rises above the hoodoos. It continues to draw some of the top physicists in the world, and yes, there's still a lot of research being done on nuclear weapons, though they don't actually explode them here anymore. Given the times, there's a lot of security. The research facilities are very much off limits and very top secret.

Of course, anyone who's ever read much about the Second World War knows that it was a conflict won thanks to superior technological development — well, superior technological development and knowing what the other guy was up to. Spying and code-breaking played almost as big a role as the technology, and one of the best of these stories involved the Navajo.

In 1942, even before the Manhattan Project was initiated, the Navajo were enlisted in the war effort in a way no one possibly could have imagined. Twenty-nine Navajo men were recruited to put together a code that was never broken by the Germans or the Japanese. These Navajo men were known as Windtalkers.

That name comes from the Navajo word for wind — *honílch'i* — which also refers to a person's soul or life force.

The code they developed consisted of two parts: a sort of alphabet based on Navajo words and a short dictionary of manufactured slang. The alphabet part worked in much the same way that military radio operators have always worked. "Alpha" stands for the letter *A*. "Charlie" stands for *C*, and so on. Now the Navajo code took that a step farther, using Navajo translations so that *A* became *wol-la-chee*, which is the Navajo word for *ant*. *B* became *shush*, or *bear* in Navajo. *C* became *moasi*, the Navajo word for *cat*.

To make things run more quickly, though, a list of common words was drawn up and coded into an invented slang. A bomb in the Windtalker code became *a-ye-shi*, which in Navajo means "egg." A fighter plane was *da-he-tih-hi*, "hummingbird," and a tank was *chayda gahi*, "tortoise." For the navy a battleship was *lo-tso*, "whale," while a destroyer was *ca-lo*, "shark," and a submarine was *besh-lo*, literally "iron fish."

After the war, it took a long time for the Navajo Windtalkers to be recognized. The code was kept officially classified until 1968, and it wasn't until 1981 that the Navajo part in the war was formally honoured. Many of the Windtalkers (and there were almost four hundred of them by the end of the war) died without receiving any sort of military pension. But their part in the war effort was enormous. The code played a huge role in campaigns such as the Battle of Iwo Jima. It was used right until the end of the war when two very big "eggs," atomic bombs, were dropped on Hiroshima and Nagasaki.

Languages really are a sort of code, one that a set number of people have agreed upon, whether it's a few dozen Tsuu T'ina speakers, a hundred thousand Navajo, or five hundred million English speakers.

"Every language," Benjamin Whorf wrote, "is a vast pattern-system ... by which the personality not only communicates, but also analyzes nature, channels its reasoning, and builds the house of consciousness." It's those last three words that are important —House of Consciousness.

Each language *is* different. They encode things from our particular environments like snow or buffalo or corn, but it's more than that. There are subtleties in the understandings. There are metaphors, connotations, and social constructions that go far beyond the simple assigning of a word to a thing.

And that's the point. Our thinking isn't constrained by our language — there are just too many other semiotic systems at play — but our language is the central encoder and processor of the information that our brains receive from the outside world. It's the frame for our House of Consciousness. It's the load-bearing wall, and as such it helps to create our immediate personal experience of the world, our phenomenological sense of our everyday lives. It's the world we inhabit and the very root of linguistic relativity. It is, once again, our Palace of Words.

Φ

The Navajo are still a large and powerful group of people. They've managed to hang on to many of their ceremonial systems in the face of a strange new world, a realm of skyscrapers and nuclear weapons. Many Navajo continue to live in mud-walled *hogans* … and their code hasn't been broken yet.

The Navajo belief system is unbelievably complex. Even different groups within the Navajo community approach things in slightly different ways. But perhaps that's how it should be. There's nothing neat and tidy about life. Defining whole worlds can't help but get a bit messy.

There's at least one thing, though, that all Navajo would recognize, and that's the singular importance of the phrase *Są́ąh naagháí bik'eh hózhó* — the same phrase I tried out at the Navajo barbecue in Alberta with the guys in the Winnebago. I didn't know it then, but it turns out that the phrase is a textbook case of linguistic relativity. It's almost impossible to adequately translate it into English but, seeing as I'm already into it up to my eyeballs, I'll give it my best shot.

Now bear with me here.

Sǫ́ąh is a derivative of the past tense verb *to grow* or *to mature*. *Naagháí*, meanwhile, is one of about 356,200 distinct inflected forms of the verb *to go* (it's the singular form of the third person of the continuative-imperfective mode, if you really want to know), and it refers to a continuous going about and returning. When talking about a person, it means unendingly walking around, the metaphor being that we *walk* through life. *Bik'eh* is the simplest of the words in the phrase. It just means "according to" or "by its decree."

And then there's *hózhó* which, in truth, would take pages and pages of English to even come close to describing. *Hózhó* is often translated as "beauty," though it's much more than that. It includes everything that a Navajo thinks of as being good. Beauty, yes, but also perfection, harmony, goodness, normality, success, well-being, and order … an idea perhaps not unlike the Chinese concept of Tao.

So a simple translation of the entire phrase — one that leaves out all the allusions and connotations, all the richness of a thousand years of experience — would be something akin to a wish to unendingly move along a path of goodness well into one's maturity and old age.

The phrase is the centrepiece of one of the most important of all Navajo ceremonies — what in English is called the Blessingway chant. The Blessingway chant goes on for days, and it's designed to right the world, to bring the world or the individual back into balance, back into harmony and goodness.

The full phrase, though, isn't only for religious ceremonies. It's also used in everyday Navajo life. A Navajo uses this concept to express his happiness and his health. It's employed to remind people to be careful, and a shortened version of it is even used to say goodbye to someone.

To be poetic (because sometimes poetry can do things that normal prose can't), we might even reduce it all to this: "May you always walk the trail of beauty."

And that's something I like very much.

Ψ

We all walk, I suppose, down these long trails of beauty, these long lines of history. We have been cast across continents and oceans and we have named them all. We have conjured up countless worlds in a thousand different tongues.

We are symbol-smiths. We are the spinners of tales. We are the builders — and memory keepers — of entire civilizations. And with our languages we call ourselves into being and sparkle, for a time, like stars over a dark and silent world.

Epilogue: The Unimaginable Future

I've been through more than fifty countries now. I've been caught in snowstorms and lost in jungles. I've been attacked by sharks and mauled by dogs, but my most terrifying adventure was yet to come. I was going to teach teenagers. My job would be to work with immigrant kids at a high school in Calgary. I was going to teach them English.

I got ready early in the morning before the first class, practising my lines in front of the mirror. "Good morning, everybody," I would say. I would write my name in neat, chalky lines on the blackboard. Twenty pairs of eyes would look up at me and twenty young sets of minds would rip me to shreds. I was sure of it.

When they shuffled into the classroom under the buzz of fluorescent lights, though, they were even more apprehensive than I was. Rupinder, a girl from the Punjab, arrived in a flash of colour, wearing her best sari. Two girls from Afghanistan hid under their head scarves. I couldn't get them to look up. Omojok and another boy came from Sudan. They had nothing. They'd never even been to a real school before. All of them sat hesitantly, their eyes darting nervously around the classroom.

A Chinese girl, Xi Chen, sat with two sisters from Vietnam. The boys sat in clumps at the back. Some of the students spoke a little English. Rupinder had learned English in India. A few others, knowing they would be coming to Canada, had picked up what they could from American movies and magazines. Still, they were caught off guard by the reality of it all: the brick walls, the strangely pale teacher, the posters of Garfield the cat left behind by a well-meaning teacher long ago. I caught a few of the students glancing at the posters. Why was there a cat talking? What was it saying and who taught it how to stand up?

Omojok and the other boy, Keyak, came from southern Sudan. Their dark faces were empty of emotion. Not even confusion was there. Their faces were simply blank. They had a language in common, Nuer — something I'd never heard of — but even that was neither of their mother tongues. Omojok spoke a tribal language called Shilluk. It's spoken along the western banks of the Upper Nile. Keyak, meanwhile, spoke Dinka, the traditional language of the cattle herders in the grasslands.

Xi Chen, from China, had been educated in Mandarin, but her first language was really Suīxī, a dialect from the south. A couple of more kids were from Afghanistan. They spoke neither Arabic nor Farsi (what we call Persian). Instead, they only knew the language of the mountain passes behind Kabul — a language called Pashtu.

This was the real global village right here in front of me, staring at me, waiting for me to begin.

ع

"Okay," I said, "let's see what you already know. We'll start with some of the verbs. I wrote the word *walk* on the board and made a walking motion with my fingers. "Walk," I said, dutifully striding back and forth along the front of the classroom. A few of them mimicked the word. All of their eyes were on me.

Rupinder put up her hand. A few wary faces turned to her. Some, I could tell, didn't know what it meant to put up a hand. I could see them trying to work it out, glancing back at me for clues.

"Yes ... uh ..." I looked down to check the names on the attendance sheet. "Yes, Rupinder?"

"The past tense of *walk* is *walked.*" She spoke with the musical phrasing of the Indian subcontinent.

"That's right," I said, smiling. Encouraged, I blundered on. "Now, *drink* ... that one's more complicated." I cupped my palms as if to drink, slurping noisily. A few of the kids chuckled. "Drink."

"Drink," Omojok repeated. He tried out the word carefully. Keyak, beside him, was still blank.

Rupinder's hand swept into the air again, this time waving a little more insistently.

"Yes, Rupinder?" I had a keener here, I thought. Already I was thinking that it would be important to keep her in check, to allow the other kids a chance.

"The past tense is *drank.* The past participle is *drunk.*"

"Right again, Rupinder."

This girl was a walking grammar book. She looked around proudly at the other students, and I decided to steer the lesson in a different direction. I'd already made some labels. I'd put the word *clock* up on the clock. I'd put the word *desk* on the teacher's desk at the front. I gestured toward one of the labels. "I think now, class, we'll look at —"

Rupinder raised her hand. "The past tense of *think*," she said automatically, "is *thank.*"

"Well, *thank* is a different word, Rupinder." The poor girl was suddenly confused. "Like in *thank you.*"

The class bubbled up. Everyone seemed to know this one. "Thank you, thank you," they mouthed between themselves. Here was something they all knew. Even Omojok managed a smile.

"No, no ... the past tense of *think* is *thought.*" I turned to write the word on the board. "*Thought.*"

327

Expressions of confusion were all around now. I seemed to have messed things up, but what was I to do? I pushed on regardless, and somehow I made it through to the bell. The following days weren't a whole lot better, either. Rupinder continued to dominate the class, but she didn't seem to be learning anything. On a quiz at the end of the week she tried to conjugate the verb *wake*. *Wake*, she wrote. Past tense: *woke*. Past participle: *wank*.

I didn't have the heart to tell her she was wrong.

ع

Outside the windows the long grass of the playing fields called to the kids. Omojok tried out and made it onto the school soccer team. It turned out he'd been kicking a soccer ball around since he'd first learned to walk. He had astounding skills and, being a big kid with a big smile, he easily made the team despite his lack of English. His feet spoke the universal language of soccer.

All the students started to reveal their true personalities. Xi Chen displayed a remarkable aptitude for art. She folded little paper dragons and gave me one. I sent her up to the art class where she began to produce some very fine drawings.

Rupinder wore blue jeans for the first time, and all the kids tried out short phrases in English. I picked up bits and pieces of their languages, too. Right from the beginning, on any given morning, I'd be greeted in any one of seven or eight languages. Their own languages flipped from their tongues like water splashing onto hot pavement. "*Zhou sun*, Mr. Dixon," Xi would say. One of the Afghan girls called me *ma'lim*, which in Pashtu means "teacher."

I smiled and tried to answer back with a word or two in their own language. It was the least I could do to say "good morning" in Mandarin or "thank you" in Punjabi. They giggled at my pronunciation, but things were getting better, and in light of all the struggles they had to endure, my linguistic contributions were pretty modest.

I would try to catch them off guard sometimes, too. I learned how to say "Could you please be quiet" in Pashtu. I used it on a lone Afghani boy, Humayoun, who was already starting to act up. He responded first with alarm, his eyes growing wide. Then his face melted into a smile. "It good, Mr. Dixon. You speak good."

Humayoun was tall, lanky, and a bit clumsy. He'd been caught in the middle of a sort of mini civil war between the Taliban and the Hozara people — the tribal group to which he belonged. He'd witnessed a massacre. His own uncle was murdered in front of him, but he managed to escape over the Khyber Pass and into Pakistan. From there the story got even crazier. He wound up in Cambodia of all places. For a year he lived in the back alleys of Phnom Penh without identification or papers of any kind.

The strange thing is that Humayoun, for all his hardships, turned out to be the comedian of the group. It doesn't seem to matter where they come from, kids are kids, and every class has its clown. Humayoun was mine.

329

Humayoun played his first trick on me in early October. When I asked him how to say "goodbye" in Pashtu, he taught me a little phrase — *Pishte pishte*. After that I called it out to the Afghani girls at the end of the day when they were leaving, though I noticed they looked at me a little strangely when I said it.

It turned out that Humayoun hadn't taught me "goodbye" at all. He taught me a phrase used for shooing cats away. At best it translates as something like "Go on. Scoot. Get out of here." For weeks I stood at the door at the end of the day, politely intoning this phrase to the girls, who were too polite to say anything. It took me some time to realize that Humayoun, guffawing down the hall, had pulled a fast one on me.

But that was just fine with me. If they were laughing, I knew they would be all right. I knew they'd be ready to learn.

ㄱ

One morning, still early in the year, with the days beginning to darken, I arrived at the school and unlocked the door to my classroom. I went across to the staff room to get a coffee, and when I returned, I found three of my students standing at the window at the back of the room. Something had caught their attention, and there they stood, wide-eyed and silent.

Omojok was there with Keyak, and the third, a girl, was from Vietnam. I stood behind them, coffee in hand, and it took me a minute to realize what they were staring at. It was snowing. Great gentle flakes were drifting down. None of the three had ever seen snow before.

Omojok turned to me, his face shining. He spoke a word he'd learned only a day or two before, forming it carefully on his lips, his eyes beaming. "Beautiful," he said. "Beautiful."

It was a start.

Ω

Throughout the year new students kept coming — often arriving at the most inopportune times. I'd get a call from the secretary, and down I'd go to the office to meet with another overwhelmed and bewildered immigrant family. I'd try to explain about bus routes and library cards. I'd go slowly through the classes their sons and daughters would need, pushing forms at them, explaining where they needed to sign, trying to get them to relax, to see that everything was all right.

In late October a new girl arrived from Mongolia. I was quite excited. I'd never had a student from there before. The girl's name was a convolution of syllables, but the mother, who spoke a bit of English, asked me to call her Sodah. It was an approximation of the first couple of syllables, anyway. "Like

Coca-Cola," the mother said, trying out a smile. "You can call her Sodah."

Sodah had the round moon face I'd become familiar with in Tibet. It was the same part of the world — the high plateau north of the Himalayas. Home for Sodah had been Ulan Bator, the capital of Mongolia. She arrived in the first blast of really cold weather, but that wasn't a problem for her. The climate on the steppes of Mongolia is quite similar to ours. Even the geography of the prairies is much the same. Sodah had been educated in a Russian school, and her eyes showed a quick intelligence. She took everything in, surveying this new world with interest, even enthusiasm.

Her first day of classes was to be October 31. What I hadn't counted on was that her first-class teacher decided to dress up as a witch for Halloween. Mrs. Taylor met us at the door. She wore a high pointed black hat, a long black cape, and a smear of mascara around her eyes. And she didn't break character for this new student. "Come in, come in," she cackled, and I saw poor Sodah's eyes widen. Was this how teachers dressed in Canada? What sort of strange rabbit hole had she fallen down?

331

Φ

At Christmastime I put up a little Christmas tree in the classroom. I wasn't really supposed to. The school board was now calling it the winter break, but I thought that was garbage. The students had asked me about Christmas, and I couldn't think of any good reason why I shouldn't tell all about the traditions I'd grown up with. Just as I was trying to understand their cultures, they were trying to comprehend mine. That was what it was all about. So I had them come up one by one and put an ornament on the tree. Rupinder put the angel on the top.

I was astounded when Xi Chen and the Vietnamese girls broke into a squeaky version of "Jingle Bells."

"We learned it in our country," they told me happily. "Everyone knows this song. But, Mr. Dixon, what is a jingle bell?"

Into the new year they came bundled against the deep Canadian winter, and the riddles of Canadian life began to unfold for them. They asked me about bank machines and driver's licences. A boy from India started to cheer for the Calgary Flames hockey team, announcing the scores proudly to me each morning before class. He began to wear a big team jersey that floated around his skinny shoulders. He still wore his turban, but the jersey was like a signal to the Canadian-born kids in the school. This was, after all, still a regular high school. The so-called "regular" students now talked with him in the hall. They called out to him, "Hey, Gurdip, how'd we do last night?"

"Two nothing," Gurdip replied. "We clobbered them."

Clobbered, I thought. I knew I hadn't taught him that word. It seemed that my students were acquiring English from all sorts of sources. They were soaking up Canadian television programs and reading Canadian magazines. And most of all they were listening carefully to the other students in the hallways, drawing out language like "Awesome" and "Catch you later" and "What's up?" — words far more useful than the ones I was giving them on their vocabulary lists.

After school one day, I discovered that someone had written something on one of the desks. It was an English word, all right, though it was misspelled. "Fuk," it said in tightly pencilled letters.

Humayoun, I thought instantly. *That looks like his handwriting.*

Ψ

Early in the spring I started an art class. Xi Chen had inspired me. The art teacher was raving about her, and already there was talk of her going to art college. My kids had been squirming in their desks for sometime now. There were only so many grammar exercises they could take. So for an hour a day I took them up to the art class to do some drawing and painting.

Most of them took to it easily. Only one boy, Keyak, still seemed to struggle. He had never seen things like scissors or Scotch tape, and his hands weren't used to holding them. He sat by himself in the corner and didn't really talk to anyone. Omojok, meanwhile, had blossomed in this new world, but Keyak remained closed off. He had, I learned, walked several hundred kilometres by himself to get to a refugee camp along the Ethiopian border. His family was gone. They had dropped off one by one on the long march and he alone had survived. Keyak smiled in a kindly way when I tried to help him, but he seemed resigned to doing poorly. Sometimes he just sat and stared at nothing.

The others tumbled joyfully through their projects — drawing animals and buildings and rocket ships. I showed them three-point perspective and explained colour theory, and they ate it up. There was a slight lurch with the Muslim students when we learned how to draw human faces. Such representations aren't allowed in mosques, and in their stead a great tradition of abstract tile work has grown up. So I gave the Muslim students the option of drawing these abstract designs. They didn't like that much, though. In the end, they all went home and came back the next day with notes from their parents, allowing and even encouraging them to draw whatever was normally drawn in "English" art classes.

One day Zeeshan, the boy from Pakistan, wrote out the Prophet Muhammad's name in a beautiful ornate Arabic script. It filled the paper in tight curlicues, and I accepted it for extra marks, then put it on the wall.

Many weeks later, when it was time to change the displays, Zeeshan asked about the paper. "What you do now?" he asked. Something was bothering him.

"Well, we'll just put the paper in the recycling bin with the other papers … unless you want to take it home."

333

"No, I no take it home. But, Mr. Dixon ... recycling no good also."

I held the paper uncertainly. I wasn't sure what he was trying to say.

"It is the name of Muhammad," he went on seriously. "We cannot ..." He didn't quite know how to continue. "We, uh, we are not allowed to put this name in the garbage. Do you understand?"

"Oh ... then what should I do?"

"In our tradition, for respect, you must burn the paper, so it not touch garbage. So that it not ... unclean. You understand?"

"Yes, yes, I understand."

So later, out around the back of the school, where the bad kids went to sneak cigarettes, I found myself hunched over the paper with a pack of matches. Hidden from view, I lit the paper and watched it curl up in a tight ball of flame. How would I explain this if anyone happened along? What was a teacher doing lighting fires behind the school?

ع

When spring came, we moved onto clay sculpture, and the kids got up to their elbows in the wet, cool clay. This was something more familiar to a lot of them. They made little bowls and figurines. Zeeshan put together a set of chess pieces. They were really quite good.

Off in the corner, Keyak began to take an interest. He worked over his glob of clay, pinching and pulling at it, and when I went over to see what he was doing, he held the form up to me. It was the figure of an ox, perfectly fashioned, its stylized horns and square body the very image of his traditional culture. "Oh, Keyak," I said, "that's beautiful."

The other students gathered around to admire the ox, and for the first time Keyak broke into a wide, toothy grin. We fired his little ox in the kiln and glazed it so that it shone. At the end of the semester Keyak gave it to me. "In my language," he told me, "it is called a *yok*. It is worth … everything."

I still have Keyak's figurine on my mantelpiece among all the other treasures I've accumulated from around the world. It's the only one that isn't from a far-off country. Except, though, it is.

ㅋ

At the very end of the year we had a final exam. My students had to write an essay on "setting goals." What was it they wanted to do in the future? Where were they going now that they had settled into this new country, this strange new language? Some of them wrote about wanting to go to university, wanting to be doctors one day or engineers. Omojok told me he wanted to be a teacher. Well, he wanted to be a professional soccer coach, but if that didn't work out, then he wanted to be a teacher. "Just like you, Mr. Dixon," he said. "Just like you."

335

Humayoun played his final card of the year. "The most important thing," he wrote in the very first sentence, "is setting your goals." Only he didn't write it quite like that. His lazy pen forgot to cross the *t*'s. Instead, the blue ink strayed across and crossed the *l* on the word *goals*. So what he really wrote was this: "The most important thing is *selling your goats*."

I couldn't be sure if he'd made an honest mistake or whether this was his last chance to make a joke. I think, though, that I caught the flash of a smile as he walked out of that final class.

Ω

These students of mine are the unimaginable future. What they do with their lives and their languages will, most likely, be a complete surprise … even to them. New meanings will emerge. New Ways of Being will unfold.

We are already living in a postmodern world where we speak easily of reheating pad thai in our microwaves, of flipping past Bollywood movies on our television sets. The world has come to us, and we can't expect that things will ever be the same. After all, they never have been.

A bright new world is emerging, despite all news reports to the contrary. Humans are meaning-making creatures, comfortable in a wild array of different conceptual systems. Yet we still feel sadness and love. We all experience fear, regret, hope, and joy. We are all concerned with "selling our goats."

So, though we come from different places, from completely different worlds, we all still pull to the sense of human touch. We all eat and sleep and dream in much the same way. To understand this is to reach the top of the Tower of Babel where nothing like mere words can prevent us from understanding one another.

Bibliography

Abley, Mark. *Spoken Here: Travels Among Threatened Languages*. Toronto: Random House Canada, 2003.

Belsey, Catherine. *Poststructuralism: A Very Short Introduction*. Oxford, Eng.: Oxford University Press, 2002.

Bergreen, Laurence. *Marco Polo: From Venice to Xanadu*. New York: Alfred A. Knopf, 2007.

Boroditsky, Lera. "Linguistic Relativity," in L. Nadel, ed., *Encyclopedia of Cognitive Science*. London: Macmillan, 2003.

Boroditsky, Lera, and D. Casasanto. *Time in the Mind: Using Space to Think About Time*. Cognition.doi:10.1016/j.cognition. 2007.03.004.

Bringhurst, Robert. *A Story as Sharp as a Knife*. Vancouver: Douglas & Mcintyre, 1999.

Brosnahan, Tom, and Pat Yale. *Turkey: A Travel Survival Kit*. 5th ed. Hawthorne, Australia: Lonely Planet Publications, 1993.

Bukkyō Dendō Kyōkai. *The Teachings of Buddha*. Tokyo: Kosaido Printing Company, 1966.

Campbell, David A. *Greek Lyric Poetry, Volume I, Sappho and Alcaeus.* Cambridge, MA: Harvard University Press, 1982.

Campbell, Joseph. *The Power of Myth.* New York: Doubleday, 1988.

Carroll, John B., ed. *Language, Thought, and Reality.* Cambridge, MA: Massachusetts Institute of Technology Press, 1956.

Chandler, David P. *The Land and People of Cambodia.* New York: J.B. Lippincott, 1972.

Clark, Virginia, et al. *Language: Introductory Readings.* New York: St. Martin's Press, 1985.

Coe, William. *Tikal: A Handbook of the Ancient Maya Ruins.* Philadelphia: University of Pennsylvania Press, 1988.

Cook, Eung-Do. *A Sarcee Grammar.* Vancouver: University of British Columbia Press, 1984.

Crystal, David. *Language and the Internet.* Cambridge, Eng.: Cambridge University Press, 2006.

Davies, Philip R., et al. *The Complete World of the Dead Sea Scrolls.* London: Thames and Hudson, 2002.

Das, Lama Surya. *Awakening the Buddha Within: Tibetan Wisdom for the Western World.* New York: Broadway Books, 1997.

Department of the Navy. *Navajo Code Talkers' Dictionary.* Naval Historical Center. *www.history.navy.mil/faqs/faq6104.htm*, June 15, 1945.

Descola, Philippe. *The Spears of Twilight: Life and Death in the Amazon Jungle.* New York: New Press, 1996.

Dixon, Glenn. *On Thinking in a Second Language: Towards a Phenomenological Accounting of Second Language Consciousness.* Calgary: University of Calgary, 1996.

Dorje, Gyurme, trans. *The Tibetan Book of the Dead*. New York: Penguin, 2006.

Edwards, Steven. "Unravelling the Inca Code." *Calgary Herald*, July 12, 2003.

Ferrell, Robert H. "Truman and the Bomb." The Truman Presidential Museum and Library. *www.trumanlibrary.org*, August 30, 2002.

Geary, James. "Speaking in Tongues." *Time*, July 7, 1997.

Goodwin, Bill. *Frommer's South Pacific*. 11th ed. Hoboken, NJ: Wiley Publishing, 2008.

Hall, Stephen S. "Last of the Neanderthals." *National Geographic*, October 2008.

Hilton, Isabel. *Spies in the House of Faith: The Best American Travel Writing 2000*. New York: Houghton Mifflin, 2000.

Homer. *The Odyssey*. Trans. Robert Fagles. New York: Penguin, 1996.

_____. *The Odyssey*. Trans. Robert Fitzgerald. New York: Farrar, Straus and Giroux, 1998.

Hooker, Richard. *Arete: Virtue, Excellence, Goodness*. *www.wsu.edu/~dee?glossary/arete.htm*, December 2002.

Hreinsson, Vidar. *The Complete Sagas of the Icelanders*. Reykjavik: Leifur Eiriksson Publishing, 1997.

Hynes-Berry, Mary, and Basia C Miller. *Responding to Literature*. New York: McDougal, Littell, and Company, 1992.

Janson, Tore. *Speak: A Short History of Languages*. New York: Oxford University Press, 2002.

Kahn, David. *The Codebreakers*. New York: Macmillan, 1967.

Kazutoshi, Hando. *Japan's Longest Day*. Tokyo: Kodansha International, 1968.

Kluster, Paul. "Endangered Speech." *Avenue*, April 2007.

Lakoff, George, and Mark Johnson. *Metaphors We Live By*. Chicago: University of Chicago Press, 1980.

Laye, Bill. *First Nations: Settling the Land Before Time*. Calgary: Sun Media, 2005.

McWhorter, John. *The Power of Babel: A Natural History of Language*. New York: Harper Perennial, 2001.

Mydans, Seth. "Cambodian Aesop Tells a Fable of Forgiveness." *New York Times*, June 28, 1997.

Nuñez, Rafael E., and Eve Sweetser. "With the Future Behind Them: Convergent Evidence from Aymara Language and Gesture in the Crosslinguistic Comparison of Spatial Construals of Time." *Cognitive Science Journal* 30:3 (May 2006), 401–50.

O'Grady, William, and Michael Dobrovolsky. *Contemporary Linguistic Analysis*. New York: Copp Clark Pitman, 1987.

Owen, Richard. "Art Master's Wall Sketches Unveiled." *Calgary Herald*, April 16, 2003.

Peritz, Ingrid. "Where Words Define the 'Perfect Citizen.'" *Globe and Mail*, April 3, 2004.

Pinker, Steven. *How the Mind Works*. New York: W.W. Norton and Company, 1997.

_____. *The Stuff of Thought: Language as a Window into Human Nature*. New York: Penguin, 2008.

Pirsig, Robert. *Zen and the Art of Motorcycle Maintenance: An Inquiry into Values*. New York: Bantam, 1974.

Pullum, Geoffrey. *The Great Eskimo Vocabulary Hoax and Other Irreverent Essays on the Study of Language*. Chicago: University of Chicago Press, 1991.

Quarrington, Paul. "All You Need Is Love and Joy, and ..." *Globe and Mail*, September 13, 2008.

Shanks, Hershel. *The Mystery and Meaning of the Dead Sea Scrolls*. New York: Vintage Books, 1998.

Shorris, Earl. "The Last Word: Can the World's Small Languages Be Saved." *Harper's*, August 2000.

Theroux, Paul. *The Happy Isles of Oceania*. New York: G.P. Putnam's Sons, 1992.

Watzlawick, Paul, et al. *Pragmatics of Human Communication*. New York: W.W. Norton, 1967.

Witherspoon, Gary. "Language and Reality in Navajo World View," in *Handbook of North American Indians*. Ed. Alfonzo Ortiz. Vol. 10. Washington, DC: Smithsonian Institution, 1983.

Wittgenstein, Ludwig. *Philosophical Investigations*. London: Basil Blackwell and Mott, 1958.

Acknowledgements

This book, of course, owes its existence to those I met along the way. Some of you appear in the book (and, except in one instance to protect his safety, I haven't changed your names), many others don't appear directly, though your voices and thoughts resonate on every page. You told me your stories and answered with delight the many questions I had about your languages and cultures. I thank you and hope you are all well.

I would like to thank the professors I had while doing my graduate work. You fostered well the philosophical turns I took and always pointed me toward the right books and theories. Equally, I would like to thank my students and fellow teachers at the Calgary Board of Education. Many of my students came from war-torn countries, and they told me much about places to which even I dared not go.

For my family, especially my parents, I'm indebted beyond repayment for their endless support and encouragement ("Where's he off to now?").

For my editor at Dundurn Press, Michael Carroll, who saw the promise of the book proposal and continued to support and advise me through the long process of publication, I'm also thankful.

Finally, I thank my friends for their love of adventure and intelligent conversation, with special thanks to Dr. Charlene Elliott for her editorial comments on every one of the several hundred drafts of this book that I managed to fumble my way through.

Index